Crisis & Renewal

THE MANAGEMENT OF INNOVATION AND CHANGE SERIES

Michael L. Tushman and Andrew H. Van de Ven,
Series Editors

Emerging Patterns of Innovations: Sources of Japan's Technological Edge
Fumio Kodama, with a Foreword by Lewis M. Branscomb

Crisis & Renewal: Meeting the Challenge of Organizational Change
David K. Hurst

Crisis & Renewal

MEETING THE CHALLENGE OF

ORGANIZATIONAL

CHANGE

DAVID K. HURST

HARVARD BUSINESS SCHOOL PRESS
BOSTON, MASSACHUSETTS

. . . .

Library of Congress Cataloging-in-Publication Data

Hurst, David K.
    Crisis & renewal : meeting the challenge of organizational change
    / David K. Hurst.
       p.   cm. (the management of innovation and change series)
    Includes bibliographical references and index.
    ISBN 0-87584-582-7 (acid-free paper)
    1. Organizational change—Management. 2. Corporate
reorganizations. 3. Crisis management. I. Title. II. Title:
Crisis and renewal. III. Series
HD58.8.H865 1995
658.4'063—dc20   95-1246
                                                  CIP

The paper used in this publication meets the requirements of the American National Standard
for Permanence of Paper for Printed Library Materials Z39.49-1984.

To The Goddess

Contents

・ ・ ・ ・ ・ ・ ・ ・

Acknowledgments

EARLY IN 1980, the company I was working for was taken over in a crazy, wildly overleveraged buyout. What followed was nearly four years of chaos in our organization. The experience, which is described in Chapter 3 of this book, changed my life. I could neither make sense of the events nor comprehend exactly how we had got out of the mess we were in. I set out to understand what had taken place. This book is an attempt to explain what I discovered. I have the feeling, however, that I did not really write this book so much as I was the place where everything happened!

During the past twelve years, I have spent most of my discretionary time (as well as a good deal that wasn't) on reading and writing. At times, I got lost, but something or someone always appeared to show me the way. In that process, I have placed considerable strains on my wife and family and my business colleagues.

My acknowledgments need to go back at least twenty-five years to my first managerial mentors—David Richardson, James Mackness, Morris Cowley, and Hugh McGregor. David Richardson displayed the most wonderful sense of humor even when the world was collapsing. James Mackness gave me all my early opportunities. He was responsible for sending me to business school at the University of Chicago, where my eyes were first opened to the fascinating study of the universe of business organizations and the behavior of people within them. Morris Cowley taught me about the great gulf that lies between theory and practice, and Hugh McGregor persuaded me that philosophy matters— even in a practical field such as management. I also owe a huge debt to Wayne Mang and my former colleagues at Russelsteel, where many of the early ideas and practices were tried out. Wayne sponsored my activities and experiments for many years, and I am profoundly grateful to him.

Several academic institutions were of great assistance after I left the steel business to write this book. I am especially grateful to Deszo Horvath at York University's Faculty of Administrative Studies, Adrian Ryans and Nick Fry at Western Business School, and Murray Bryant at the University of Toronto. Many members of the academic community have been enormously supportive of me and my work. Rod White and Jim Rush at Western Business School have been a continual source of ideas and encouragement and for several years kept me in contact with what was happening in the academic world. Many of the concepts used in this book emerged from my collaboration with them. The more radical models in this book were first outlined and developed in papers written with my colleague Brenda Zimmerman while I was at the Faculty of Administrative Studies at York University. Her ideas have been a great source of inspiration to me.

It is hard to say where one gets many of one's ideas and impetus, but in addition to those mentioned above and cited in the Bibliography, the following people have all contributed in many different ways to the project: Debbie Ackley, Harvey Babiak, Stafford Beer, Pat Bradshaw, Mary Crossan, David Ewing, Gordon Forward, Peter Foster, Peter Frost, Mike Greene, Charles Hampden-Turner, Anne Huff, Norm Katzman, Harry Lane, Clyde Mahon, Jim McKay, Henry Mintzberg, Gareth Morgan, Alan Pearson, Margaret Power, Bob Quinn, Dan Schendel, Don Schuelke, Al Shkut, Karl Weick, and Al Ziven.

The extended team at the Harvard Business School Press has played a central role in bringing this book into being. Alistair Williamson and the anonymous reviewers spent much time and effort challenging me to make myself clear. Once the conceptual framework was in place,

Marjorie Williams took over to make the book coherent and readable! Her comments and suggestions have been insightful and enormously helpful. Once the text was settled, the teamwork continued with Barbara Roth, managing editor, Susan J. Cohan, copyeditor, and Kathy Massimini, indexer, making continual improvements to produce the high quality product that you now have in your hands. I really appreciated the dialogue with all these people: they have improved the book almost beyond recognition.

Finally, I cannot thank my family enough for their sustenance over the past twelve years. For much of that time, I have been either physically or mentally absent from home. My wife, Diana, who has believed in the project from the very beginning, has maintained and supported me unflaggingly through the most difficult journey I have ever undertaken.

Thank you.

Oakville, Canada
February 1995

In order to arrive at what you are not

You must go through the way in which you are not.

And what you do not know is the only thing you know

And what you own is what you do not own

And where you are is where you are not.

T. S. ELIOT, "East Coker"

Introduction

THIS BOOK is about organizational renewal and the essential role of crisis in the process of renewal. Renewal is concerned with the revival in mature organizations of the values, feelings, excitement, and emotional commitment often experienced only in the beginning of an organization's life. Renewal is about the restoration of something of value, something important, that has been either lost or forgotten as an organization has grown and prospered. Renewal, then, is about values and the central role that they play in the lives of organizations undergoing renewal. For during the process of organizational renewal, values are necessary—critical to the process—not just

---

Excerpt from "East Coker" in *Four Quartets*, copyright 1943 by T.S. Eliot and renewed 1971 by Esme Valerie Eliot, reprinted by permission of Harcourt Brace & Company. Excerpt also from *Collected Poems 1909–1962*, reprinted by permission of the Eliot Estate and Faber and Faber Ltd.

nice. Renewal is thus about how we make sense of our lives and those of our organizations: it is about the restoration of meaning to work.

This book is practical, written from a manager's perspective—from the point of view of a participant in the management of organizations rather than that of a spectator. It deals with the changes that take place in the role of the manager as an organization evolves. It argues that, to a considerable and unacknowledged extent, modern business organizations advance strategically by accident, economically by windfall, and politically by disaster. This does not mean that events in organizations are random or capricious or unmanageable. It does mean that a manager's influence is often occasional, indirect, and delayed rather than constant, direct, and immediate. It recognizes that managers may often be constrained in their ability to act and confused as to what to do. But this book shows them that they are never powerless.

This book tells stories: it tells of change through time. It looks at the evolution of a variety of organizations over long periods of time in different places and at different times. It sets organizational change in the context of the development and history of organizations. More precisely, it deals with how organizations are conceived, born, and grow to maturity, and how, as they age, they become both systemically vulnerable to catastrophe and ready for renewal. Stories help us to put together these long sequences of events in a coherent way. These days, many managers are so bombarded with information that meaning becomes fragmented. Often they understand only individual events, not what has happened. Stories allow us to reconnect events, to reconstruct meaning, and to understand what has happened.

This is a radical book. First, it is radical in the original meaning of the word. It goes to the roots of organizations and the practice of management. And it tries to understand how that practice is affected by organizational history and context. It is also radical in that many of its conclusions and recommendations run counter to conventional wisdom. Much management writing has been concerned almost exclusively with rationality in management and stability in organizations. This book is also concerned with the role of instability—crisis—in organizations and the nonrational aspects of management. It suggests, for example, that contexts arise in every organization that so constrain managers that their only course of action is to destroy the system— creatively—in an act of what I call "ethical anarchy."

This is an ambitious book. It is written both for managers and for academics. It uses a series of conceptual frameworks in an effort to reintegrate the practice and theory of management. In a modest way, it tries to restore management to life—to reintegrate it with the humanities, by reconnecting it with literature, philosophy, history, and art. The humanities do not make progress in the way that science does. They begin and end with the human experience. Their great advantage over the sciences, however, is that they deal with ultimate concerns. They wrestle with the important questions. The issues are huge but clear, even if the priorities conflict with each other. In management, it is the loss of the big issues, the absence of our concern for the important, that has made us slaves to the urgent.

Finally, this is a personal book. It is written with a certain passion. It began with a takeover deal and the subsequent "meltdown" and renewal of an organization of which I was a member. The four years that followed that transaction were some of the most intense and exciting times I have ever experienced as a manager. After the turbulence died down, I tried to understand what had happened to us. I could not find a framework in my business training that described the dynamics adequately. I found the first clues to a structure, or rather a process, in Chinese Taoist philosophy and, much later, in the study of nonlinear dynamics and complex systems. The watershed experience in the early 1980s had begun what was (and still is) an obsession to understand in a more fundamental way the processes that underpin human behavior.

ORGANIZATIONAL RENEWAL: BACK TO THE FUTURE

To renew an organization is to restore or revitalize it in some way. The concept of organizational renewal assumes that in the beginning of an organization's life, at its founding, there was something of value, some shared experience that was authentic and meaningful. Over time, this original feeling of authenticity, of meaning, has either faded or been lost. Renewal involves going back to the founding values to reconnect the past to the present, to rediscover the old in the new.[1]

Renewal is about the future—it requires a social vision of the future, of what society could be—but it is firmly rooted in the past:

> We do not know the future at all except by analogy with the past, and the future that will happen will not be much like anyone's vision of it. This gives our social ideals the intensity and purity of something that does not exist, yet they are born out of analogy with what has come to us

through tradition. So all visions of a social future must be rooted in the past, socially conditioned and historically placed.[2]

Thus, renewal is about continuity amid change and about patterns that repeat themselves—the rhythms of life. It helps to remember these patterns as we travel forward, for if we can recognize them, we know whether we are headed in roughly the right direction. Thus, renewal is about how we need to go backward in order to go forward—to travel back to the future. And the cycles of these movements are in the patterns of the stories that we tell. They are the rhythms of renewal.

MANAGEMENT FROM THE PERSPECTIVE OF A REFLECTIVE PRACTITIONER

I began my management career in the 1960s, an era of unparalleled economic growth and optimism about our abilities as managers to control our own destinies. At that time, it was widely believed that a good general manager could run anything, whether it was a conglomerate or an economy. There was a good deal of evidence that such managers "knew what they were doing." The formal business education that I received in the early 1970s tended to support this belief, although, to be fair to the University of Chicago, it never claimed to teach me business, only the disciplines that would allow me to learn from my experience. To the extent that this book is effective, perhaps that goal has been achieved.

Almost immediately upon my graduation, however, the world for which my business education had prepared me changed. The first oil shock of 1973 and subsequent market disruptions destroyed the illusion that one could forecast the future with any precision. Although initially this did not appear to matter in the soaring inflation that followed, the discontinuities of the new era were reinforced by a series of severe recessions in the 1980s and 1990s. The social and political turmoil of more recent times and the ferocious competition in many global markets have only validated the transformation in the managerial world.

This book is written from the viewpoint of a reflective practitioner, a manager who participates in an ongoing stream of action and then reflects upon his or her role in those events in order to understand it better and improve upon his or her performance. From this perspective, experience is usually something that one gets about ten minutes after one really needed it! For managers often don't know exactly what they are doing at the time they are doing it. But afterward they can try to find out exactly what they did. Even then, their knowledge may still be imperfect.[3]

This is not the way that I was taught to manage: in fact, it's the opposite of what I was taught. The instrumental, rational decision-making model, which we'll examine more closely in the following section and which still dominates the North American business schools, implies that calculated thought should *always precede* effective action and that the action should be taken with a clear business objective in mind, such as increasing market share or reducing expenses. Every manager knows that this is not always the case in practice. My experience has convinced me that often this *should not* be the case—even in theory.

MODELS OF MANAGEMENT ACTION

This book begins with practice and ends with practice. I believe that in management, practice comes first and last, but that in between there has to be theory. Theory is not currently fashionable in management. For the past decade, the English-speaking management world has been preoccupied with the practices of "excellent" companies and managers to the exclusion of theory. But if we are to learn from experience, whether our own or that of others, we have to have theory. Without theory, it is all too easy to overdose on anecdotes.[4] For without theory, it is impossible to guess what is generalizable from a situation and what is specific to it. Without theory, we as managers run the risk of becoming totally incoherent, confused in perception and muddled in practice. Unable to understand the relevance of techniques to our own particular situation, we introduce one initiative after another to our dazed organizations. Incapable of distinguishing inputs from outputs, we end up slaves to fad and fashion, trying to replicate the practices of "excellent" companies in contexts we cannot fathom. The psychologists who work with rats would call it "superstitious behavior."

In this book, I present the following three perspectives on management action:[5]

1. *Rational action:* Action is purposive and rational; it is directed toward the achievement of goals. In this view, managers think rationally, making clear choices before they act. The connection between means and ends

is very close, and their action can usually be justified technically as maximizing some well-defined objective such as profits. Traditionally, this kind of means-end rationality has been associated with classical economics.[6] This assumption is buried deeply in modern Western culture, so it is not surprising that management education in North America has been founded on this perspective. It is the perspective on action with which most of us have grown up.

2. *Constrained action:* Action is externally constrained and situationally determined. Although individual actors may believe that they are acting with purpose, their actions are in fact constrained by the circumstances in which they find themselves. In this view, any rationality is retrospective in nature; it represents an attempt to give meaning to and a sense of control over the world. In the academic world, this perspective is usually associated with population ecologists,[7] who explain organizational forms as resulting from a selection process imposed by the environment. If taken literally (and if it applied everywhere and at all times), this perspective implies that managers really cannot do very much to affect organizational outcomes. Perhaps this is why it has not been a popular view among managers, except, of course, when the organization's results are poor. Then the constrained actor model is often used to explain the "circumstances beyond our control" that led to the disaster.

3. *Emergent action:* Action is emergent from a process that is almost random in nature; it unfolds over time, and rationality, goals, and purpose are emergent from the process. In this perspective, managers are free to act but don't know what to do! Their behavior is not goal-directed; rather, it is goal-interpreted retrospectively.[8] This third perspective agrees with the retrospective nature of rationality developed in the second view, but it denies that knowledge of external constraints is sufficient to predict action. This third model is the most difficult one to explain, yet it seems to me to capture the essence of some of the real dilemmas that managers face. For example, how does one take effective action in real time in shifting, ambiguous situations that defy definitive analysis?

My central conceptual theme in this book is that, in the management of organizations, the rational model isn't wrong: it just isn't enough. In my view, we get into trouble when we claim or imply that it is. The rational model needs to be examined more closely, supplemented with the additional perspectives I've described, and placed in a broader context.[9]

My argument is that the key question is not which of these three models of action is right, or even which is better, but *when* and under what circumstances they are useful to understand what managers should do. Modern organizational life is characterized by oscillations between periods of calm, when prospective rationality seems to work, and periods of turmoil, when nothing seems to work. Although effective management often does demand individualistic, firm, top-down direction, in certain cases a more sensitive, collective, nurturing approach is required. At some times, analysis is possible; at other times, only on-the-ground experience will do. If the oscillations are random, then they are impossible to understand. Integration of these models requires that there be patterns to these oscillations. These patterns are the rhythms of renewal.

DEVELOPING A VALUES-BASED RATIONALITY FOR CHANGE

In some deep way, Western technical rationality is uneasy about change and has been so since its origins in Greek philosophy. Parmenides (540–470 B.C.) was one of the first Greek philosophers to argue that change was an illusion.[10] Indeed, Parmenides was one of the first to advance the theory that one could not obtain the pure knowledge of reason about things that were in a constant state of change. About them, all one could get was delusive opinion. This is understandable. If something is solid and stable, one can take it apart, analyze its parts, and put them back together again. It is no coincidence that the words *understand* and *substance* share the same roots. Things that move—processes—do not allow us to perform these functions, and our language reflects our annoyance at this fact: we call them "insubstantial," "erratic," and "infirm."

Nevertheless, in management, frameworks for the rational, objective management of change are everywhere these days. Whether the slogan is "continuous improvement," "worker empowerment," or "process reengineering," each of them purports to offer the user a logical framework from which to manage the change process. The promises of process reengineering are particularly seductive in this regard, suggesting that organizations can redesign their systems from scratch.

The most popular models of change in management theory get change over with as quickly as possible. They also leave the manager of change comfortably outside of the change process. These models are variations of Lewin's famous tautology "Unfreeze-Change-Refreeze."[11] The manager changes the organization much as a craftsperson uses a tool to work some material. The tool changes the material but not the craftsperson. The implication is that managers can manage organizational change in much the same way as they maintain organizational stability. Change is seen as a technical problem requiring technical solutions.

In my view, it is here—at the intersection of technical systems and their users—that the fatal flaw lies. The apparent objectivity that these rational frameworks give their users undermines the very social dynamics that lead to really fundamental change. Indeed, the intellectual detachment of the designers and managers of change from the process itself should be identified as a leading cause of the failure of such change efforts.

In this book, I will be developing frameworks that point to the importance of another kind of rationality in management. It is a values-based rationality, in which action is taken not because it is instrumental in the achievement of some technical goal but because the behavior is seen as *intrinsically* valuable. People feel that it expresses their beliefs irrespective of the instrumental outcomes. This is in contrast with instrumental rationality, in which behavior is seen only as a means to an end. Indeed, *it is the absence of a means-end rationality and "clear goals" from these other kinds of rational activities that allows outcomes to be creative, that permits novelty to emerge.* It will become apparent that the two kinds of rationality are often in tension with each other.[12]

THE CONTENT OF THIS BOOK

Three aspects of the book need to be outlined here: the organization of the topics; the diagrams and metaphors used throughout the book; and the role of the notes which accompany the text.

ORGANIZATION

This book consists of a series of stories in contexts that get progressively more complex. In the first four chapters, each story is used to develop a conceptual model of one kind or another. In the first part of the book, the evidence is used inductively to build the models. From Chapter 5 onward, the conceptual models are used deductively to suggest management action: the stories are used to illustrate management practice.

Chapter 1 is the interpretation of a report that I first read in *Scientific American* several years ago. The report detailed the rapid cultural transformation of the nomadic Bushman hunters of the Kalahari Desert to settled farmers and herders on the fringes of their ancestral hunting grounds. In this chapter, I explore the apparently self-organizing dynamics that sustained each type of society and the factors that precipitated the change from one structure to another. I make the case that the Bushmen's story is our story.

In Chapter 2, I track the evolution of an entrepreneurial firm from its creative beginnings through the institutionalization of its success. We follow its development from a learning organization to one dedicated to performance. I will argue that the processes involved in such developments are very similar to those found in the transformation of nomadic hunting societies into herders and farmers. The tension between performance and learning resembles that between herding and hunting. It seems that although young organizations may start off as informal and nonrational, their success requires that they become both formal and rational!

In Chapter 3, I begin to discuss the possibility of reversing what appears to be a natural evolutionary process. Can bureaucracies (herders) be changed back into entrepreneurial organizations (hunters)? The vehicle for this discussion is the actual experience of a management team (of which I was a member) in the sharp economic downturn of 1982. The key features of this successful transformation are identified and discussed, particularly the apparent role of crisis in precipitating change by shattering the logic of the previous organization.

In Chapter 4, the social dynamics of innovation and learning are examined in much greater detail, but in a radically different setting— that of the English industrial revolution. The renewal process began in crisis—the aftermath of the English Civil War. I maintain that it was the "hunting" social dynamics with which dissenting religious groups such as the Quakers responded to the crisis that contributed to their enormous success as social reformers, scientists, and business entrepreneurs. They were led by their vision of a new society and lived their plain values in every aspect of their lives. In the process, they renewed an entire society. I use the story of the Quakers' involvement in the industrial revolution to describe a model of organizational change.

In Chapter 5, I show how the model described in the previous chapter was derived from ecology—the study of how complex natural systems evolve. This model, the organizational ecocycle, captures many of the concepts of change that have been developed in management writings. Based on some of the most recent thinking from the study of nonlinear dynamics or chaos theory, this model also allows us to understand how successful mature organizations become systemically vulnerable to catastrophe. It also supplies a new perspective on what managers actually do as well as what they ought to do.

In Chapter 6, I begin to focus on the management implications of the ecocycle model. This chapter deals with the most controversial recommendation—that managers of mature organizations need to create deliberate crises if they are to preserve their organizations from destruction. I show how crisis is intimately associated with creativity in organizations. The rise of the Japanese auto industry and the renewal of its American counterpart are plotted onto the organizational ecocycle. New insights are gained into the dynamics of the shift from craft production to mass production and, more recently, to lean production. Sources of management-induced crisis are discussed.

Chapter 7 addresses the serious ethical implications of requiring crisis for organizational renewal. I deal with the need for constructive damage to the status quo and for managers to live their social visions of the future. These activities are illustrated with experiences from organizations for which I have worked as well as with vignettes from the experience of others. The problems encountered underscore how difficult it can be to renew established organizations. The chapter concludes with the argument that we have to create contexts in which people and organizations can be self-organizing. I argue that there are models for these in our past, in the social dynamics of the original nomadic hunting organization and egalitarian groups such as the Quakers.

DIAGRAMS AND METAPHORS

A picture may be worth a thousand words, but nobody seems to know why. My speculation is that a good diagram does more than illustrate the verbal material. It outlines the structures and indicates the dynamics that underpin and integrate our use of language.[13] I believe that our ability to create, recognize, and retain visual patterns is much more fundamental a mental process than our ability to work with words. It is the capacity that we call intuition, and it emerges from our ability to generate such patterns from the huge interconnected neuronal network that comprises our nervous system. Good diagrams, which embody powerful patterns, communicate in a very intensive way, and by arousing and resonating with the patterns in our minds (in-forming us), they pack far more "information" than many thousands of words.

Working rather less obviously than the diagrams in this book are the metaphors.[14] Metaphors are powerful, not only because they, like diagrams, are also miniature models, but because they are so inconspicuous. They help us organize our thoughts—create maps of the territory—but they often add unobtrusive features that limit our ability to explore any further. Worse still, we often confuse our abstractions—the maps—with reality, a largely unexplored territory. One cannot avoid metaphors—indeed, I believe that they are essential to creativity in management—but one must be aware of their power.

NOTES

This book is the product of more than twelve years of intensive study and reading, woven together with experience. Although the book itself is written for practicing managers, I have attempted, via the notes, to support many of the assumptions made and conclusions reached. I have tried to make the notes as interesting as possible, and they are designed to be read with the chapters. If the book is a forest and the chapters are trees, then the notes represent a thick underbrush of ideas, capable of generating many forests under the right conditions. Managers will know soon enough whether the book helps their practice, and the notes will point them to readings and ideas that I have found to be helpful. Academics, of course, will want to know whether the ideas work in theory! I hope that the notes will be helpful to them, too.

WALKING THE WALK

When members of the Society of Jesus, the Jesuits, seek renewal, they try to understand how the values of their founder can be realized in the new contexts in which they find themselves.[15] To this end, they go through the "exercises" developed by Ignatius of Loyola nearly five hundred years ago, either doing the exercises themselves or supervising someone else going through the process. By "walking the walk," stepping in the footsteps of their founder, they participate in the activities that led to the founding of their institution. This is not an intellectual activity. They develop no logic, no "map" of how to proceed. But the feelings, the appreciation of the founder's values, generated by this participation act as a compass needle, giving them a continual sense of the direction in which to head. Indeed, this is probably one of the roles of ritual in all organizations, religious and secular—to re-mind one of the living presence of the past in the present.

Good stories perform the same function for us. They allow us to step in the steps of others who have gone before us. They allow us to participate in the meanings that they made—to see the world through their eyes. Often set in different times and places, these stories usually do not and cannot supply a "map" of the territory—lists of specific things to watch out for and do. But they should give us a general sense of direction. Like a true compass, a good story says to its readers, "Follow me." I hope that the stories in this book are up to that task.

1

The Wisdom of the Hunters

THE FIRST story about organizational behavior and change is drawn from the recent history of the San people, or Bushmen,[1] of the Kalahari Desert in southwestern Africa. Indeed, it was the account of the rapidly changing culture of this desert population of something less than fifty thousand people that was one of the inspirations for this book.

The Bushmen's story is of interest to modern managers because their original hunting-gathering structure was one of the most successful social adaptations ever developed, and humans and their forebears lived successfully in this way for millions of years. For the nomadic hunting band was dynamically stable: capable of adapting to changing

---

In this chapter, I have relied on several sources. The original article (Hurst 1991) was based on Yellen's article in *Scientific American* (1990). Other sources not quoted directly are Chance 1988; Lee and DeVore 1968 and 1976; Lewis-Williams and Dowson 1989; Power 1991; and Vinnicombe 1976.

and often hostile environments without losing its coherence. The absence of technology and the apparent simplicity of the organization allow us to see with great clarity the social "glue"—the basic social dynamics—that can hold an organization together without the use of hierarchy. The hunting band also models many of the desirable features that managers are currently trying to introduce into their modern organization structures: absence of hierarchy, multiskilling, open communication, mutual trust, and individual empowerment. In addition, the recent transformation of the Bushmen from nomadic hunters to settled herders and farmers seems to parallel the familiar evolution of successful entrepreneurial organizations into stable, but often rigid, bureaucracies. If we can understand this latter transformation process better, it will be easier to grasp what is needed to reverse the shift—how to renew established organizations.

In short, because of its longevity and capacity to cope with a variety of circumstances, the hunting band can be thought of as the original "learning" organization. Up until about ten thousand years ago, all of us lived in this way. This was a time when the different world cultures must have been much more similar to each other than they are today. The hunting band is thus the common root of our many national cultures. It is the original cradle, the container of the creative process called learning. I will argue that it is to this cradle that all organizations must return in some way—to revisit—if they are to renew themselves.

FEATURES OF A HUNTER-GATHERER CULTURE

There are only about half a dozen hunter-gatherer societies left in the world,[2] and as one might expect, they inhabit relatively inaccessible places. The nomadic Bushmen of the Kalahari are one of this group, all of whom live in what are known as immediate-return economic systems. That is, returns to labor are direct and immediate.[3] Little investment or even preparation is needed to generate a return: hunters do not have to build elaborate animal traps or storage devices. Weapons and tools are simple, and although requiring skill to make, they are constructed of easily available materials. The proceeds of effort, whether from the hunt or from foraging activities, are consumed immediately and not stored for any significant length of time.

The Kalahari Desert, located in the southwestern region of southern Africa, comprises an area of roughly 220,000 square miles—about half the size of a combination of the Chihuahuan, Mojave, and Sonoran Deserts in the southwestern United States. This makes it one of the largest continuous expanses of sand in the world. For the Kalahari is a landlocked basin of sand, bounded on its southern edge by the great Orange River and in the north by the Okavango swamps and Lake Ngami. To the east, the desert becomes the wide veldt of Botswana and South Africa. In the west, it changes into the stony Nama and Damara foothills of Namibia. With an average elevation of 3,000 feet, the land slopes from east to west, dipping in the north to the swamps and lakes.

In general, with less than 9 inches of rain a year, the Kalahari is arid with few permanent water holes, for the sand allows water to drain away and any surface liquid is quickly evaporated by the searing heat. Nevertheless, the region's geology does hold water below the surface, and it is this feature that allows the Kalahari to support a wide range of vegetation and animal life. This, in turn, allows humans to live in the desert.

The Bushmen are probably the original human inhabitants of southern Africa, and until the middle of the last century, they were distributed widely over the subcontinent. Here they are thought to have lived a nomadic hunting mode of life for well over fifty thousand years. With the twin invasions of their hunting grounds by Bantu tribes from the north and Europeans from the south, many were systematically exterminated or taken into slavery. The survivors were steadily driven from the more fertile lands in the east to the deserts in the west. Until recently, the inhospitable Kalahari has been the last refuge of this culture, preserving it from destabilizing contacts with the outside world.

In their hunting mode of operation, the Bushmen's society consisted of loose coalitions of open, assertively egalitarian communities known as bands. Membership of the bands was governed by ties of family, kinship, and even friendship, and there was a continual flux and flow in the membership of any band. Band territories overlapped with each other, and the territories were not defended because the resources were widely dispersed and often seasonal. As a result, no band could stay in one place for any length of time.

As they roamed the desert, a Bushman family had a relatively wide choice of whom to travel with. Unencumbered by possessions, they had great physical mobility and were able to switch easily from less attractive bands to those with more to offer. This mobility was encouraged by the environmental conditions. The wild animals that they hunted were mobile, and the bulk of their diet consisted of vegetables, fruits, and nuts, which were widely located and seasonal in their yield. During the rare times of plenty, when heavy rains made water generally available, the Bushmen bands fragmented and spread out across the desert to exploit the new wealth of resources. Every winter and especially in times of drought (which occurred about two years out of every five), the families tended to come together and did not stray far from the permanent water holes.

ABSENCE OF HIERARCHY

Although these flexible dynamics[4] of the hunting society were suited to the Bushmen's physical needs, they were not determined by the physical environment. Their major function was to prevent hierarchical relationships from forming between people.[5] The Bushmen hunters felt a strong hostility toward anyone who aspired to hierarchical authority. Any evidence of a desire for wealth or power was likely to eliminate an individual from consideration as a leader: "None is arrogant, overbearing, boastful, or aloof. In [Bushmen] terms these traits absolutely disqualify a person as a leader and may engender even stronger forms of ostracism."[6] As a last resort, those who felt uneasy about a relationship with such a person could easily move away and join another grouping. The ease of their exit from the situation thus prevented hierarchical relationships from forming. Would-be hierarchical leaders could easily lose their followers! Thus, the flex and flow in the bands was subversive of authority, maintained individual autonomy, and minimized the buildup of aggression in the society. As we shall see, it also ensured that the organization could continue to adapt effectively to the demands of the environment.

EMERGENT STRATEGY

Each extended family was autonomous and self-sufficient, and the individuals who comprised it had each learned the variety of skills necessary to survive in the desert. It was this autonomy of the small groups composed of multiskilled individuals that allowed the society to spread itself out in its search for the dispersed resources. Effectively, this gave the Bushmen the ability to cover large areas of territory without losing the flexibility to capitalize on success wherever it was found. As soon as anyone in the scattered coalition had success, the Bushmen's easy rules of association allowed the dispersed families to reaffiliate to form a larger-scale organization. Using modern business concepts, one would describe their "strategy" as opportunistic and emergent rather than deliberate and planned. Strategy developed from a series of rapid responses to exploit activities that showed promise.

COOPERATIVE VALUES

The flexible band system was complemented by values that stressed the ethic of sharing, both of meat and of possessions. Not only did this ensure equal distribution of food, but—extended to kin outside of the band—it led to a system of delayed reciprocity between neighbors. For instance, when a hunter's kill was more than enough to feed him and his immediate family, the meat would also be used to feed neighbors against the day when they would make similar kills and reciprocate. The distribution was initiated by a custom that awarded the ownership of a dead animal (and thus the right to distribute its meat) to the owner of the first of the poisoned arrows to effectively penetrate its skin. Arrows were freely exchanged among members of the band, either as gifts or as loans, so the owner of the meat might not even be a member of the hunting party.

The ultimate effect of this intricate system of distribution was that the rewards of the hunt accrued to the band as a whole: successes belonged to the team and not to the individual, one might say. Indeed, successful hunters did not enjoy a higher status than anyone else, and because up to 90 percent of the Bushmen's food intake came from foraging, the band was in no sense dependent on the hunters for their survival. Meat was greatly prized, however, because it added strong flavor to what could become a rather boring diet at some times of the year.

Although men hunted the larger game and women did most of the foraging, there was no status distinction between the two activities. Men and women were regarded as equals: the women were not possessions. This egalitarianism extended to marriage: adult women usually gave themselves in marriage, or if given by their male kin, they had the right to refuse any particular union. They could also initiate divorce if they were unhappy. Men had no socially sanctioned rights over women, and the women did not wait on them. As if to underscore this, when couples married, they lived with the bride's extended family, where the man performed so-called bride service by hunting for his new in-laws and their kin.

The custom of gift giving ranked second only to meat sharing in importance within the Bushman community. They regarded trading among each other as undignified and as likely to lead to bad feelings within the community. So artifacts and utensils of all kinds made a slow rotation among members of the society. The unwritten rules of this activity were that no Bushman could refuse a gift and that he or she had to reciprocate: although the delay between receipt and response might range from weeks (anything less might look like trading) to years. Thus, through meat sharing and gift giving, the Bushman bands were held together by webs of mutual obligation. At any given point in time, everyone within the society owed someone else a favor.

OPEN COMMUNICATION

The hunting society's social values were reflected directly in their physical living arrangements, as shown in Figure 1-1. The Bushmen's temporary camps consisted of grass huts arranged in a tight, circular pattern with all entrances facing toward the center of the circle. From his or her doorway, each resident could see everyone else across the small communal area. The cooking hearths were placed just outside the hut

Figure 1-1 A Bushman Hunting Camp in 1944

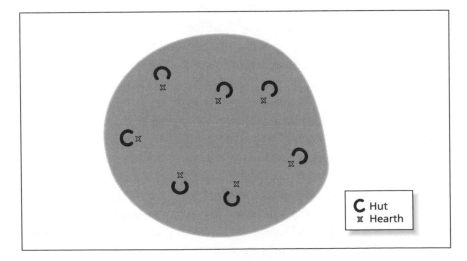

C Hut
x Hearth

Source: Adapted from Yellen 1990 (104). Reprinted by permission of *Scientific American*.

entrances. Contrary to what one might expect, their way of life did not demand that the Bushmen spend all their time searching for food.[7] Hunts might last for several days, but they were relatively infrequent events. Usually, the Bushmen spent only a few hours each day gathering food and fuel. This left plenty of time for talking and socializing.

The "open-door" layout of the Bushmen's living space encouraged openness and interaction, most of which took place around the cooking fires. Everyone knew everyone else's business; indeed, the hunters lived their whole lives in full view of the rest of the band.[8] When she first saw the brown, clustered encampments and the activities that went on within them, anthropologist Lorna Marshall was reminded of a swarm of bees:

> The [Bushmen] are the most loquacious people I know. Conversation in a[n] encampment is a constant sound like the sound of a brook, and as low and as lapping, except for shrieks of laughter. People cluster together in little groups during the day, talking, perhaps making artifacts at the same time. At night, families talk late by their fires with their children between their knees or in their arms if the wind is cold. . . . There always seems to be plenty to talk about. People tell about events with much detail and repetition and discuss the comings and goings of their relatives and friends and make plans. . . . [T]he men's imaginations turn to hunting. They converse musingly, as though enjoying a sort of daydream together, about past hunts, telling over and over where the game was found and who killed it. They wonder where the game is at present and say what fat bucks they hope to kill. They also plan their next hunts with practicality.[9]

The dialogue around the campfires was conducted with an intensity that is matched on few occasions in a Western culture. The Bushmen were what behavioral psychologists would call "active" listeners: "While a person speaks the listeners are in vibrant response, repeating the phrases and interposing a contrapuntal 'eh.' . . . [T]he 'ehs' overlap and coincide with the phrase, and the people so often talk at once that one wonders how anyone knows what the speaker has said." Apart from promoting consensus building and allowing the emergence of plans, these conversations maintained community bonds and surfaced incipient social problems. Cooperation was essential to survival in the desert—the nuclear family could not survive alone—and the Bushmen had a horror of direct argument or fighting. They had to belong to a band and were acutely aware of any hint of rejection. Meat sharing kept concern over food at a low intensity, while gift giving reduced jealousy and built relationships. The maintenance of peaceful social relations was a constant preoccupation, and face-to-face communication played a major role in their preservation. According to Marshall: "Getting things out in words keeps everyone in touch with what others are thinking and feeling, releases tensions, and prevents pressures from building up until they burst out in aggressive acts."

SHARED VISIONS

The physical living arrangements that facilitated such intimacy could probably not be better calculated to foster a sense of belonging among the members of the Bushman community. Yet the processes active round the Bushmen's campfires went well beyond the physical and social bonding activities described so far. Although events and plans were discussed and developed at the conscious level, these activities took place against a vast, mythological backdrop that brought meaning to the Bushmen's daily routines.

The hunting Bushmen had no sense of past and future to frame their activities in the way in which modern humans do. They could not remember back more than two or three generations, and there was no concept of the future beyond the expected cycle of the seasons. They were engaged totally in the here and now. The only way to make sense of their existence was to live it! So round the campfires, especially during their larger gatherings in times of plenty, the Bushmen enacted in story, song, and dance the rituals that reminded them of the origins of their universe and their place within it.[10]

Their mythology was rich in the details of the provenance of every element and inhabitant of the desert, explaining both their roles and their relationship with each other. It was this mythology—this shared vision, if you will—that located the Bushmen in a web of meaning, descriptive of what their role had been and prescriptive of what it ought to be. Nothing they did was trivial or unimportant: everything played a role in the overall system. In consequence, they were acutely sensitive to everything that happened in the context in which they lived their lives and were capable of responding rapidly to unanticipated events:

> The world, then is seen as a gigantic version of a self-regulating
> life-support system in which component subsystems, themselves self-
> regulating within certain limits of tolerance, interact to correct perturba-

tions. . . . The [Bushmen] see their culture as plastic; old knowledge is lost and new discoveries take its place. There is more than one way of doing something, more than one way of solving a problem, and more than one problem in a situation. . . . New means can be discovered to attain the same ends, or the same means may be used to attain new ends.[11]

In effect, then, their mythology constituted a web of significance, a cognitive framework, that allowed the Bushmen to make sense of and negotiate what to outsiders looks like a dangerous, unpredictable environment—an environment that the Bushmen were comfortable in calling their home.

STABLE STRUCTURES

The most prominent feature of the Bushmen's hunting culture is their "systems view" of their world[12] and its apparently natural balance—a woven blend of stable structures and flexible processes that allowed them to follow and capitalize upon the natural rhythms of their desert home. In fact, one might say that the hunting Bushmen were not so much *in* the environment as they were *of* the environment. They blended in so naturally that they were almost indistinguishable from it. The most striking of the structures was the physical living arrangement, which facilitated the social processes, allowing the Bushmen to both frame and resolve issues without engaging in overt "decision making." That is, the intense social interaction and deep dialogue allowed members of the community to identify and articulate issues as they arose, usually resolving them well before they became "problems" requiring "decisions."

A second stable structure in the Bushmen's hunter culture, which is less obvious than the one just discussed, is the mythological framework, or shared vision, within which they operate. Unlike modern Westerners, the hunting Bushmen did not regard their mythology as a fiction to be contrasted unfavorably with historical facts; rather, they regarded their mythology as an extraction of the essence of role behaviors that have worked at all times. Thus, their mythology informed their daily activities by supplying helpful information about elements of their environment (such as the habits of animals and the characteristics of plants) and helped them coordinate their experience—to derive meaning from their lives. As Northrop Frye[13] has pointed out, myths play a leading role in early societies by giving them a shared possession of knowledge, essential instruction in what everyone in the society has to know. It is this function of the myth in the present tense that generates meaning for the members of the society by showing how every element of the environment is related, each to the other, and imbuing every activity with significance.

THE HUNTING BAND AS A LEARNING ORGANIZATION

By now, the reader may be wondering in what sense the hunting band can be thought of as a learning organization. After all, the hunters made no progress, at least as we understand it, in this form of organization. They remained at the same level of social evolution for thousands of years. They developed no technology, built no permanent structures, accumulated no possessions, and left no literature and little art, other than their masterful rock paintings and their stories. In short, they created little, if any, economic surplus. Today there are very few of them left, and it is unlikely that they will be with us for long.

Yet the nomadic hunting organization survived successfully, preserving their vision and their values for an immense period of time in climates and physical environments that differed greatly from each other and must have fluctuated considerably. If learning, at a minimum, means the ability to survive, then the hunting band qualifies. In addition, all our modern organizations have in some sense evolved from the hunting bands. Are we not their inheritors—the evidence of their success? After all, what is the "it" in a modern organization that stays the same and thus allows us to say that such and such an organization has evolved, changed, been renewed, or survived? "It" is not the people or their possessions, the customers, or suppliers. "It" is not the physical or legal structures, the products, or the technologies. All these can and will change. "It" can only be nonphysical "things"—the shared beliefs, the stories, the memories, the visions, and the values. Thus, to the extent that our modern organizations and societies share—if only as visions and aspirations, mythologies and religions—the open, egalitarian, cooperative values of the hunters, then the hunters *have* survived, and we are their direct descendants and the heirs to their ability to learn and survive.

FEATURES OF A HERDER CULTURE

Despite an immensely long period of cultural stability lasting thousands of years, the Bushmen's nomadic hunting society has changed dramatically during the past twenty to thirty years. The hunting bands have been largely transformed into communities of settled herders and farmers. Nowadays many Bushmen live in villages, keep cattle and donkeys, and raise goats and chickens. Their vegetable diet includes cultivated corn rather than the wild roots and tubers they have traditionally eaten. Young men are no longer taught how to hunt, and the bows and arrows that they construct are made only for the curio trade.

This type of cultural change has occurred in many societies throughout history; nevertheless, the precise reasons for such cultural shifts continue to puzzle anthropologists. For a time, it was believed that the diet of farmers was nutritionally superior to that of nomads and hence offered agricultural societies an advantage in the struggle for survival. It now appears, however, that, if anything, the opposite is the case: the hunters' diet actually yields a more balanced intake than that of the farmers. In addition, in the case of the Bushmen, the hunting mode of life suited them ideally. In a drought-prone region, communities relying on water-dependent herds and crops have little to fall back on when disaster strikes; the hunters can always move on. With their generalist strategy and keenly honed skills, the Bushman foragers could find water where none was known to exist, and in the absence of game, they could survive on a wide variety of reptiles and plants.

POSSESSIONS

Why did this cultural change take place so fast (fast, that is, by anthropological standards)? The anthropologists now suggest that it was the exposure of the Bushmen to material wealth that catalyzed the transformation.[14] The emergence of a market economy on the fringes of the Kalahari allowed the Bushmen, for the first time, to become collectors of possessions. Not only did these possessions hamper their physical mobility, but more important, the ownership of possessions ran directly counter to their ethic of sharing. It seems that as the Bushmen accumulated material wealth, they felt increasingly uncomfortable exposing their new possessions to the scrutiny of the rest of the band, let alone sharing their good fortune with them. In the past, the relative scarcity of goods had encouraged their communal use, as they were passed from owner to owner in the form of gift giving. Now the relative abundance of goods meant that everyone could aspire to have his or her own. And so the Bushmen began to hoard goods and, ashamed of their reluctance to share them with others, arranged their living spaces to give themselves maximum privacy so that others could not see what they possessed. As will become apparent, in that process, they lost their ability to talk to each other face-to-face in open dialogue. And when this kind of communication was no longer possible, the whole society was transformed.

BREAKDOWN OF COMMUNICATION

One of the most striking aspects of the Bushmen's transformation has been the change in the architecture of their living spaces. For the circular patterns of the hunting camp have given way to the linear, boxlike arrangements of the farming village.

Figure 1-2 shows the layout of the more permanent living arrangement of the herders in 1982. The herding camp is larger in size than the hunting camp, with the huts spread out and the doorways turned away from each other. Most of the cooking hearths have either been brought inside or grouped in a specialized "cooking" area (see top

Figure 1–2 A Bushman Herding Camp in 1982

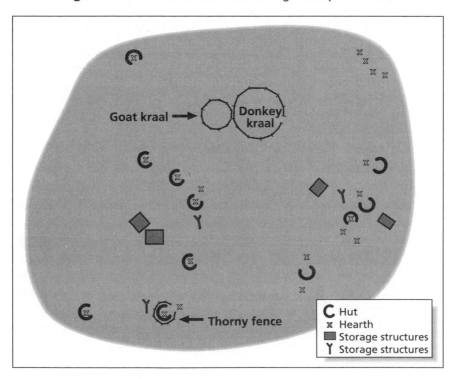

Source: Adapted from Yellen 1990 (104). Reprinted by permission of *Scientific American.*

right). There is no longer a central communal space. Storage structures for goods are located around the camp, and the goats and donkeys are corralled behind thorny fences. One family (bottom of the diagram) has gone so far as to encircle its hut with a thorny fence. Indeed, many Bushmen now live in permanent mud-walled huts with doors across their entrances.

The herding camp, then, is laid out for privacy rather than intimacy, and in consequence, the Bushmen do not meet around their campfires, either to discuss community events or to reach consensus on band activities. Of course, these activities no longer have any survival value. Individuals are now dependent on a large-scale economic system for their livelihoods and are required to do work for which their hunting-foraging skills do not equip them. The band no longer functions as a coherent whole, and the ethic of sharing is waning fast. There is certainly no need for hunters to visualize where the game might be: the Bushmen now rely on their goats for meat.

EMERGENCE OF HIERARCHY

One of the most immediate consequences of this change in living arrangements is that the Bushmen are finding that they need a hierarchal authority to resolve disputes among themselves. Usually, they have to turn to a local Bantu chief to play this role, for they have no experience of hierarchical leadership.

In the desert, the role of leadership was not regarded as having any special status. Leadership was not centered on one person, but like the Bushmen's strategy, it emerged from the demands of the situation, as the band followed its fortunes, making the best of the environment. Once consensus on a general course of action had been reached around the campfire, leadership on the ground would move among the members of the band as circumstances dictated: at some times, it might be the best tracker who led; at other times, it might be a woman who could locate water-bearing tubers; and so on. Because all these necessary skills were widely distributed among the members of the band, anybody could lead. Each hunter-forager could switch from the role of follower to that of leader and back again without giving the matter a moment's thought.

Now, however, in the absence of the open communication within their community, consensus is difficult to reach and social tensions can grow to intolerably high levels. Without the continual dialogue around the cooking fires and the myriad opportunities it gave for people to raise delicate and difficult issues, problems fester and grow. Outbreaks of violence become common. In their hunting society, as a last resort, intractable interpersonal problems were resolved by the quarreling parties' moving away from each other, at least for a while. In their new "boxed" culture, these free-flowing processes are no longer available to the Bushmen: they are no longer mobile, and anyway they cannot survive alone. In a static society, characterized by standard routines requiring minimal interpersonal interaction and offering little opportunity for intensive, informal communication, a formal authority is required to settle disputes and maintain order.

DISASTROUS CONSEQUENCES OF THE HUNTER-TO-HERDER TRANSFORMATION

As one might expect, the consequences of this transformation have been disastrous for the Bushmen. The hunting culture is probably lost, and for them, the herding way of life is problematic at best. As hunters, the Bushmen lived self-sufficiently in a seamless universe of which they were an integral part. This is in sharp contrast with their more fragmented life as herders and farmers in which trade and barter are essential if they are to satisfy their basic needs. In the past, these kinds of transactions had always led to bad blood. Meaning must now be found in the acquisition of material possessions in a society in which laws, hierarchical authority, and the technology of herding and farming have replaced the regulatory role of mythology and the natural cycles of the climate and the environment. Although there is no doubt that this development creates considerable material prosperity, it is not costless. For apart from the susceptibility of the Bushmen's society to all the ills that attend the loss of community feeling and their identity as a people, their lack of flexibility renders them vulnerable to disastrous reversals when the recipe for success changes. Indeed, the risk is that their entire society will be destroyed.

Crowded together in the farming camps, the erstwhile hunters are exposed to a host of threats that they never encountered in the desert. Diseases ranging from smallpox and measles to whooping cough and flu often prove fatal and sometimes reach epidemic proportions. When they do, the knowledge base of the community can be decimated. In the absence of a written record, the hunting-foraging skills may already be beyond recovery. It is feared, for example, that much knowledge was lost when the bands were ravaged by smallpox in the 1950s. In addition, the herding camps are starting to show all the symptoms of societies in which people have lost the meaning of living. Drug addiction, crime, and violence are assuming the proportions found only in the inner cities and on the Native reservations of North America. This is happening in the Kalahari for the same systemic reasons it has occurred in North America. For their story is our story.

THE HUNTERS' AND HERDERS' STORY IS OUR STORY

"There are only two or three human stories," wrote Willa Cather, "and they go on repeating themselves as fiercely as if they had never happened before."[15] In this book, I contend that *the Bushmen's story is our story* and that it is told over and over again at many levels in the lives of our organizations and our societies. We start off in the beginning in small-scale, informal organizations as naive hunters, not knowing much but capable of learning every day through trial and error. With success and the learning of effective routines, we steadily become more like herders. Soon we are protecting possessions and defending territories in large-scale hierarchical bureaucracies whose social dynamics are very similar to those in the Bushmen's herding mode of living.

Such large-scale organizations flourish in delayed-return economies in which significant investments, both of capital and of time, may be required to generate a return. In the process of institutionalizing success, we build organizational structures that break down what were once novel, complex activities into simple, routine procedures. The generalists who once did these jobs are replaced by specialists and technology in many forms. The easy informality that often characterizes small, entrepreneurial organizations is replaced by formality and rigid procedures. The maintenance of these procedures is ensured by a system of hierarchical control mechanisms that require little informal interaction among organizational members. In some cases, the complex technologies used in such organizations may preclude meaningful social interaction among those who operate them.

Where knowledge of all kinds had once flowed freely through many channels, now it is restricted by sophisticated data-processing systems, which limit the type of information captured and can be used to control the numbers of people who may have access to it. There is much more data, but without the ability to integrate it, there is often less meaning. Restricted access to information creates secrets and confidentialities of all kinds, and confidentiality is the enemy of trust. Thus, a shared logic, which at first supplements and supports a system held together by shared values, gradually begins to supplant it as the logic becomes embodied in technology of all kinds.

In this organizing process, the people who perform and manage the essential tasks are endowed with a variety of possessions, both physical and psychological, that enhance their status and hence their power in the formal organization. This power increases as the organization grows and prospers. The products of success, the possessions, are protected and preserved in the boxes of the formal hierarchy, which is designed to formulate (or as will become clear, more accurately, to formalize) strategy, settle disputes, and perpetuate the static organization via a system of controls and sanctions against deviations from plan.

Like societies of herders and farmers, bureaucracies excel in low-variation environments, in which the formula for survival remains fairly stable. They are much less successful in situations in which the recipe is changing, for their very strength—their ability to maintain the status quo—reduces their capacity to change. The danger comes for them, as it does for all herders, when the environment becomes turbulent and ceases to be predictable. Then, in order to survive, they will have to recover something of their lost hunting way of life.

Thus, our search for a learning organization involves the challenge of recreating the dynamics of the original hunting band in contexts that are far removed from those in which it flourished naturally. For, I will argue, as organizations and societies build structures, develop technologies, and accumulate possessions in pursuit of progress, this sets them on an erratic course of change, with apparently smooth periods of evolution being interrupted by sudden disasters—disasters to which they become systemically vulnerable. It is during these periods of crisis that the social dynamics of the nomadic hunting band come into their own.

THE CASE FOR RENEWAL

As far as the Bushmen are concerned, the first question that strikes one is whether the shift from hunter to herder is reversible at all. The change seems to be unidirectional. With the loss of their daily enactment of the hunting way of life, the basic skills required to live in that way will soon wither through disuse. The hunting Bushmen's intimate knowledge of the particular parts of the Kalahari where they lived depended upon detailed on-the-ground experience. Because the migratory herds of animals moved constantly and other resources fluctuated in their availability, their location could not be captured and preserved on an abstract map. Indeed, maps can capture only stable structures, and in this situation, they would immediately become stale and outdated.

Without the social interaction around the campfires, the entire process of socializing the young and their inculcation with the hunting values and social dynamics will be lost.[16] Without the stories, songs, and dances, the origins and destinations of the society will soon be forgotten. Even if the shared vision is somehow remembered, the Bushmen may find it hard to shed the attachments of the settled life, although a turbulent environment will certainly help in that regard. Nevertheless, surrendering psychological possessions such as status and power is likely to be even harder than surrendering physical possessions. For even in the face of an ecological crisis, many of those higher up in the hierarchy, those who have "made it," may cling to the secrets and confidentialities that they "own" and be dismissive of the notion that a society can be self-organizing. "Who is going to resolve the disputes?" they will demand to know, and indeed, a herder may be unable even to imagine how a hunter could ever function without a hierarchy.

Thus, the Bushmen may find themselves possessed by their possessions and quite unable to summon the cultural memory of the hunting skills that ensured their survival in a turbulent past. Without either role models or their archetypes, embodied in myth and legend, there will be neither behaviors that they can emulate nor traditions to which they can appeal. If a severe environmental crisis were to strike the Bushmen in their herder mode of living, they have little resilience, and their society might well disappear, incapable of adapting to the changed circumstances. Indeed, the question is whether there is any hope of their avoiding this fate. Can they and their organization be renewed?

The case for renewal sounds daunting, yet I believe that the situation of the Bushmen, although apparently extreme, does contain all the elements of the problems faced by any established organization seeking to renew itself. This analogy, drawn from the experience of the Bush-men, gives us some clues as to what is needed to change our bureaucracies into more flexible organizations—to convert at least part of these organizations from herders back into hunters. For the challenge faced by modern organizations is, at least in some ways, even more difficult than that faced by the Bushmen. In a turbulent environment, modern managers have to preserve the core "farming" competencies, which produce a value-added surplus, while the hunting skills at the periphery of the organization are used to forage for new opportunities. These are the opportunities that do not show up on environmental "scans" or maps because they come and go like the migratory herds in the Kalahari. Until they are exploited and developed, they are unstable and not mappable. Thus, they are available only to those on the ground with an intimate knowledge of the territory. They are available only to the hunters.

I have said that the Bushmen's story is our story, but the reader does not have to take this on faith. Indeed, I suspect that many readers have an uneasy feeling about the proposition. In the next chapter, however, I will demonstrate the similarities between the evolution of a modern organization and the transformation of hunters into herders.

At the same time, the reasons for any unease may become apparent. For if the Bushmen's story is our story, this has significant implications for our theories of how managers should act. Take decision making, for example. In North American management thought, we have usually regarded decision making as being the essence of the manager's role, almost defining the function of general management. Yet the tacit assumption behind this thought is that problems exist as some sort of "given" in the environment. The Bushmen's story suggests that, in fact, problems may often be systemic in their origin—a by-product not only of interactions between the organization and the environment but also of the dynamics within the organization itself. In their hunting mode of operation, the Bushmen got by without any conscious need to make decisions. Action flowed not from abstract thought but from the demands of the whole situation, the totality of which had been exhaustively examined in the campfire dialogue. The ease with which this process operated in the hunting mode contrasts starkly with the difficulties the Bushmen now experience in their herding society, in which their problems require decision makers with hierarchical power.

There is a clear counterpart to this in modern organizations. For as every management consultant knows, one of the most prolific sources of problems in any organization is people's inability to talk honestly and openly across the boundaries that separate them. It seems that the contexts in which they find themselves inhibit the deep dialogue required to resolve the difficult issues. Such organizations "know" the answers to the problems that plague them but seem unable to summon and focus that knowledge. Effective consultants understand that their role is often to act as catalysts to help the necessary interactions take place. Their position as outsiders helps them break the constraints that inhibit open conversation. It's not a question of logic; it's a problem of process. Thus, if an organization experiences the need for constant decision making on the part of its managers, this may be a symptom of dysfunctions within the organization, reflecting the absence of social processes capable of framing and resolving emerging issues *before* they become overt problems (and the consultants are called in). The direct implication of this is that logic has its limits in management. Its use can be constrained by the physical and psychological contexts in which people find themselves.

In the next chapter, I will show how these contexts evolve, as I track the emergence of the entrepreneurial "hunters" and their development into bureaucratic "herders" in a modern business organization.

2

Learning and Performance

T HE STORY in this chapter is about the birth, growth, and maturation of a successful, modern business organization. Set in North America, it is separated by at least ten thousand years from the time when our ancestors were nomadic hunters. It would seem, however, that our social nature has changed little during this period. For I will show that, in their origins and in their development, modern organizations seem to display social dynamics very similar to those discussed in the previous chapter.

My theme is that, in their small-scale, informal beginnings, many modern organizations have social dynamics rather like those of the hunters. The emphasis in such organizations is on learning of all kinds—learning to master recalcitrant technologies, learning to respond to divergent customer needs, learning to develop sources of capital required by the young business, and so on. This learning is usually of the trial-and-error variety, and errors in an unforgiving climate are often fatal: many of these start-ups will fail. Their people, like hunters, will either join other groups that are having more success or set out on their own. The organizations that survive, however, will sooner or later start to look more and more like herders. The emphasis will move from learning to performance, from the development of routines to the repetition of routines. There will still be learning within such organizations, but even in new industries, it will be confined to progressively smaller aspects of the business as the major issues such as product features, production technology, and markets are resolved.

The most extreme statement of this view is to say that young businesses begin their lives as informal, *learning* organizations, but if successful, they become formal, *performance* organizations.[1] It is thus helpful to think of learning and performance as two ends of a continuum, with the young organizations starting off on the left-hand side and moving toward the right as they age. Learning always includes some performance: even start-ups have to pay their bills. Performance always includes some learning: mature companies are continually updating their systems and technologies. The difference between the two ends of the continuum is the scale on which learning and performance take place. In a performance organization, learning is always possible, but it is limited because it takes place *within* the framework that the organization provides and that makes performance possible. The learning that occurs is less likely to be *about* the framework.

It is important to track this organizational transition—from hunters to herders, from "mostly learning" to "mostly performance"—if we are to grasp the dynamics of organizational aging and the requirements for renewal. In this task of tracing the development of an organization from its vague, ephemeral beginnings to successful maturity, a conceptual model will be used. It will help us keep tabs on the different elements of the organization as we go. At the same time, I will illustrate the concepts by using a practical example—that of Nike.[2]

(Note: Often when writers use examples from successful companies like Nike, there is at least the tacit implication that what these organizations are doing is "right" and can be emulated consciously by managers in their own organizations. This is not my intention. I have used the Nike example as a concrete illustration that will either help to remind readers of situations in their own organizations or, more important, help them to notice aspects of these situations that they had overlooked before.)

ELEMENTS OF AN ORGANIZATION

The conceptual model used here to track the development of an organization identifies five interacting elements of an organization: people, the roles and tasks that they perform, the structural arrangement that they use, their sources of information, and the reward systems that hold the organization together.

PEOPLE

New organizations begin with people coming together round some unexploited opportunity—a "ripple" in the resource field. The opportunity could come from anywhere. It could be a latent consumer want or a need created by an environmental or a demographic change. It could be the result of a technological breakthrough or a government initiative. Or it could literally be an unexploited physical resource in the earth. Whatever the source, the people who first gather round the resource are likely to be metaphorically or even literally "prospectors." They will tend to be people with unusual combinations of skill and experience or particular passions that make them especially sensitive to anomalies and unexploited opportunities in the field. Just as is the case in the Kalahari Desert, there are no signposts or maps to guide them. They must find their own way, often in territory that has never before been mapped. In our efforts to explain how they do it, we often say that successful entrepreneurs seem to be able to "smell" the opportunities. Curiously, the hunting Bushmen say that's how they find water in the desert—by smelling it.

In the case of Nike, the first two people who came together were Phil Knight, a track star at the University of Oregon, and his coach and mentor, Bill Bowerman. Both were obsessed with improving the performance of top-class athletes and were acutely dissatisfied with the running shoes then available. Bowerman, one of the founders of the jogging "movement"[3] in the mid-1960s, was the technical visionary. He was continually tinkering with performance shoe design and manufacture, including the use of new materials. In one famous incident, he cooked up an experimental rubber compound in the kitchen and attempted to mold it in the family waffle iron (ruining the appliance in the process). Knight would later describe Bowerman as "part genius, part madman, the best coach I ever had."[4] Knight, a good middle-distance runner himself, combined his obsession with athletic performance with a CPA and an MBA. He could not understand why high-performance running shoes were made in Germany, with its high wage structure. In his view, they should be made in the Far East, following the example of so many other products whose manufacture was being moved there.

Thus began the application of high-technology, mass-manufacturing, and later on, sophisticated marketing techniques to the humble sneaker. But it was not a matter of cold calculation: it required the obsessive dedication of the founders and the mobilization of a team of like-minded individuals for its realization. Later Knight recalled, "The idea that the brains are all at the top of an organization is really kind of silly. And nobody at the top ever *does* anything—it's the folk down the line that make it work. I learned that early. I had a great concept about bringing in shoes from Japan to compete with the German shoes, but I wouldn't have gotten far with it if I hadn't bumped into Jeff Johnson. He *really* made it work. And Jeff in turn had to rely on other people. I have a lot of respect for how we did that, and I guess that's the way this company has always worked."[5]

Jeff Johnson was Nike's first employee. Over the years, he played a central role in the integration of the elements that comprised the successful business. Indeed, the concept took more than seven years to really come together. At each stage in Nike's development, key individuals with just the right skills would appear as if by magic. For example, when Knight and Bowerman started the company in 1964, they called it Blue Ribbon Sports, and the name stayed that way for over seven years. Jeff Johnson would have the *Nike* name come to him in a dream in 1972. The famous "swoosh" logo was created at about the same time by a graduate design student—for a fee of thirty-five dollars! Even at that time, no one (other than Jeff Johnson) was particularly excited about either the name or the logo. "I don't love it, but I think it will grow on me," Knight is reported to have said after seeing the logo for the first time.[6]

ROLES

These early stages in the life of Nike illustrate another aspect of a young organization in its formative years: the people attracted to the opportunity usually describe themselves as "being in the right place at the right time," for their reasons for being there are often hidden, even from them. The skills that they use and the roles that they play with respect to each other are activities that reflect their natural abilities and preferences with which they respond to what feels like an exciting opportunity. Many of them are unaware that these abilities exist within them until they encounter the opportunity. Their skills are demanded by the context, evoked by the situation. They made the opportunity, and the opportunity makes them. It is this mutual causality, this evocation by and response to a situation, that lends excitement to the entire enterprise.

When a new product or service is in the early stages of its development, the critical tasks to be performed and the skills required to execute them will be poorly understood and largely unspecified. In its early years, no one in Blue Ribbon Sports really knew what skills would be required. Bowerman and Knight just muddled along, redesigning shoes, testing them on the track, and selling them to a widening circle of track-and-field enthusiasts. Via the network of communication so created, individuals, each of whom was a "prospector" in his or her own right, could be attracted to the emerging opportunity.

There is, as yet, no "organization" to select anybody: via the interactions on the network, the people will select themselves. In a young organization that is to become successful, as each newcomer makes his or her contribution, the opportunity and the organization become a bit more visible to outsiders. There are no clear boundaries to separate the organization from "its" environment. Both organization and environment are coevolving together.

TEAMS

The unstructured and nonroutine nature of the work in a new organization requires that people work with the minimum of structure. Typically, this requirement is met by the use of informal, multiskilled teams. Like hunting bands, such teams can form and dissolve at short notice. This kind of flexible structure is essential if the myriad issues that emerge during the hectic early days of the young organization's life are to be addressed. The intensive communication and interaction on the teams allows them to deal with the complex, unstructured, "wicked" problems[7] that every young enterprise faces. These problems are unique. They are difficult to formulate. There are no right or wrong answers, and yet the answers count in real time! The nature of these issues and the timing of their emergence will be unpredictable and unforeseeable. Thus, the organization will tend to be issue-driven, moving rapidly from one predicament to another, reaching out and co-opting people and resources as required.

At this stage in the life of a young organization, the social dynamics resemble those of the Bushmen in their hunting mode. There is very little formal structure but a lot of process. In emergencies (and almost everything is an emergency in a young organization), there is no time for hierarchy or formality. Whoever has the skills should do the job. People seem to come from nowhere to address the problems and then disappear as fast as they came.[8]

These are intensely exciting times for insiders. As Nike matured, members of the organization from the early days remembered with nostalgia the spontaneous way in which they had responded to emergencies:

> In the olden days, we had shipping problems once, and Hayes and Knight and I started going over to the warehouse at night to help ship shoes. We probably f----d up more orders than we got out, but we felt great—we were *doing* something about a problem. Actually, we did get a few more shoes out, and had fun ourselves; and I think we sent a signal to some people.[9]

NETWORKS

One can think of an organization as consisting of a relatively stable set of transactions among a set of individuals. This stable set of transactions is a small, relatively tightly connected system. It is "born" when it emerges as one of a myriad of possibilities from a much vaster, loosely connected network that links many individuals.[10] One of the largest of these webs is society as a whole. Of course, society is not a uniform structure but a set of complex, nested patterns of relationships of varying degrees of looseness and tightness. How does a particular organization "condense" out of a society? It seems that, if an organization is to form, there have to be periodic gatherings, when the network participants come together for intense exchanges. These periods of "fusion" change the strengths of links and can lead to the formation of the tightly connected systems that we recognize as organizations.

In human systems, there is a huge variety of sources of these opportunities for union and reunion. We saw in the last chapter how the Bushmen came together in times of plenty to celebrate their rituals and enact their shared vision or mythology. In the case of Blue Ribbon

Sports, athletic events automatically supplied similar occasions for social fusion. At track meets, athletes would gather from all over the country to perform and exchange knowledge and information about the sport. The communication was intimate and intense among people with a shared passion. The fusion lasted a limited time, but participants left with new relationships and perspectives that would change their patterns of interaction in the extended network. Thus, several of the people who were later to become important to Nike were first attracted to Bill Bowerman and Phil Knight via athletic competition and the network of communication evolving with it.

As the young organization begins to "gel," the variety and equivocality[11] of the unstructured issues faced by a young organization require that the teams and their members be connected by denser networks carrying information about all events that occur, both inside and outside the organization. The pulse of the dynamic changes, with the periods of fusion becoming more extended. People spend more and more time together. With limited criteria for classifying the relative importance of equivocal information and the intense interaction demanded by the ambiguous situations, there will be few if any confidentialities or secrets within the fledgling business. Communication will be free and open and characterized by a continual sharing of individual views and opinions among all members of the organization. Like the Bushmen's campfire dialogues, the communication will reflect the full range of the participants' feelings, concerns, and aspirations.

This open communication is very evident in the early Nike: "In the old days . . . people drifted into the top management area after five and talked over the day. As a result, people knew enough about what others were doing. . . . When Nike was a small company, communication used to just happen—in the hallways, over a beer on the way home, at the basketball game."[12]

RECOGNITION

In the early stages of the start-up, cash is likely to be at a premium and profits will be scarce. The reward systems that bind the members of the organization together will be psychic and subjective rather than financial. Since they have self-selected themselves to join the fledgling business, this is not surprising. They have come together first because of a shared interest (in the case of Nike, a shared passion) in the activities of the organization. There will be the external recognition, shared by all of them, of the opportunity to be exploited as well as the internal, mutual recognition of each other's individual contributions to the overall effort. They are doing what they love to do. For some, the thought that they might get paid for doing this seems superfluous, if not outrageous. Many of them will either be moonlighting or have part-time jobs, upon which they will rely for their basic financial needs.

It was a long time before Nike became self-financing, and its early years were punctuated by repeated cash crises. Bowerman and Knight formed Blue Ribbon Sports (BRS), the predecessor company, in 1964, but Knight did not work in it full-time until 1969. Indeed, for the first eight years, the business of BRS consisted of athletes selling performance shoes to athletes. The reward system that held the organization together during these early years was clearly not based on financial remuneration. Rather, it seems to have been based on strong bonds and trust developed between people with mutual interests—the camaraderie and team spirit between fellow athletes and a shared desire to achieve peak performance.

INTERACTION OF THE ELEMENTS OF AN ORGANIZATION: MISSION EMERGES

In the past few pages, I have described the evolution of the elements of a new organization serially. In practice, all the elements evolve together. More correctly, they coevolve, with each affecting the others and in turn being affected by them. At the same time, the organization is coevolving with what *will become* its environment. For the environment and the organization are not distinguishable from each other until there is a definite boundary between them. And the boundary itself evolves.

Figure 2-1 shows how these elements of what I shall call a young "learning" organization—people, roles, teams, networks, and recognition—can be thought of as interacting to form a coherent system.

One of the earliest and most significant developments in the life of a young organization is the emergence of a shared sense of purpose among its members that transcends individual ambitions. This feeling of mission, which engages everyone in the organization, is the central set of values to which anyone can refer, either as a guide to action or as a justification for having taken action. In effect, it permits coordinated individual initiative without formal control: it empowers individuals

Figure 2-1 A Learning Organization

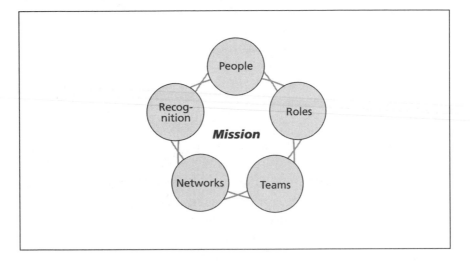

to act, but in harmony with each other. "The team on the run," Phil Knight would say. "Everyone up to speed. Everyone on the same squad."[13] The pioneers in a young organization learn the values from each other by watching and doing. Soon these behaviors are embodied in stories and spread throughout the company in face-to-face dialogue. Like the Bushmen's mythology, these stories contain the essence of practices and attitudes that have worked in the past and are thought to exemplify the very best the organization has to offer. Just as is the case with the Bushmen, the stories inform people's actions and help them coordinate their experiences, bringing meaning to their lives.

The emergence of this sense of mission is often catalyzed by a vision of the future held by a single person—usually, the founder. The vision is generally the articulation of some transcendent, over-the-horizon goal. In the case of Nike, the mission that emerged early in the young company's existence was expressed as "enhancing people's lives through sports and fitness." This sounds abstract, but it was coupled with a fierce dedication to "authenticity" and a corresponding affection for the "bad boys" and iconoclasts of big-time sports. In tennis, Ilie Nastase, Andre Agassi, and John McEnroe were obviously "Nike people." McEnroe, with his antielitist, antiestablishment attitude, clearly embodied Nike's fierce sense of authenticity and corresponding hostility toward the "country club" set. From its very beginnings, Nike has always been "an athlete's company," servicing the serious athlete who dwells in the minds of all of its customers, even if it does not live in their bodies! Nike's transcendent goal, first articulated in 1977, was familiar to anyone who had ever competed seriously. Quite literally over-the-horizon, it read, "There is no finish line."

FROM HUNTERS TO HERDERS: MISSION BECOMES STRATEGY

Many readers will accept that trust among the participants is an emergent quality in young organizations and perhaps that mission is similar in character. Most would probably argue, however, that strategy is not an emergent quality of any organization. They would contend that it has to be externally formulated and imposed. Indeed, this is what most North American business schools have been teaching for the past thirty years. Superficially, there would appear to be evidence in the case of Nike to support this view. After all, Phil Knight had written a paper in 1962 at Stanford suggesting that running shoes should be made in the Far East rather than Germany. The Harvard case study, in common with many other reports on the company, plays up this rational aspect: "The Nike story—a graduate school paper transformed into a company within shooting distance of a billion dollars—is a fairytale example of entrepreneurial success."[14]

Yet I will argue that the insights in the paper did not constitute strategy. They were a recognition of a trend that could perhaps constitute a vision of the future. Certainly, the paper offered no guidance on how to proceed, and as an insight, it was available to many other people. Its role in Nike's subsequent success was probably as a rationalizer of what the company was doing—a communication device to explain to outsiders what was happening. It supplied a logic for the sustained success of the business that could be used to build legitimacy with bankers and other suppliers of resources.

Instead, I want to make the case that strategy in learning organizations is emergent.[15] For with the emergence and articulation of a shared organizational purpose—the mission—coherent organizational action starts to become possible on a systematic basis. As knowledge about cause and effect is acquired, behavior within the organization becomes rationalized. People begin to appeal to a framework of logic to justify their actions. Patterns of action that have proved consistently successful are repeated. Grouped into coherent, conceptual patterns, they are identified and named as strategy.

In the beginning of a new organization's life, the formulation of strategy is the culmination of a process of retrospective sensemaking[16] whereby activities *that have already proved successful* are identified and articulated. Strategy is the "hard" counterpart to mission: it makes the mission operational. If the mission and the values it reflects act as a "compass," then strategy is the "map." A compass gives a general sense of direction in an uncharted territory. A map reflects actual encounters with the territory and identifies aspects of it thought to be important. Strategy, then, does not create new businesses; it rationalizes them retrospectively. The rationalization process is accomplished by re-stricting the movements of people, by placing boundaries on all the elements of the organization. These restrictions are instituted for the very best of reasons—to perpetuate success and to make routine opera-tions more efficient. With these restrictions based upon what the or-ganization has learned, the young, learning organization becomes transformed into a performance organization. The social dynamics of the hunters start to shift into those of the herders.

With the articulation of strategy—the lessons learned in the learning organization—the pace of rationalization picks up as the products of individual learning in an organizational context are encoded[17] and formalized in a hierarchical structure—as the products of trial-and-error learning are converted into performance routines. The people are no longer pulled into the future by their shared vision and sense of mission: they are now also driven by a successful past—propelled by the organization and its strategy. The individual elements of the learning organization, presented earlier in the chapter, begin to crystallize into stable entities.

ROLES BECOME TASKS

The roles that were once chosen by the members of the young organiza-tion now become tasks, defined by job descriptions and standard operating procedures. The skills required are now increasingly well understood, and performance can be evaluated against established standards. People can be selected for jobs with some precision, and as they move through the organization, they are replaced with people who have similar abilities. In the early years, people might have been hired just because they believed passionately in the organization's mission. Their technical abilities were a secondary consideration. Now they are hired for instrumental reasons—to perform a particular function, to get a designated job done. Now ideals often become a secondary consideration as the organization becomes preoccupied with the routines and techniques necessary to deliver reliable performance. The original fervor of the founders starts to become diluted.

In its early years, Nike (BRS at that time) had not had the funds to hire experts, and in any event, there was no traditional industry from which to hire expertise. It simply hired good generalists (often accountants and lawyers) who were attracted to the business. As the business grew, however, operations became more specialized, and efficiency became a concern. Nike had to hire managers with specific skills and expertise: "There's a limit to the sins you can cover up with enthusiasm," Phil Knight commented at about that time.[18]

TEAMS BECOME STRUCTURE

As the successful organization matures and the routines are defined and their elements analyzed, the tasks themselves and the responsibility for their performance become fragmented and embedded in formal, hierarchical structures designed to ensure their repetition. The easy informality of the participative, multiskilled teams is gradually replaced by specialized departments whose activities are coordinated by rules, procedures, formal planning processes, and a hierarchy of administrators. This hierarchy is visible not only in the formal organization structure but also in technology, where routines become buried in manufacturing processes, embodied in data-processing systems, and cast in concrete in the form of physical facilities. Hierarchy (not to be confused with bureaucracy) is the essential accompaniment to the survival of any complex system. It reflects the progressive mastery and reduction to subconscious routines of the multitude of activities that have to happen automatically every day if the organization is to stay in business. If these activities were not buried subconsciously, then the management would be able to do nothing except fight fires. In short, in complex systems, hierarchy is history, and no successful modern organization can avoid accumulating it.[19]

The emergence of hierarchy is probably the most insidious of the aging processes in a maturing organization. On the one hand, it is essential for control of the productive processes and technologies that allow people in an organization to produce valuable goods and services.

On the other hand, it also acts as a major constraint, preventing them from easily changing the processes, technologies, goods, and services. The struggle of Nike's founders against a formal organization structure illustrates how their growth and success have made it increasingly difficult to avoid:

> Our early years were characterized by no structure—period! This was an incredibly effective approach for a while. We attracted people who weren't necessarily good "managers," but who were excellent team players and good performers. . . . Then things changed. The business got so large and so complex that it was impossible for Phil [Knight], or any of us, to play the same role. We started to lose our hands-on feel for the business. Yet we haven't formalized things. We knew that we were lacking structure and systems, and we knew that we weren't as efficient as we could have been.[20]

NETWORKS BECOME SYSTEMS

As the organization matures, the dense, rich networks, whose function it was to generate "thick" information for a young organization in search of meaning, become attenuated and slender as they are replaced by systems designed to work with "thin" information.[21] The informal "grapevine" will survive as a remnant of the original learning network, but its functioning will be hampered by the absence of opportunities for face-to-face communication. In extremely formal organizations, the content and process of the grapevine may be dismissed as "gossip and politics" by members of the formal hierarchy. That is, the grapevine will be seen as threatening to the organization's identity, which is now firmly established. The close camaraderie of the early years is no longer possible in the large, dispersed workforce. If the founders of the business are still around, it is inevitable that people will see less and less of them, as their time becomes more fragmented. Information is increasingly used for control purposes—to detect deviations from preset objectives and standards.

Organization and environment are now clearly separated. The organization has learned which aspects of the environment to pay attention to, as well as which to ignore, by developing a series of frames and templates to lay over what was once a confusing jumble of messages.[22] Many of these cognitive frameworks, these constructions of "reality," may become incorporated into the organization's identity in the guise of strategy, definitions of "What business we are in," and so on. If this happens, the organization's self-referring processes will tend to maintain the cognitive frameworks, even in the face of evidence that tends to disconfirm them. This is what happened to Nike when, in the early 1980s, it was blindsided by Reebok's entry into the aerobics market. Nike totally misjudged the market potential and initially defined itself out of that arena. Its macho, jock image and rage for authenticity undoubtedly contributed significantly to this failure. "Nike will never make shoes for those fags who do aerobics," a senior manager was heard to proclaim at the time.[23] Between 1981 and 1987, Reebok's sales grew by nearly a thousandfold! It would take Nike years to catch up and a huge effort to regain its lead.

RECOGNITION BECOMES COMPENSATION

With the material success of the organization growing steadily, the informal, psychic rewards are at first augmented but eventually may be all but replaced by financial rewards determined by formal, objective compensation systems. Tasks are well defined, skill sets can be identified, and progress toward goals can be assessed. Formal job evaluation procedures may be introduced at all levels of the formal hierarchy. Career paths and career planning become possible. In addition, members of the successful organization will begin to accumulate the visible trappings of success. The "old-timers" will want to distinguish themselves from the "newcomers," and this will accelerate the development of a formal process for the allocation of rewards and add subtle nuances to the emerging pecking order.

When Knight appointed a president in 1982, an attempt was made to formalize the company's chaotic business practices. A Policy and Procedures Committee was established to sort out the emerging inconsistencies in the ways in which people were treated. One of the most contentious issues was salary policy, which had been based on a "pay the person not the job" philosophy. As the business and the industry grew, this had led to widespread inequities across the system and, apart from upsetting people, had made Nike employees more likely to be "poached" by competitors. Competitors, of course, had not been a problem in the early years: their evolution is a feature of a maturing industry. Eventually, Nike decided it had to introduce a formal system similar to the Hay system to address these problems. The easy atmosphere began to become constrained.

PEOPLE CHANGE

Earlier in the chapter, in discussing the elements of an organization, I began with people because their coming together to capitalize upon some unexploited opportunity represents the very first stirrings of an organization. Now, in discussing the transformations by which mission becomes strategy, I will end with people because they are the last and perhaps the slowest element of an organization to change. For those who have been inside the organization since the beginning, the changes that have taken place are just so many indicators that things are not the way they used to be. Often the founding members, bored with the routines that they have created and independently wealthy, decide to leave for greener pastures. Their places are often taken by professional managers. People may now be replaced, at even the most senior levels, without changing the organization's identity.

Nevertheless, with the advent of the professional manager, the organization often "dies" a little. For the new managers will have powerful ambitions and purposes developed in contexts outside of the organization they now enter. Frequently insensitive to the organizational culture, they will usually reinforce the focus on efficiency and performance using a panoply of techniques learned in business schools and practiced in other organizations for which they have worked. With no shared memory of the past among new members of the organization, its original meaning is inaccessible to them. A process of legitimation is required to explain and justify the institutional order—a process that places knowledge ahead of values.[24] The organization's visions and values and, by extension, the purposes of the senior management become tacit and undiscussable. The sense of shared mission is not as vibrant as before. Performance is now the primary focus of action.

Nike was not immune from this phenomenon. Jeff Johnson, the company's first employee, left in 1982. "I don't feel I'm contributing," he said. "I am not a manager. What the company needs now is managers."[25] By 1988, all the vice presidents who had been with the company in 1981 had gone. Some retired as wealthy individuals from the proceeds of the equity they sold when Nike went public. Others left when they became unhappy, either at the distribution of the shares or at the amounts of money others were getting. Like the Bushmen, when they had nothing, they had shared everything. Now, in a time of abundance, the inequalities rankled and divided them.

FROM TENTS TO PALACES: PERFORMANCE LEADS TO SUCCESS

All the elements of the strategy[26]—people, tasks, structure, systems, and compensation—support each other in the cause of performance (Figure 2-2) in exactly the same way that those of the learning organization supported each other in the cause of learning.[27]

The organization is now mature in the sense that it can replicate itself: it has a "formula" that allows it to make copies of itself. Given the right conditions, the performance organization may now go through considerable growth via geographic expansion. In this process, it will become further entangled with the conservative institutions of society. It will be listed on stock exchanges, become a force in local communities; its executives will join the boards of local institutions; and so on. With each of these contacts, the organization will be socialized to conform with the status quo around it. A stock exchange listing will be a major factor in this process. Finance for growth will now be contingent on the company's meeting the expectations of thousands of new stakeholders. The board of directors, articulate strategies, quarterly earnings, annual reports, and statutory filings will now assume an importance never before required for internal purposes. Members of external institutions will, in their turn, be invited to sit on the board of directors, reflecting the importance of the access to resources that they bring to the organization.

Figure 2-2 A Performance Organization

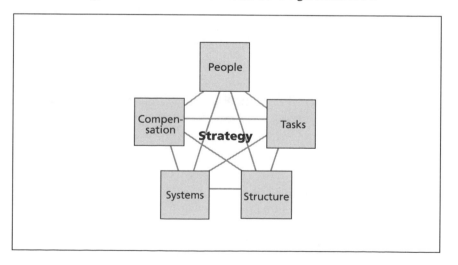

Where once only the young organization had stood, an industry may have grown up. In the case of Nike, by the end of the 1970s, it had spawned an industry. Alumni of Nike left both to found competitive businesses (such as Avia) and to work for competitors. Techniques that had once been proprietary and unique become standards for the industry. People now enter the organization with experience directly relevant to their jobs. They are there not to innovate but to perform. The organization may have increasing difficulty in playing a maverick role: it has been woven into the tightly connected threads of a tapestry of a larger pattern and is being regulated by society as a whole.

One of the most obvious marks of achievement at this stage of an organization's progress is the move of its people from the humble, crammed, "temporary" dwellings, where they have all lived cheek by jowl, to fancier quarters. Those who perform the corporate duties—raising money, reporting results to shareholders and bankers, talking to lawyers and accountants—usually make the first arguments for this move. Their reasoning is impeccable. The corporation is now part of a market economy and must compete for funds with everyone else. Appearances matter when wooing investors, and social legitimacy is important: "It's not for us, you understand; it's for them." A building that "makes a statement" would be helpful, and anyway, the real estate would be a good investment, a useful diversification. . . . The move is made.

I will argue later in the book that the physical layout of facilities and offices can be one of the major barriers to open communication and dialogue in an organization. Its impact is totally underestimated and often ignored. As such, the purchase and development of new executive quarters often represent the apogee of the corporation's trajectory. For the typical executive offices are designed to ensure that nothing novel enters the corporation's routines.

In the early 1990s, Nike consolidated its many facilities scattered all over Beaverton, Oregon, and moved into the magnificent new Nike World Campus, located on 74 acres. The buildings are stunning, each named after one of the Nike heroes. They are more like shrines than offices, for each contains statues of the hero, texts on the hero's personal history, and relics from his or her struggles. The unanswered question is how the social dynamics will work. Will the setting encourage the formation of open hunting circles or defended farming squares? It is too soon to tell, and by the time the company knows, it may be too late. The nostalgia for bygone days among the old-timers is very real. "I do miss the old days," Knight remarked. "Those early entrepreneurial days, frankly, were more fun. . . . [W]e were so footloose in those early days."[28]

To outsiders, however, by the time of the move into the "palace," organizations like Nike will have developed what appears to be a "recipe for success." It is usually at this stage in its life that the successful business is discovered by academics and consultants and proclaimed to be "excellent." But if the evolutionary process presented here is correct, often all that the outside observers are looking at is the organizational equivalent of fossil remains. For the hard structures and routines that now characterize the organization's performance mode give little indication of how the successful strategies were learned in the first place: the flesh may have long since departed from the bones.

PERFORMANCE VERSUS LEARNING

It will be apparent to the reader that, if this description of the evolution of a successful organization is accurate, then it has some striking parallels with the change of hunters into herders described in the preceding chapter. Although learning evolves into performance, at the extremes, the two processes tend to preclude each other. The dynamics of the learning process hamper performance by discouraging the establishment of routine, whereas the demands of performance inhibit learning by institutionalizing routine. The locus of control is different in each case. The learning organization is internally controlled during its process of emergence. It is pulled by the visions and shared sense of mission of its founders. The performance organization, on the other hand, becomes increasingly externally controlled—constrained—as it becomes successful.

Although investors may applaud the replacement of the entrepreneurs by professional managers, the risk is that the performance structures that managers perpetuate may render the organization dangerously insensitive to subtle changes in the environment. Short-term results may be excellent, but the seeds of failure may be hidden in the fruits of success. The reasons for this are discussed in Chapter 5.

In business practice, the mutual interference between learning and performance is further aggravated by all kinds of fluctuations in the economy. Ideally, the product of learning, strategy, should be expressed in performance, and the results of that performance should be fed back into the learning organization, as shown in Figure 2-3.

Optimal learning takes place when the gap between action and result is as short as possible in time and space. Then cause and effect can be closely linked and mistakes easily learned from. In practice, however, this virtuous cycle is interrupted by the alternating periods of growth and decline that characterize all economies. During periods of extended growth—whether they be cyclical or secular, economywide or restricted to an industry—it is very difficult for either managers or anybody else to distinguish objectively between performance that is due to the upcycle and performance that is due to genuine competitive advantage. This gives us some insight into the lopsided attribution to individuals of responsibility for organizational success and failure so often seen in the business press. In business booms, managers will naturally tend to take the credit for the excellent performance of their organizations. Their belief in their ability will almost certainly be reinforced by the workings of the formal compensation system and the applause of the investment community. The genius of the strategy will be confirmed.

Thus, periods of economic growth interrupt the feedback from performance to learning, preventing organizations from evaluating the effectiveness of their strategies. Healthy skepticism about managerial

Figure 2-3 Learning and Performance in Theory

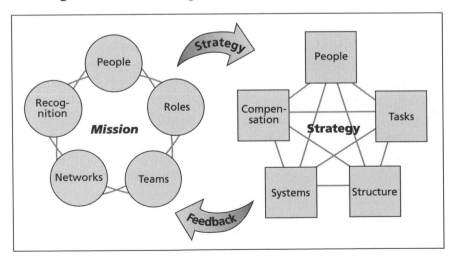

abilities is swept aside by the tangible evidence of what seems to be sustained success. This will be particularly true in organizations that emphasize financial performance over other measures.[29]

The situation is just the reverse in periods of economic decline. Now organizations are overwhelmed by feedback from every action taken during the long upcycle. Panicked by the sudden reversal in their fortunes, unable to assimilate all the information, yet still confident in the appropriateness of their strategies, managers are likely to expend their efforts on frantic attempts to maintain performance rather than cycle through a learning process. Of course, the imperative to maintain performance will be even more urgent if the organization has taken on substantial financial commitments during the good times.

Thus, the long and variable delays between action and result, which are a by-product of the business cycle, create conditions highly unfavorable to learning. The net result is that many organizations, studied longitudinally, display a pattern of apparently outstanding performance followed by steep decline (Figure 2-4). The managerial challenge is to dampen this erratic progress—to sustain performance. A key issue in this challenge is whether it is possible to reverse what appears to be a unidirectional, evolutionary process. Is renewal possible? Can herding organizations learn to behave like hunters again? How can this be done while protecting the core value-adding processes? Can it be done in modern contexts?

All these issues will be addressed in the chapters that follow. The subject of the next chapter is the renewal of an organization in a

Figure 2-4 Learning and Performance in Practice

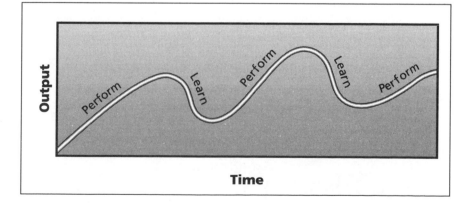

business as far removed from Nike's as one could imagine. It is a mature organization selling a commodity product in a humdrum industry. I had the good fortune to be working for it when we were suddenly pitched into a situation that threatened us with destruction. In our efforts to save the business and our livelihoods, we found ourselves on a pathway to renewal.

3

Boxes and Bubbles

T HE STORY in this chapter is a personal recollection of the experience of a group of managers in a mature organization undergoing profound change. It was this experience that supplied the raw material from which this book began. In the years that have elapsed since the events described here, I have continually gone back to try to understand what happened—to extract the meaning from what at the time was a hectic series of activities offering little opportunity for such reflection. I have used the models of performance and learning organizations developed in Chapter 2 to organize my thoughts, for this is the story of how a performance organization became (at least partially) a learning organization. The precipitating event in

This chapter is an extensively revised version of an article written for the *Harvard Business Review* (Hurst 1984). It has been revised to reflect additional interpretations over the past ten years and to fit in better with the sequence of ideas in this book.

this change was a serious business crisis. The structure of the story is expressed diagrammatically in Figure 3-1.

THE WAY WE WERE

When I joined Hugh Russel Inc. in 1979, it was a medium-sized Canadian distributor of steel and industrial products. With sales of CDN$535 million and three thousand employees, the business was controlled by the chairman, Archie Russel, who owned 16 percent of the common shares. The business consisted of four groups—the core steel distribution activities (called "Russelsteel"), industrial bearings and valves distribution, a chain of wholesalers of hardware and sporting goods, and a small manufacturing business.

The core steel distribution business had its origins in the trading activities of several families of Scottish heritage, who emigrated to Canada in the eighteenth and nineteenth centuries and made their living by trading goods between the "old country" and their chosen land. Over the years, these trading activities developed into local distribution businesses, often dealing in iron, steel, and manufactured goods.

One such family, named Russel, had been in trade for over a hundred years before one of its members founded a small steel distribution business in Montreal in 1936. In 1962, when the company went public, the organization structure was a simple one. Two brothers, Guy and

Figure 3-1 A Performance Organization Becomes a Learning Organization

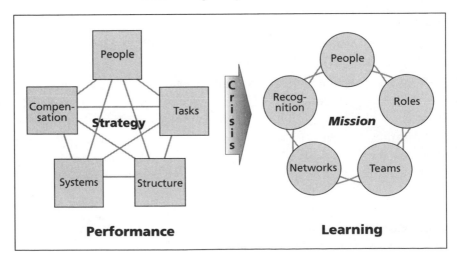

Archie Russel, together with two managers and a controller formed the management team. The company was housed in an old, cramped building in Montreal with the executives and the salesmen (there were no women in sales) crushed together on the same floor.

The old-timers who remembered those days were real "characters." They talked with nostalgia of the informality of the organization, of their various antics, of the laughter and the camaraderie, and of how hard they worked and how little they earned. To me, the social dynamics sounded like those of a hunters' camp. There was no hierarchy, and if anyone tried to pull rank, the office had multiple subtle and not-so-subtle ways of signaling its displeasure and taking revenge. Everyone lived in everyone else's pocket, and no secrets, personal or corporate, could be kept so for long. At the time, Russelsteel was an upstart maverick in the industry, and its people saw themselves as members of a small, aggressive, irreverent, elite group of supersalesmen, capable of outperforming their larger bureaucratic competitors at any time. In short, in those early days, Russelsteel appears to have had all the hallmarks of a learning organization.

Over the next three years, however, Archie Russel became preoccupied with growth and diversification outside the core business. The company had gone public to allow Guy Russel to liquidate his holdings, and Archie was to become the dominant voice. In 1965, as Guy Russel withdrew from day-to-day activities, Archie Russel augmented the management team with the addition of Peter Foster. Foster, an aeronautical engineer and Harvard Business School graduate, had spent fifteen years with Procter & Gamble before running a small conglomerate. He would be responsible for the diversification of Hugh Russel Inc. into areas other than the distribution of steel. The first of many acquisitions outside the core steel distribution business came in 1965.

The company grew in scale during the next few years, and several reorganizations took place as the organization developed into a divisionalized bureaucracy. By 1975, a fully divisionalized organization had emerged, with the Metals Group itself being divisionalized and replicating the structure of the parent company.

The company was structured for performance, and the performance model developed in the previous chapter can be applied to it directly. The management was professional, with each of the divisional hierarchies headed by a group president reporting to Peter Foster in his capacity as president of the corporation. Jobs were described in job descriptions, and their mode of execution was specified in detailed standard operating procedures. Three volumes of the corporate manual spelled out policy on everything from accounting to vacation pay. Extensive accounting and data-processing systems allowed managers to track the progress of individual operations against budgets and plans. Compensation was performance-based, with return on net assets (RONA) as the primary measure and large bonuses (up to 100 percent of base) for managers who made their targets.

At the senior management level, the culture was polite but formal. The board of directors consisted of Archie's friends and associates together with management insiders. Archie and Peter ran the organization as if they were majority owners. Their interaction with management outside of the head office was restricted to the occasional field trip. The head office was the site for the annual five-year planning exercises and the budgeting process, during which the financial targets were negotiated between the divisions, the groups, and the corporate office. The emphasis at these meetings was on performance and growth. The five-year plans had to be formulated within a strategic framework that showed growth opportunities, priorities, and action plans for their achievement. Notwithstanding the espoused rationality of the process, the planning and budgeting sessions were highly stressful events for all concerned. The corporate office tried to set "stretch" targets, raising the sales and profit numbers to which divisional managers "committed," whereas the managers tried to lower these quantities, to get numbers that they could "live with."

It is clear that, by the time I joined Hugh Russel in 1979, the original "hunters" had long since become "herders." People were dedicated to the protection and incremental improvement of existing businesses. Growth prospects for most of these operations were modest, constrained by both competition and the mature nature of the Canadian economy's industrial sector. To achieve their growth targets, senior managers sought to make aggressive acquisitions of other "herding" operations and territories. Once acquired, these operations were often merged with similar existing businesses with the objective of pursuing economies of scale to achieve greater efficiencies.

Although these economies of scale, prominent in the corporation's espoused strategy, were appealed to in the initial justifications of investments, they proved very difficult to realize in practice. Nevertheless, the size of the organization and its impressive financial results, fueled by the business booms of the 1960s and the early 1970s, seemed to justify all that had been done. The senior management, now removed from day-to-day operations, believed that its strategy had been fundamentally correct and that all was now a question of implementation and execution.

CRISIS

Nine months after I joined the company as a financial planner, we were put "in play" by a raider and, after a fierce bidding war, were acquired in a hostile takeover. Our acquirer was a private company controlled by the eldest son of an entrepreneur of legendary wealth and ability, so we had no inkling at the time of the roller-coaster ride that lay ahead of us. We were unaware that not only did the son not have the support of his father in this venture but he had also neglected to consult his two brothers, who were joint owners of the acquiring company! As he had taken on $300 million of debt to do the deal, this left each of the brothers on the hook for a personal guarantee of $100 million. They were not amused, and it showed!

Within days of the deal, we were inundated by waves of consultants, lawyers, and accountants: each shareholder seemed to have his or her own panel of advisers. After six weeks of intensive analysis, it was clear that far too much had been paid for us and that the transaction was vastly overleveraged. At the start of the deal, the acquirer had approached our bankers and asked them if they wanted a piece of the "action." Concerned at the possible loss of our banking business and eager to be associated with such a prominent family, our bankers had agreed to provide the initial financing on a handshake. Now, as they saw the detailed numbers for the first time and became aware of the dissent among the shareholders, they withdrew their support and demanded their money back. We needed to refinance $300 million of debt—fast.

The good news was that, as far as management was concerned, we seemed to be "it." The acquiring business had been run in autocratic style, with seven hundred people apparently reporting to one man! We might be fired individually, but at least the acquirer did not have a management team waiting in the wings. That was the only good news, for interest rates continued to rise, and shortly after the takeover, the Canadian economy fell into a deep recession.

CHANGE

The takeover and the subsequent merger of our new owner's moribund steel-fabricating operations into Hugh Russel changed our agenda completely. We had new shareholders (who fought with each other constantly), new bankers, and new businesses in an environment of soaring interest rates and plummeting demand for our products and services. Almost overnight, the corporation went from a growth-oriented, acquisitive, earnings-driven operation to a cash-starved cripple, desperate to survive. Closures, layoffs, downsizing, delayering, asset sales, and "rationalization" became our new priorities.

In the preceding chapter, we saw how each of the elements of the organization changed as Nike made the transition from being a predominantly learning organization to being a predominantly performance organization: roles became tasks, teams became structure, networks became systems, recognition became compensation, and people changed. The following subsections trace how the elements of Hugh Russel Inc. changed during the converse of that process—as we attempted to make the perilous transition from performance organization to learning organization.

TASKS BECAME ROLES

At the head office, the clarity of jobs vanished. For example, I had been hired to do financial forecasting and raise capital in the equity markets, but with the company a financial basket case, this clearly could not be done. For all of us, the future looked dangerous and frightening as bankruptcy, both personal and corporate, loomed ahead.

And so it was in an atmosphere of crisis that Wayne Mang, the new president (Archie Russel and Peter Foster left the organization soon after the deal), gathered the first group of managers together to discuss the situation. Wayne Mang had been in the steel business for many years and was trusted and respected by the Hugh Russel people. An accountant by training, he used to call himself the "personnel manager" to underscore his belief in both the ability of people to make the difference in the organization and the responsibility of line management to make this happen. The hastily called first meeting consisted of people whom Wayne respected and trusted from all over the organization. They had been selected without regard for their position in the old hierarchy.

The content and style of that first meeting were a revelation to many! Few of them had ever been summoned to the head office for anything but a haranguing over their budgets—"To have the shit kicked out of us," as they put it. Now they were being told the complete gory details of the company's situation and, for the first time, being treated as if they had something to contribute. Wayne asked for their help.

During that first meeting, we counted nineteen major issues confronting the corporation. None of them fell under a single functional area. We arranged ourselves into task forces to deal with them. I say "arranged ourselves" because that was the way it seemed to happen. Individuals volunteered without coercion to work on issues in which they were interested or for which their skills were relevant. They also "volunteered" others who were not at the meeting but, it was thought, could help. There was some guidance—each task force had one person from the head office whose function it was to report what was happening back to the "center"—and some members found themselves on too many task forces, which required that substitutes be found. But that was the extent of the conscious management of the process.

The meeting broke up at 2:00 A.M., when we all went home to tell our incredulous spouses what had happened.

Gradually, as the situation evolved, each of us started to play distinctive roles at these meetings and on the teams. My role became that of facilitator-networker-framemaker: I would develop the team agendas, sit in on the meetings, and frame the process, explaining how I thought the situation was evolving. I became adept at making graphic presentations to bankers, suppliers, and shareholders and dealing with the press.

Every member of the senior management team found himself in a new hyphenated occupation. For example, Al Shkut, a gentle giant of a man from operations, excelled at the execution (literally, in many cases) of our plans to close, downsize, and rationalize many operations. He became our organizer-operator-executor. The team could give Al a general direction on an issue, and he would come back with deadlines, responsibilities, and contingency plans all perfectly laid out. He implemented the plans personally, and they worked flawlessly.

Wayne was our entrepreneur-negotiator-inspirer. In the 1960s, he had had a similar experience with a feuding family in trouble with its bankers, and he knew enough to "expect" the unexpected. On the one hand, there were the shareholders and their families, fighting with each other but individually dangerous and likely to combine at any time against outside threat, imagined or real, to the family. On the other hand, there were the new bankers, with the realization slowly dawning on them that their loans were less than safe. Wayne had a chameleonlike quality that always made you feel that he was on *your* side. I would be at meetings and marvel at his giving what I came to call a "multidimensional" speech. This was a speech in which everyone who listened to it—supplier, banker, shareholder—came out with a very different understanding of what was said, but each feeling curiously comforted that his or her interests had been addressed! A rare gift, but it was enormously helpful as we navigated our way through the political minefields trying to build a consensus for coordinated action among people and groups who had very different interests and priorities.

Looking at this aspect of our experience from the learning/performance perspective developed in Chapter 2, the breaking of the daily routine and the scrapping of our job descriptions freed each of us to "be ourselves," playing roles for which we felt best suited as individuals. The departure of the chairman and his president shattered the old hierarchy, and the formation of all the project teams blurred the boundaries further. On some teams, "senior" managers followed the lead of far more "junior" people. Like the Bushmen in their hunting-foraging mode, leadership within the organization was now much more widely dispersed and emergent, depending upon the situation and the skills needed to deal with it.

STRUCTURE BECAME TEAMS

The cross-functional project team rapidly became our preferred method of organizing new initiatives, and at the head office, the old formal structure virtually disappeared. The teams could be formed at a moment's notice to handle a fast-breaking issue and dissolved just as quickly. We found, for example, that even when we weren't having formal meetings, we seemed to spend most of our time talking to each other informally. Two people would start a conversation in someone's office, and almost before you knew it, others had wandered in and a small group session was going. Later on, we called these events "bubbles"; they became our equivalent of the Bushmen's campfire meetings.

A bubble is a minimalist organization: there is a transparent boundary that separates the inside from the outside, and that's it. Bubbles are temporary, transparent, soft, almost playful structures that cluster together to form easy alliances with each other. In short, they were everything that our old "boxes" were not.

Later, when I became executive vice president, Wayne and I deliberately shared an office so we could each hear what the other was doing in real time and create an environment in which "bubbles" might form spontaneously. As people wandered past our open door, we would wave them in to talk; others would wander in after them. The content of these sessions always had to do with our predicament, both corporate and personal. It was serious stuff, but the atmosphere was light and open. Our fate was potentially a bad one, but at least it would be shared. All of us who were involved then cannot remember ever having laughed so much. We laughed at ourselves and at the desperate situation. We laughed at the foolishness of the bankers in having financed such a mess, and we laughed at the antics of the feuding shareholders, whose outrageous manners and language we learned to mimic to perfection.

I think it was the atmosphere from these informal sessions that gradually permeated all our interactions—with employees, bankers, suppliers, everyone with whom we came into contact. Certainly, we often had tough meetings, filled with tension and threat, but we were always able to "bootstrap" ourselves back up emotionally at the informal debriefings afterward.

I remember one incident, when Wayne had a heated shouting match on the telephone with a senior executive of the bank. It seemed that the banker was threatening to call our loan. The exchange went on for thirty minutes. Through Wayne's open door, the sounds of his voice echoed through the office. Soon everyone's stress level was rising as the ferocity of the confrontation grew. But by the time Wayne slammed down the receiver, two of our colleagues had prepared large scorecards similar to those used by judges at skating and gymnastic events. They awarded him only a "3" for technical merit but gave him a "6" for artistic impression! The rest of us fell about laughing.

We were amazed at the responses of the people on the myriad task forces we had set up. There had been some apprehension at the outset that we would have resignations en masse when people heard about the company's financial condition. Instead, they tackled their projects with a passion we had not seen before, and we lost no one we didn't want to lose. In the old days, the strategic plans had been stamped

"Confidential," and their circulation had been restricted. But now we recognized that this was totally unproductive; the task forces had to know everything. Secrecy is the enemy of trust, and the reaction of our people encouraged us to spread the network of communication even further.

The old divisions had thoroughly distrusted the head office (for good reason!) and had kept it at a comfortable distance. These attitudes softened considerably as we walked around soliciting people's views, listening to what they had to say, and incorporating their concerns into our plans. For the first time, divisional people felt that they were not just an item on someone else's agenda. The old territorial boundaries began to blur.

Perhaps the best example of both the change in structure and the blurring of the boundaries of the organization was our changing relationship with our bankers. In the beginning, at least for the brief time that the loan was in good standing, the association was polite and at arm's length. Communication was formal. As the bank realized the full horror of what it had financed (a process that took about eighteen months), the relationship steadily grew more hostile. Senior executives of the bank became threatening, spelling out what actions they might take if we did not solve our problem. This hostility culminated in an investigation by the bank for possible fraud (a standard procedure in many banks when faced with a significant loss).

Throughout this period, we had seen a succession of different bankers, each of whom had been assigned to our account for a few months. As a result of our efforts to brief every new face that appeared, we had built a significant network of contacts within the bank with whom we had openly shared a good deal of information and opinion. When no fraud was found, the bank polled its own people on what to do. Our views presented so coherently by our people (because everyone knew what was going on), and shared so widely with so many bankers, had an enormous influence on the outcome of this process. The result was the formation of a joint company-bank team to address a shared problem that together we could solve. The boundary between the corporation and the bank was now blurred: to an outside observer, it would have been unclear where the corporation ended and the bank began.

The use of the informal team as our primary vehicle for organizing gave us a flexibility that would have been unattainable with the old bureaucracy. People could come together and redeploy at very short notice, and given the broad sharing of information, minimum briefing was required to get everyone up to speed. In addition, people who experienced problems of any kind on one team could easily switch to another. This substitution of one player for another became essential as teams made progress on their projects and the mixture of skills required began to change. Effectively, we began to function like bands of nomadic hunters. Spread out over the landscape in our issue-driven teams, we could rush resources to any one of them and have people up to speed and functioning with a minimum of delay.

SYSTEMS BECAME NETWORKS

Our corporation had extensive formal reporting systems to allow the monitoring of operations on a regular basis. After the takeover, these systems required substantial modifications. For example, we had to track and forecast cash on a weekly basis. Each of our different audiences seemed to want information in its own idiosyncratic format, and cash conservation became our single most important priority. The management of payables, for example, became a science of its own as we "zoomed" in on the intricacies of the payment process to streamline the collection of cash. But the major change in our use of information was created by our need to address a slew of audiences we had never had to face before.

The primary cause of this was the company's preferred shares, which continued to trade on the stock exchange. Although we had tried to buy them back from the holders at the time of the deal, we had not succeeded in getting them all. This meant that we had to report our results to the public every quarter at a time when we were losing nearly two million dollars a week! We knew that unless we got to our suppliers ahead of time, they could easily panic and refuse us credit. Hasty moves on their part could have had fatal consequences for the business.

In addition, our closure plans for plants all over Canada and the United States brought us into contact with unions and governments in an entirely different way. We realized that we had no option but to deal with these audiences in advance of events.

I have already described how our relationship with the bankers changed as a result of our open communication. We found exactly the same effect with these new audiences. Initially, our major suppliers could not understand why we had told them we were in trouble before we had to. We succeeded, however, in framing the situation in a way that enlisted their cooperation in our survival, and by time the "war story" was news, we had their full support. Similarly, most government and union organizations were so pleased to be involved in the process before announcements were made that they bent over backward to be of assistance. Just as had been the case with the bank, we set up joint task forces with these "outside" agencies to resolve what had become shared problems. A significant contributor to our ability to pull this off was the high quality of our internal communication. Everyone on the teams knew the complete, up-to-date picture of what was happening. An outside agency could talk to anyone on a team and get the same story. In this way, we constructed a formidable network of contacts, many of whom had special skills and experience in areas that would turn out to be of great help to us in the future.

The addition of multiple networks to our information systems enhanced our ability both to gather and to disseminate information. The informality and openness of the networks, together with the high volume of face-to-face dialogues, resembled the Bushmen's meetings held around their cooking fires. We had an early warning system with which to detect hurt feelings and possible hostile moves on the part of shareholders, suppliers, nervous bankers, and even customers. This information helped us head off trouble before it happened. The networks also acted as a broadcast system through which we could test plans and actions before announcing them formally. In this way, we not only got excellent suggestions for improvement, but everyone felt that he or she had been consulted before action was taken.

PEOPLE CHANGED

The most striking feature of the transformation that was taking place in the corporation was the changing attitude of the people. We found this happening both inside and outside the organization. It was first brought home to us when we were out in Winnipeg, reporting our terrible financial results to a mass meeting of all the people in one operation. About fifteen minutes after the meeting ended, one of the lead hands in the warehouse approached Wayne Mang and said, "Look, I've been talking with the boys and we wondered whether it would help if we took a 10 percent reduction in pay?" The offer made no logical sense: the savings were minuscule compared with the sums of money we needed, but it spoke volumes about the commitment that the group felt to the company. Such behavior was based upon shared values rather than logic, and the story of it spread around the organization like wildfire, bolstering the "volunteer" spirit among all employees. The corporation's predicament and our requests for help seemed to have evoked a new cooperative atmosphere in the organization.

We had a similar experience with a group of people outside the company during the hectic last six months of 1983, when we were trying to finalize a deal for the shareholders and bankers to sell the steel distribution business to new owners. The group of people in question comprised the secretaries of the numerous lawyers and accountants involved in the deal. If one thinks about it, it takes only a moment to realize that many professionals are not the managers of their time. They do the work—reading and writing documents, researching points of law and principle, briefing clients—but they do not determine their priorities in real time. This is done by their secretaries, who largely determine to whom they speak, what documents get on their desks, and when things happen.

We made these secretaries part of the network, briefing them in advance on the situation, explaining why things were needed, and keeping them updated on the progress of the deal. We were astounded at the cooperation we received: our calls were put through, our messages received prompt responses, drafts and opinions were produced on time. In the final event, a complex deal that should have taken nine months to complete was done in three. All of this was accomplished by ordinary people going far beyond what might have been expected of them.

The change we observed in people's behavior was their response to the breaking down of their boxes—the boundaries that isolated them in their specialist functions. Like the Bushman hunters, by becoming involved in the different activities of the various teams, they had the opportunity to learn from others and practice new skills—to become multiskilled and play leadership roles. Some, for the first time in their working careers, felt that they were making a real contribution to an organization that actually needed them. We were asking people to think, to engage their whole brain, and they responded with enthusiasm.

COMPENSATION BECAME RECOGNITION

The company's formal compensation system had been performance-based, with significant bonuses to be made from hitting RONA targets. Base salaries were adjusted after formal annual performance reviews.

This compensation system collapsed very quickly. The recession and the rationalization of operations removed any possibility of bonuses. Performance reviews were suspended, and across the company, base salaries were frozen and, in some cases, rolled back. Yet the organization did not disintegrate. If anything, morale went up.

The team had discussed the implementation of the freezes and rollbacks with trepidation. The money saved made very little difference to the corporation's ability to survive, and the fear was that people would be totally demotivated. Nevertheless, we had to send the bankers and shareholders a message that we were serious, and the cuts were implemented.

Probably because the freezes and cuts were implemented across the board, there was a sense of shared contribution. I think every manager finds that it is *relative* compensation that causes all the problems in an organization. You can get away with paying people in the company at the fortieth percentile for their jobs and they will accept it. But let them find out that one of the group is getting a thousand dollars a year more and it corrodes the whole structure. Thus, the fact that we had made a *shared* sacrifice softened the loss of the real dollars.

In some perverse way, the place was fun to work in by now. Many of us felt part of an exciting adventure in which everything we did or saw was potentially significant. Every day one looked forward to coming in to follow the twists and turns as the story unfolded. There was a shared recognition that this was an extraordinary time and that we were learning both as individuals and as an organization.

It was the *shared* nature of the hardship that probably accounted for the favorable effects of the across-the-board freezes. The move underscored the fact that, like the Bushmen, we were mutually dependent, each on the other. Our fate would be a shared one. In the past, it had often seemed that the upper levels of the hierarchy were insulated from hardship; now it was clear that no one was exempt. We were a much more egalitarian community than we had ever been before, and this new ethos was affirmed daily by our behavior.

STRATEGY EMERGED

We had been thrust into crisis without warning, and our initial activities were almost entirely reactions to issues that imposed themselves upon us. But as we muddled along in the task forces, we began to find that we had unexpected sources of influence over what was happening.

The changing relationship with the bank illustrates this neatly. Although we had no formal power in that situation, we found that by framing a confusing predicament in a coherent way, we could, via our network, influence the outcomes of the bank's decisions. The same applied to suppliers: by briefing them ahead of time and presenting a reasonable scenario for the recovery of their advances, we could influence the decisions they would make.

Slowly we began to realize that, although we were powerless in a formal sense, our networks, together with our own internal coherence, gave us an ability to get things done invisibly. As we discussed the situation with all the parties involved, a strategy began to emerge. A complicated financial/tax structure would allow the bank to "manage" its loss and give it an incentive not to call on the shareholders' personal guarantees. The core steel distribution business could be refinanced in the process and sold to new owners. The wrangle between the shareholders could be resolved, and each could go his or her own way. All that had to be done was to bring all the parties together, including a buyer for the steel business, and have them agree that this was the best course to follow. Using our newfound skills, we managed to pull it off.

It was not without excitement: at the last minute, the shareholders raised further objections to the deal. Only the bank could make them sell, and they were reluctant to do so, fearful that they might attract a lawsuit. Discreet calls to the major suppliers, several of whose executives were on the board of the bank, did the trick. "This business needs to be sold and recapitalized," the suppliers were told. "If the deal does not go through, you should probably reduce your credit exposure." The deal went through. By the end of 1983, we had new owners, just in time to benefit from the general business recovery. The ordeal was over, for a while.

SUMMARY OF THE CONDITIONS UNDER WHICH CHANGE OCCURRED

The experience of Hugh Russel Inc. from 1982 to 1983 does represent a significant organizational transformation, but in some ways, it was a limited one. Although the change seemed wrenching and pervasive, the focus of all the change attempts was on the corporate vehicle and its holdings, and essentially, it was only the corporate office that underwent the change. The head office of an organization is inherently less routinized than most of its other parts, particularly the roles of senior managers. Some basic routines were changed, but they involved paper flows, form designs, and some minor computer programs.

In operations, the great integrated routines that underpin any efficient bureaucracy remained intact. The technology, systems, and procedures for buying, storing, processing, and selling steel stayed the same. Even the formal organization structure, which had been softened somewhat by the new attitude at the head office, remained in the background at all times. In retrospect, it is clear that we had been through a relatively "easy" transformation. As we will see in the later chapters, the comprehensive renewal of an entire organization is much more challenging!

Although the scale of the transformation was modest, the conditions under which the change took place do bear examination. These conditions were as follows:

1. *Crisis:* There was a manifest failure of the status quo that could not be rationalized away or denied. The organization could not sustain itself financially without radical change. Smaller crises helped catalyze action throughout the period of instability.
2. *Removal of the old guard:* Archie Russel and Peter Foster, who dominated and sustained the organizational hierarchy, left the scene fairly quickly. This shattered the routines of the head office and allowed new processes a free rein.
3. *Emergent leadership:* Wayne Mang had credibility with the people in the organization as well as a large network of contacts, and he had developed some essential skills in situations similar to the one facing the corporation. His leadership was authoritative rather than authoritarian. During the teamwork that followed the crisis, similar leaders emerged on a smaller scale all over the organization.
4. *Open communication:* Communication in the old hierarchy had been vertical and highly restricted. Much confidential information was held at the top. This changed with the need to brief the myriad task forces and to respond to the many pressing issues.
5. *A shared mission:* Out of the intensive communication and the work done together in teams, there emerged a deep sense of shared purpose among everyone involved. No one had any doubt as to what the mission was—to rescue the good businesses and refinance them—and we all pulled toward its achievement.

6. *Flexible people:* The people central to the change process were versatile, with a number of task and process skills. When they did not have a required skill, their flexibility extended to being able to co-opt and work with those who did and to defer to the leadership of others who were better equipped to deal with the situation at hand. Like the hunting Bushmen, they could flip from leader to follower without feeling demotivated.

7. *Cross-functional teams:* The teams that were formed to deal with issues were usually composed of people from a number of different functions and levels in the formal organization. The pervasive use of these teams had the effect of "delayering" the hierarchy. In combination with the broad communication, this meant that many more decisions were made lower in the formal organization.

8. *Blurring of the boundaries:* A key to the transformation process was the blurring of boundaries, both within and outside the organization. This had the effect of redefining the organization. Groups that would otherwise have pursued their own separate, often mutually destructive goals made common cause with each other.

9. *Networks:* Extensive networks were developed based on shared purposes and mutual reciprocity. This evoked a spirit of cooperation and trust. Significant contributors toward the development of trust were the elimination of secrecy, the sharing of personal feelings, and the use of humor to defuse tense situations.

In short, Hugh Russel Inc., the quintessential herder, had become a hunter—at least at the head office. *Although the change seemed to be as much spontaneous as planned, the key had been the fact that management responded to crisis by creating new contexts for action and that senior management had modeled the desired new, egalitarian behaviors.* The social dynamics that emerged closely resembled both those of the Bushmen in their hunting mode and those of enterprises such as Nike in their entrepreneurial, learning phase.

LEGITIMIZATION OF A NEW CORPORATE CULTURE

We emerged from the crisis with a sense of coherence and identity as an organization that none of us on the team had ever experienced before. We had a shared sense of mission and purpose that "infected" everyone who came into contact with the organization. When we looked at our old Russelsteel logo, we decided that it no longer reflected who we were or what our objectives were, so we came up with a new one, which soon appeared everywhere to reflect our new corporate identity (Figure 3-2).

The legend beneath the new logo read:

> Steel in its many shapes and sizes provides the inspiration for the Russelsteel Inc. logo, but the shapes have a deeper symbolic meaning. The alchemists of the Middle Ages regarded the squared circle as the ultimate unity in which all opposites were joined.
>
> For us at Russelsteel our logo also represents the unity of opposites for which we all strive: product and service, quality and value, price and performance.
>
> This is achieved by the unity of opposites in our management approach: by the use of teams we bring out the best in everyone.[1]

The new ways of behavior were legitimized at first by the behavior of the senior management team, but after a while, they became supported conceptually by the development of new language, culminating in the development of the new logo. There were the informal "bubble" processes that contrasted with the formal, hierarchical boxes. When trying to reach consensus on complex issues, we found that we often had to wait to allow key players to come on board. We called this a "creative stall." When faced with what appeared to be outrageous proposals in a task force, we learned to "hum" a lot, to give the idea

Figure 3-2 The Two Logos

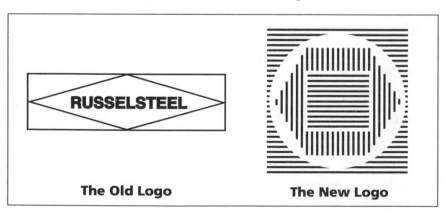

The Old Logo   **The New Logo**

a chance to evolve. Our new peripatetic management style was dubbed "managing by wandering around," and so on.

In short, it seemed that in response to the crisis, we had created a "microclimate," a context in which a new culture had flourished. There were new norms of behavior—such as being able to wander into an office while a meeting was in progress—and new ways of thinking about the world. The new culture did not replace the old hierarchy, but it was thoroughly interwoven with it.

What was even more surprising was how naturally everything had happened. Once we had created the "right" climate, the system seemed to organize itself. This was most noticeable at times when events seemed to flow without our intervention. In the old days, via action plans and artificially imposed deadlines, we had "ridden herd" to get projects done on time. Things certainly happened, but often the outcomes were less than satisfactory. Now, in the new climate, things just seemed to work out without our intervention. In retrospect, this was the first time that we became aware of the self-organizing properties of human systems, without being able to name the phenomenon explicitly.[2]

AN EMERGING MODEL OF CHANGE

The story of the renewal of Russelsteel resonates with the account of the hunting Bushmen and the sad tale of their transformation into herders and farmers. In our case, we were able to reverse the aging process, at least for a while. For it seems likely that renewal is not a one-shot affair but an ongoing process—a continual struggle. We can start to develop a model of the process of organizational change, a rhythm of renewal. Presented in a preliminary way here, the model shown in Figure 3-3 will be developed throughout the remainder of the book.

The model consists of two loops that intersect to form an infinity symbol. The loop with the solid line is the conventional S-shaped life cycle. The dotted line is a reverse S: it represents the process of renewal. To illustrate how the model works, it is helpful to track the progress of Russelsteel around the entire cycle.

In the early years, in the crammed offices in Montreal, there is a simple rationale to the steel business, together with a culture and an environment that encourage spontaneous behavior and learning. Activities seem to be emergent rather than planned (stage 1). The

Figure 3-3 A Model of Organizational Change

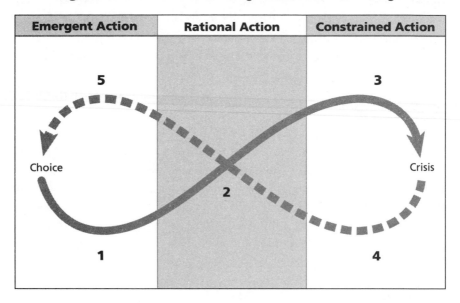

Emergent Action	Rational Action	Constrained Action

business prospers and grows, becoming larger and somewhat more structured in the process. After a few years, a new logic is imposed from the top by senior managers—a deliberate strategy of diversification and growth through acquisition (stage 2). This is followed by significant growth in revenues and income, accompanied by a steady increase in the scale of the organization (the business had grown from CDN$14 million in sales in 1962 to CDN$535 million when I joined in 1979). Eventually, this leads to a loss of control on the part of the managers within Hugh Russel, when the company is acquired by an outsider.

The behavior of all actors, including that of the bankers, becomes constrained soon after the acquisition, as the company gets into problems (stage 3) brought upon it by the uncompetitiveness of many of the individual operations, excessive reliance on debt, and a severe economic recession. This leads to a major financial crisis that threatens the survival of the organization.

The crisis seems to shatter all kinds of constraints on the actors (stage 4): hierarchy is flattened within the business, the bank scraps its policy manuals, the unions decide to support the management in its efforts to save the company, new information channels are opened, and so on. This is accompanied by a radical "downsizing" as the newly defined "noncore" operations are either closed or sold and the "core" operations are reduced in size (by the time they were sold at the end of 1983, the core operations had sales of only CDN$220 million). In the resulting "space," management action seems to take on an emergent character again (stage 5). There is a renewed devotion to the old business of steel distribution reminiscent of the way things were in the early 1960s. The capacity to choose is now restored, although the business is significantly larger in scale than it was in those early years.

During the renewal cycle, there is little hierarchy and no shared logic to coordinate the organization. Why do people stay together during the traumatic transition from stage 3 to stage 5? The short answer, based upon our experience at Hugh Russel, is "leadership" and "shared values." But these are descriptions rather than explanations. What is "leadership"? How do values become "shared"? In the next chapter, I will explore these questions in a very different, much larger scale context during one of the most innovative periods in the history of business—that of the English industrial revolution.

4

Hunters of the Spirit

T HE PREVIOUS chapter told the story of the radical change in an organization from a performance-focused bureaucracy to an open, flexible structure more oriented toward learning. After precipitation by a crisis, the process of renewal was begun by the introduction of social dynamics very similar to those found among the Bushmen in their hunting mode.

This chapter tells a story of organizational renewal on a broader canvas in a different place and at another time. It is an examination of the part played by the Quakers—or the Society of Friends, as they came to be known—in the English industrial revolution. Its value to managers is that it shows us how a social and political crisis (the English Civil War) allowed "hunting" social dynamics to be realized in a very different context. The broad perspective gives us a more comprehensive view of the process of renewal.

At the same time, the story of the Quakers makes it clear that the study of the contexts of large-scale renewals such as the English industrial revolution has been much neglected. Our retrospective explanations of the causes of this radical change in a whole society—the Protestant ethic, high achievement motivation,[1] a zeal for education[2]—have been uniformly unsatisfactory. They are overly rational, too individualistic, and worst of all, impossible to replicate in modern contexts. For unless these traits have genetic roots, appeals to them are descriptions, not explanations.

What were the contexts that evoked such behaviors from ordinary people? Under what circumstances did the revolution begin? How was it sustained, and why did it eventually slacken? I will argue that the social dynamics are critical to an understanding of all these questions. For the Quakers did not start off with an intellectual vision of how the world should look. They did not set out either to accumulate material wealth or to be spiritually saved. Instead, they had a *social* vision of how people should behave toward each other, and they set out to live their assertively egalitarian "hunting" values every day. Along the way, they came to exemplify what Max Weber would later call the "Spirit of Capitalism." That is why I have called them "hunters of the spirit."

THE ENGLISH INDUSTRIAL REVOLUTION

The English industrial revolution is recognized as one of the most profound societal transformations in history:

> In a short span of years . . . the face of England changed. Areas that for centuries had been cultivated as open fields, or had lain untended as common pasture, were hedged or fenced; hamlets grew into populous towns; and chimney stacks rose to dwarf the ancient spires. Highroads were made. . . . [T]he North and Irish Seas, and the navigable reaches of the Mersey, Ouse, Severn, Thames, Forth and Clyde were joined together. . . . [I]n the North the first iron rails were laid down for the new locomotives, and steam packets began to ply on the estuaries and the narrow seas.
>
> Parallel changes took place in the structure of society. The number of people increased vastly. . . . [T]he growth of communities shifted the balance of population from the South and East to the North and Midlands. . . . [W]ork grew to be more specialized; new forms of skill were developed. . . . [L]abour became more mobile. . . . Capital increased

in volume. . . . [T]he currency was set on a gold base; a banking system came into being. . . . Ideas of innovation and progress undermined traditional sanctions: men began to look forward, rather than backward, and their thoughts as to the nature and purpose of social life were transformed.[3]

Why did this change happen, at that time and in those places? Many reasons have been advanced. The best known of these is the "Protestant ethic," first proposed by Max Weber.[4] The shorthand version of this view is that capitalism was invented by people who had strong beliefs about the accumulation of possessions as a sign of God's blessing and worked hard in order to be saved.[5] As will become clear, this does not explain the behavior of the Quakers.

A second problem is that the term *Protestant* is at once both too narrow and too broad. It is too narrow in that many non-Protestant cultures and groups have been involved in the evolution of capitalism.[6] So clearly, Protestant beliefs are not a necessary precondition. In the case of the English industrial revolution, the term *Protestant* is far too broad—at least, as we understand it today. For the dominant roles in the revolution were played by people who had protested against Queen Elizabeth's compromise religion. They were the Puritans, later described as Dissenters or Nonconformists, and the large part they played in the transformation of English society was out of all proportion to their numbers in the population. It is estimated that over a third of the innovators during the industrial revolution in Britain were Nonconformists of various kinds; yet Nonconformists comprised less than 8 percent of the population.[7] According to a random survey of successful entrepreneurs taken in England at the end of the eighteenth century, 49 percent were Dissenters.[8]

The main dissenting denominations were the Presbyterians, the Congregationalists, the Baptists, and the Quakers. Although the Quakers were one of the smallest of the Puritan sects and never comprised much more than 1 percent of the total population, they were to make one of the largest contributions of any religious denomination to the English industrial revolution.

The backdrop to the industrial revolution was forty years of political, religious, and social turmoil that culminated in the Civil War of the 1640s and the execution of Charles I in 1649 (one way of getting rid of the old guard!). Politically, the struggle had been between absolutist monarchs, who insisted on their rights, and Parliament, which was no longer prepared to be ignored. The religious situation was more complicated. Henry VIII had started the English Reformation for religious, political, and personal reasons (his wish to divorce his first wife, Catharine of Aragon). His daughter by Catharine, Mary Tudor (also known as Bloody Mary), had reversed the process and changed the state religion back to Catholicism. Elizabeth I, his daughter by Anne Boleyn, had switched it back to Anglican again.

To make matters even more confusing, a significant group of people (the Puritans) felt that the Anglicans had retained far too much of the Catholic doctrine, rites, and organization. The Puritan sects focused on the ancient doctrine of the Christian calling and the direct relation between God and the individual. They rejected the rituals and sacraments of the established church and refused to acknowledge the authority of the bishops.

Add to this scene a severe agricultural depression, and the social consequences can be imagined. The society was in a ferment, and the countryside was full of strangers. Radical religious and political groups such as the Arians, Anabaptists, Baptists, Diggers, Fifth Monarchy Men, Levelers, Ranters, and many others flourished. The times were full of portents, and itinerant preachers delivered their apocalyptic visions to receptive audiences.

One such preacher was George Fox, a charismatic leader and a brilliant, fiery preacher with a new vision for society. From 1650 onward, he traveled around the north of England, gathering followers who were attracted everywhere to his simple message and its radical implications for how people should live together. With Robert Barclay and William Penn,[9] Fox would become the spiritual leader of the Society of Friends—or Quakers, as they were initially called.

QUAKER BELIEFS AND VALUES

Robert Barclay once wrote that there were three forms of Christianity: Catholicism, Protestantism, and Quakerism.[10] In his view, the first depended upon the authority of the church and the second upon the authority of the text (the Old Testament), whereas Quakerism depended upon the authority of the spirit. The Quakers believed that what counted was the individual's experience of the spirit, unmediated by priest or text, and that this experience could be realized only in a group context.[11]

The Quakers were also fond of calling themselves "New Testament" Christians, contrasting their egalitarian treatment of men and women with the patriarchal habits of the Protestants, which, the Quakers contended, stemmed from their reliance on the Old Testament. Their favorite gospel was John, particularly the Sermon on the Mount, for in their view, the other three gospels were too concerned with the historical Christ.[12] Only John wrote of an eternal Christ available to all in the here and now. A direct consequence of this belief was the characteristic structure of all Quaker meetings (no distinction was ever made between business and religious meetings): there was no agenda, and the meeting remained in silence until a member felt moved by a "concern" to speak.

To modern managers, with our packed agendas and prepared statements, this sounds like an incredibly inefficient way to run meetings, but efficiency was not the objective. The structure ensured that issues of genuine importance were raised and discussed in open dialogue. The absence of an agenda prevented predigested issues, historical structures, and verbal formulations from dominating the dialogue. George Fox rejected the reliability of intellectual, "head knowledge" as he called it: every Quaker had to "feel" his or her own way to the spirit.[13]

It is this emphasis of Quakerism on nonintellectual modes of understanding that gives it much in common with Eastern religions. Indeed, it is this feature that also interferes with the ability of our Western minds to appreciate Quakerism.[14] The Quakers were to take their values of honesty, equality, simplicity, and peace and live them absolutely. And it was their devotion to their values that would change the structure of society.[15]

This attitude would often have unexpected effects. Quakers would not tolerate dissembling behavior of any kind. For them, acting and the law were suspect professions, because both actors and lawyers were required to behave unauthentically—to project views that they did not truly hold and emotions that they did not really feel. It seems that the Quakers had the surprisingly modern view, reinforced today by TV dramas, that the playhouse and the courthouse were one! Thus, the first Quaker shopkeepers felt it was dishonest to bargain over prices, to put a false price on goods, or to charge two customers a different price for the same goods. This policy was greeted with scorn and derision by their competitors when it was first introduced. But the customers beat a path to the Quakers' stores, and soon everyone had to follow suit. Thus, the Quakers may have invented the concept of the price tag and the market price. It is interesting to note that although these innovations were *sustained* by market forces, they were *initiated* by ethical considerations.

REJECTION OF AUTHORITY

The Quakers rejected established authority of all kinds. They would not pay tithes to the church or take their hats off to acknowledge superiors (perform "hat honour," as they called it).[16] Neither would they swear oaths, many of which were required at the time. Their rejection of what they saw as a pagan past even extended to changing the names of the days and months. Sunday became First Day; January became First Month.

It was their refusal to swear oaths and pay tithes that got them into trouble with the authorities. While Oliver Cromwell (1599–1658) was alive, even the most radical Puritans were somewhat protected from sanctions, but with the Restoration of the monarchy, persecution began in earnest. Quakers were arrested and imprisoned for their failure to pay tithes, and their possessions were confiscated. The Quakers quickly gravitated toward trade and the towns: tithes were levied on land, and penalties for nonpayment took the form of the confiscation of animals and implements. The delayed nature of the returns from farming meant that periods of imprisonment could occur at critical times. Trade, in contrast, offered faster returns and was less vulnerable to disruption: inventories could be replaced, and a man's wife could carry on the business while he was in prison.

Their refusal to swear oaths meant that the Quakers could not hold university posts or trade in incorporated towns. Neither could they use the courts to collect monies owed to them. As a result, the Quakers moved away from the southeast of England to the noncorporate towns of Birmingham, Bristol, Liverpool, Manchester, and York. These places were usually Nonconformist and freethinking, and far away from the establishment influences of London. Here they traded with people they knew they could trust to pay their debts. Lacking faith in joint-stock corporations, they preferred partnerships. Their partners were usually fellow Quakers.

ASSERTIVE EGALITARIANISM

With the Quakers' rejection of authority, there went an assertive egalitarianism. In their view, because of their focus on the individual, anyone of whatever religion could have access to the spirit. This was a major break with the beliefs of other Puritans.[17]

I have already mentioned the equality between men and women. Many Quaker women played a prominent role in business, often learning to do so on the job, while their husbands were in prison. With no priests, marriages were conducted before the meetings and sealed by affirmation. Women could refuse any union and did not take a vow of obedience to their husbands. Although the Quakers' philosophical insistence on equality between men and women may have been limited in practice, it is undeniable that Quaker women performed astonishing feats for that (and most other) times. They preached, wrote tracts, traveled in the ministry, often to far-off lands, and later on, played leading roles in social reforms of all kinds.[18]

Quaker egalitarianism extended to all vocations, and none was regarded as menial. There were no class distinctions. Within their comprehensive apprenticeship system, Quaker apprentices could, upon graduation, aspire to marry their masters' daughters, and many of them did. This had the effect of extending the Quaker network.

FLEXIBLE DYNAMICS

George Fox set the model for the Quaker dynamic with his travels all over the north of England speaking to "Seekers" in many places. Quakers were encouraged to travel in the ministry, and by 1654, there were at least sixty preachers traveling in England and Wales. The wool farmers in the hills of this region, unlike crop farmers, were not self-sufficient and needed to exchange their wool products for other necessities. As a result, each market town had a small trading network centered on it. The Quaker "teams" (they often traveled together) on their regular travels were ideally situated to integrate these networks to form larger systems. The Friends soon developed a unique source of news and ideas available only to members of the Society.

We talk today of the age of information, contrasting it with the age of the machine, but it seems that information must have played an enormously significant role in the Quakers' success in the industrial revolution! Perhaps things do not change as much as we think they do.

Social fusion came from two sources and was intensified by political persecution. The first source of fusion was the Quaker meetings, which emerged from the need to coordinate the activities of some of the more radical Friends and to take care of the dependents of those who were in prison. Soon weekly, monthly, quarterly, and annual meetings were instituted. Groups of Friends would come together to discuss both spiritual and secular matters. The practice of visitation—attending meetings outside of one's own area—became common. Wherever they were from, Friends were always welcome at meetings.

The other source of fusion was the regular imprisonment of Quakers for offenses of all kinds. Friends were likely to be incarcerated with other Friends as well as with the persecuted of all religious backgrounds. It would seem highly likely that these periods of imprisonment offered tremendous opportunities for Quakers both to bond with each other and to spread their views.[19]

The picture that one has of the social dynamics of the early Quaker community is rather like that of the Bushman bands in their nomadic hunting mode. The "structures" are stable, but the elements that comprise them are in a constant state of flux and flow.

MUTUAL DEPENDENCE

The Quakers' group dynamics emerged directly from their religious beliefs, as they sought to avoid both pure individualism and majority rule. Quaker meetings never voted, for this would have short-circuited the process of finding the "sense of the meeting" and placed too heavy an emphasis on verbal formulations. Instead, they waited—"waiting upon the Lord" was the phrase used most often to describe the process.[20] Their communion with the spirit did not take place via external sacraments but was with each other, as they searched for that feeling of unity and mutuality that they sometimes called a "gathered" meeting.

The relationship that the Quakers sought between individuals is best described by what existentialist philosopher Martin Buber has called an "I-Thou" or "I-You" relationship (the Quakers always used "thou" when addressing each other).[21] The "I-You" is a subject-subject relationship. This is in contrast with the subject-object, "I-It," relationship (and its corollary "I-I"), with which we are more familiar.[22]

In short, it is a relationship of mutual dependence. The relationship is not only capable of changing its polarity but is *defined* by its capacity to do so. This is unlike the "I-It" relationship, which always runs in the same direction: an "It" is always an "It." The relationship between Quaker individuals thus resembles that between leader and follower in a nomadic hunting band: sometimes I lead, sometimes it's you.

It may seem strange to the reader for me to be discussing religious feelings in a management book, but the Quakers did not distinguish between religion and business. Their business meetings were not secular, but a special kind of worship that, like all other meetings, began in silence. The mutual dependence of Quakers, each upon the other, was always expressed in their behavior at the meetings and had been underscored in the early years by their persistent persecution and imprisonment. Funds raised at monthly and quarterly meetings were regularly used to replace tools and inventories confiscated by the authorities. As persecution began to diminish, the meetings became sources of advice and counsel from people in the same trade, with the concern that trade practice always reflect principles of Quaker belief. If a Friend were to get into financial trouble, a small group would analyze the books of the business and, like management consultants, advise on the best course of action. For outsiders, who were not familiar with the value system, the requirements of the meetings for honesty, plain dealing, and trading within one's capital became their assurance of the enterprise's trustworthiness.

The Quaker meetings became developers of people under the "care of the meeting." In trade, apprentices would be taken on as shop assistants, and funds were supplied by the meeting for their training. When they were qualified, funds would also be made available to be used as working capital to set them up in their own store.[23]

One can see, then, in the Quaker business meetings, the direct expression of their values, especially that of mutual dependence. The reliance of outsiders upon this process probably constitutes the origins of our modern corporate system of governance in the Western world. In many, if not most, companies today, however, the values behind the process seem to have been lost. We have retained the methods but forgotten the principles. This exploration of the founding belief system helps one realize how much has been lost.

INDIVIDUAL SELF-DIRECTION

Individual self-direction in the Society in matters both spiritual and practical was inculcated from the beginning. With no professional clergy, every woman and man was encouraged to find her or his own way to the inward light. Quakers rejected the doctrine of original sin and hence the need for baptism. In their view, children were born innocent and remained in that state until they reached an age of reason.

As one might expect, however, the education of their children went far beyond the teaching of "head knowledge." The onus on the parents was first to set good examples because learning by watching and emulation was far more powerful than exhortation. Far more than book learning, education meant the acquisition of virtuous habits. It took place in a secluded environment, first in the home and later in a meeting-controlled school with a Quaker teacher and Quaker classmates.[24]

In practical matters, the training for self-direction and learning by watching and doing were most evident in the Quakers' comprehensive apprenticeship system. They rejected the authority of the churches in this area and made the training of apprentices the business of the monthly and quarterly meetings, paying particular attention to the employment of poor children. This process turned out to be a forerunner of what we would today call the development of human resources—except that, in the case of the Quakers, the process served not a single organization but an entire network of enterprises. The apprentice system became the primary source of young, well-trained, ethically sound people who were to sustain Quaker businesses from generation to generation.

Thus, toward the end of the seventeenth century, a fringe community operating on the social and geographical margins of English society began to build an extensive network of information and trade, underpinned by shared values and mutual trust. They would exercise an influence out of all proportion to their numbers, with this network playing a central role in innovation, both of products and of services. The Quakers took the lead in the development of the most important technologies of the times and created some of the first consumer mass markets that society had ever seen. Nowhere is their influence clearer than it is in the spiritual birthplace of the revolution, in Coalbrookdale.

COALBROOKDALE: THE "SILICON VALLEY" OF THE REVOLUTION

In the eighteenth century, Coalbrookdale,[25] located in Shropshire on the river Severn, was the most heavily industrialized valley in the world. It was also a hotbed of innovation, the Silicon Valley of the English industrial revolution. Of course, back then the new "miracle" material was not silicon; it was iron. Iron had been made and used for centuries, but the methods of manufacture had not changed much, and it was both expensive and of indifferent quality. In Coalbrookdale, the manufacture of iron would be revolutionized, and its use would become widespread. For over 150 years, from the early 1700s onward, products and innovations from the valley would have a profound influence all over England and the industrializing world.

Throughout this period, several generations of a Quaker family by the name of Darby were involved with Coalbrookdale and the production of iron. Four of the men in the Darby "dynasty" were named Abraham. Their involvement was not continuous; Abrahams I and III died before they were forty, and Abraham II lived for only fifty-two years. As a result, upon their deaths, their children were too young to succeed them. Management of the enterprise during these periods was given to other members of the family until the young Darbys were of an age to get involved in the business. All of these managers were Quakers. Indeed, until the nineteenth century, the entire management group as well as some of the workers were Quakers. This fact in itself is probably a clue to the sustained creativity of the business: throughout this period, management was always in the hands of young, well-trained people who, although they shared the values of the founders, had little investment in the status quo. This trait, coupled with Quaker curiosity, inculcated from the start of their education, led them to spend their time in incessant tinkering and experimentation to improve the business.

Abraham Darby I (1678–1717) started the business in 1709. The son of a clockmaker, he had been apprenticed at Bristol in the malting business. Although the Quakers frowned upon the use of hard liquor, they were great brewers, and the grains used to make beer had to be malted before use. Part of this process involved kiln drying of the crop, using coke as a clean-burning fuel. It is highly likely that this is how Abraham I initially became familiar with the use of coke in this way. His location in Bristol would also have given him invaluable introductions to the network of Quaker traders there. An unincorporated town, Bristol had attracted Quakers from the beginning. Its location on the west coast of England made it a center of the wool trade and commerce with the Americas. Situated in the estuary of the river Severn, it had made that river one of the busiest waterways in the country. The Quaker traders in Bristol would become some of Coalbrookdale's largest customers for the export of iron products all over the world.

Once he had finished his apprenticeship, Abraham Darby became involved with several local Quakers in the setting up of a brassworks. Why he should have done this is unclear. Perhaps, in Bristol, he had met members of the Champion family, Quakers who were already heavily involved in the brass business. Later they would become one of his major customers. In any event, this curious cross-industry experience would allow Abraham Darby to revolutionize the production of iron and its manufacture into all kinds of products. For in the early eighteenth century, iron was still made using charcoal as a fuel. As the demand for iron grew, the forests were being depleted at a huge rate, requiring ironmakers to forage farther and farther afield to feed their furnaces. The price of charcoal was soaring, and indeed, the British Navy was concerned that it would not have enough oak trees to make warships. In those days, wood was a strategic material! Thus, iron was expensive and used mainly in bar form for nails, horseshoes, chains, door hardware, and swords and muskets. No one knew how to cast it into thin-walled hollowware.

In 1705, Abraham Darby traveled to Holland to study the casting of pots and pans in brass. In England at that time, pots and pans of brass were imported from Holland, where the Dutch were masters of brass founding. These utensils were incredibly expensive, often being specifically named in wills so that they could be passed on as heirlooms. Perhaps this spurred Darby on, for in 1707, he patented a process for casting good-quality, bellied pots in iron. In combination with the use of coke as a fuel, he now had all the ingredients to set up an iron production process in Coalbrookdale. Here he would construct one of the world's first continuous production processes, with the raw materials being fed in at one end and finished products flowing out at the other.

DEVELOPMENT OF THE CONTINUOUS PRODUCTION PROCESS

If you stand today in the Quaker burial ground high up on the side of Coalbrookdale and look to the south, you can see the flow of the process just as Abraham Darby I must have visualized it. The deposits of iron ore, coal, and limestone were up in the hills to the east. The narrow Coalbrook stream and its numerous small tributaries cut down through the dales toward the Severn. Dammed at regular intervals, the brook was made to flow over the waterwheels, which were, in turn, used to pump the bellows of the furnace air blast. The raw materials were brought down by packhorse and dumped above the furnaces. Here the coal was burned in great heaps to turn it into coke. Limestone, also carried in by packhorses, was piled nearby. Men charged the furnaces from above with measured loads using wheelbarrows. The molten iron was then cast into pigs, which would later be remelted in air furnaces farther down the valley and cast into pots, kettles, fire grates, and numerous other items. These finished goods were transported a few hundred yards downhill to a wharf on the Severn for shipment to ports all the way to Bristol. In some sense, Abraham Darby I, by harnessing the natural forces in Coalbrookdale, created a gravity-feed production and distribution system over a hundred miles long!

When iron was made using charcoal, a furnace could remain in blast for thirty weeks or less until supplies of charcoal ran out. It would then take another three months to repair the brickwork inside the furnace while sufficient charcoal was gathered for the next campaign. The use of coal in the form of coke to make iron opened up England's huge deposits of coal for large-scale exploitation and laid the foundation for the transformation of a batch production process into a continuous flow.

With the problem of fuel solved and the production process being steadily improved, Abraham Darby bumped into the next major constraint—the seasonality of the water supply. The Coalbrook is a fast-running stream when there is plenty of rainfall, but it dwindles to a trickle during times of drought. There was a limit to the size of the dams, and as a result, the waterwheels did not have enough power to drive the furnace bellows during much of the summer. After campaigns averaging forty weeks in length, the furnaces would have to be shut down, with all the attendant damage to the brick interiors that this entailed. This problem was tackled by Richard Ford (1689–1745), Abraham's son-in-law, who succeeded him on his death in 1717. Ford placed some of the newly developed horse-driven water pumps below each of the furnaces so that the water, once it had done its job of driving the waterwheels, could be returned to the upper pools to be reused. Now the air blast could be sustained for much longer periods of time—up to four years. This not only improved productivity and quality but avoided the need for frequent, expensive furnace relines. Horsepower proved to be only a temporary solution, for soon the pumps were to be powered by the first steam engines, another invention in whose development Coalbrookdale was to play such an important part.

DEVELOPMENT OF STEAM ENGINES AND TRAMWAYS

Many people do not realize that the evolution of the steam engine from its initial role as a supplier of pumping power to that of driving a railway locomotive took nearly a hundred years. A similar, somewhat shorter development process took place in the use of iron rails. Coalbrookdale was to feature prominently in both innovations.

Newcomen had patented the first viable steam engine in 1715. These engines were to become essential to the mining industry. Initially, the cylinders for the engines, like earlier household pots and skillets, were made from brass and imported from Holland. These were prodigiously expensive, but they could be cast thin, and brass cooled quickly, which made the engines fairly small and reasonably efficient. What iron lacked in efficiency, however, it could now make up for in size and cheapness. In 1722, Coalbrookdale began to cast the first of the enormous iron cylinders that came to characterize the Newcomen.

The first steam engines supplied linear rather than rotary motion so that they could not be attached directly to anything that needed to turn. When, in 1743, Richard Ford and Abraham Darby II installed the first Newcomen engines, they used them to replace the horses on the water pumps: the waterwheels were still needed as an intermediary device to transmit the power to the rotary cams that moved the bellows. It would take nearly another forty years for inventors to redesign and improve Newcomen's engine, culminating in the efforts of James Watt. Indeed, it was not until 1781 that Abraham Darby III was able to connect the new steam engines directly to the bellows. By then, however, there were furnaces all over England, and the individual furnace could put out nearly ten times as much product as the 1709 model built by Abraham I.

Another great innovation with which Coalbrookdale was involved was the development of tramways. It seems to have begun in various ingenious attempts to solve the transportation problems. Packhorses could not carry more than two or three hundred pounds each. In addition, they were expensive and reduced the roads to mire. By the late 1740s, Abraham II had begun to lay wooden tramways around the property to protect the roads and allow carts and wagons to be drawn. The wood rotted and wore out quickly, and in 1767, Richard Reynolds, Abraham II's son-in-law, struck upon the idea of making the tramways out of iron plate. Some say that the inspiration for this was a slump in the demand for iron in the aftermath of the Seven Years' War (1756–1763). Making iron plateways would have kept the furnaces busy, and when demand picked up, the plates could be smelted down again.

In any event, this was the first time that iron had been used for this purpose, and it proved astoundingly successful. By 1785, there were over twenty miles of tramways in the dale, designed for use by wagons with flanged iron wheels. A horse could pull a 15-ton wagon running on an iron rail. The wagons would have to be reinforced to carry such loads, with wheels and axle trees of iron rather than wood. Naturally, Coalbrookdale pioneered in the manufacture of these products.

DEVELOPMENT OF CANALS, BRIDGES, AND RAILWAYS

By the middle of the eighteenth century, the use of coke to make cheap, high-quality iron at Coalbrookdale had spawned a variety of industries as consumer and commercial demand for the newly affordable iron products boomed. Previously, the country had operated as a myriad of small, separate economies. Now the rapidly growing scale of the iron industry and the markets it served demanded that these microcosms be connected. All over the country, the requirements for bulk transportation soared, both for finished goods and for raw materials, especially in the mining industry. There were about a thousand miles of navigable rivers in England at this time, but often they did not connect the right centers, and the seasonality of their flow together with obstruction from other users made them unreliable. Tramways laid on the roads helped somewhat but did not provide the scale of carrying capacity now needed.

The first solution to the transportation problem was the building of barge canals.[26] The canal offered huge gains in the efficiency of transportation, particularly of bulk goods. A horse could carry 300 pounds on its back and pull 3 tons on a road wagon or 15 tons on rails, but it could draw, at the same speed, up to 100 tons loaded in barges. Over the next eighty years, the canal network would grow to over 4,000 miles in extent. This basic network was supplemented by innumerable small "feeder" branches, usually consisting of horse-drawn wagons running on iron tramways. Richard Reynolds and later his son, William Reynolds, became sponsors of canal construction to serve the needs of both Coalbrookdale and its neighboring enterprises.

The undulating landscape of Shropshire posed a number of special problems for the canal builders and taxed the ingenuity of another emerging class of specialists who would become known as civil engineers. Canals demanded a steady supply of water to maintain a constant depth and to feed the locks used to raise and lower barges over short distances. Canal bottoms had to be sealed with clay to prevent leakage into the mine workings, and pumps had to be added to offset the effect of droughts and consumption by the locks. Canal beds had to be level, so tunnels and cuttings were needed to go through hills, and aqueducts, supported on stone pillars, were required to carry the canals across the deeper valleys. The aqueducts themselves, like the early barges, were often made of iron plates riveted together to form tubs. Coalbrookdale made many of these.

Valleys like the Severn River Gorge were far too wide and deep to be crossed by aqueducts, and barges could not be lowered to the river by locks, for the slope was too long and steep for locks to be economical. The solution to this was the so-called inclined plane. This usually consisted of twin rail tracks on which barges could run, sitting on trolleys of some kind. Two trolleys could be connected by rope or chain via a giant pulley at the top of the plane. Full barges could be lowered while drawing up empty barges at the same time. Later on, steam engines were used to drive the process. One of the forerunners of the railway, this system was pioneered and developed by William Reynolds and widely adopted by the canal companies.

By the latter half of the eighteenth century, Coalbrookdale became a major producer not only of the iron pots, skillets, and fire grates with which it had begun the business but of iron products of every kind (other than cannon, shot, and war materials). The latter prohibition turned out to be fortunate, as it forced the enterprise to focus on rapidly growing markets in other technologies and protected them somewhat from the cyclical booms and busts of the military hardware business, although it was still exposed to the wide fluctuations in the price of iron.

Abraham III continued the close involvement of Coalbrookdale with the development of the steam engine. But his crowning achievement was the construction across the Severn River of the world's first iron bridge. It was erected in three months in 1779 without accident. Using 400 tons of castings, it arched in a single, graceful span 100 feet wide at a height of 50 feet above the river. It captured the imagination of all who saw it, attracting industrial pilgrims who came from all over Europe to marvel at it. It still does so today, but back then, in the eighteenth century, it made real the possibility of constructing buildings of iron instead of wood and stone. For his efforts, Abraham III was awarded a gold medal from the Society of Arts.

More important, Coalbrookdale, via the Quaker network, was a center for entrepreneurship of all kinds. The Darbys and their extended family seem to have been associated with every important innovation in the use of iron for 150 years, either working closely with the leading inventors or developing the technology themselves. William Reynolds, for example, kept close ties with the developers of the steam engine, especially with Matthew Boulton and James Watt. Their double-acting machines with mechanical speed governors and rotary transmissions became the dominant design. Coalbrookdale cast and bored many of the cylinders and pump barrels for them and also used such engines to direct-drive their furnace air blasts. Later, after the turn of the century, when Richard Trevithick finally succeeded in reducing the huge scale of the steam engine to a size that could be used to drive locomotives and boats, it was to Coalbrookdale that he came to have many of the parts made. Thus, the Darbys were involved in the first use of steam power to drive both railway engines and riverboats.

And so it continued in Coalbrookdale for another seventy years. In the great flood of 1795, all the bridges across the Severn were severely damaged, with only the iron bridge surviving unharmed and intact. This confirmed the superiority of iron construction to other methods and boosted demand tremendously. For decades, Coalbrookdale made iron bridges to be installed all over England and shipped to other countries as far away as Jamaica. By the turn of the century, the first "fireproof" iron buildings began to appear, with iron columns and iron beams. This development opened up yet another fast-growing market for iron products.

The involvement of the Quakers with the early railroads kept Coalbrookdale in the thick of developments in that industry. When the railroads first emerged as a viable method of transportation, many people thought that they would be used only to replace the tramway feeders to the canals. After all, the mines, factories, and warehouses were all situated on canals and could not relocate easily. As a result, the first railroads were seen as highly speculative investments. But what seems speculative to an individual may not seem at all risky to a network of entrepreneurs who are already trading with each other. When Edward Pease, the Quaker engineer who surveyed the first railroad line in 1820, could find no one to invest in it, he turned to the Quaker network for financing. Pease was a close friend of George Stephenson, the developer of the "Rocket" locomotive, and knew that the scheme was technically sound. The Quaker network would make it commercially viable. Thus, the Stockton and Darlington railroad, the first in England, became known as the Quaker Line. It was a huge financial success: the price of coal in Darlington fell by over half shortly after the line opened, and customers flocked to use it. The early locomotives could pull as much as a barge horse but at considerably higher speeds. In addition, a railroad was much cheaper to build and maintain than a canal. There began a railroad building boom that, in its size and duration, soon eclipsed that of the canals.

QUAKER ACCOMPLISHMENTS

I have called the Quakers' achievements "accomplishments" because the original Friends did not set out to achieve anything for themselves; they set out to change the world. They lived their values, and as the saying goes, "By doing good, they did very well."

ECONOMIC

During the English industrial revolution, the astonishing success of the Coalbrookdale enterprise was repeated over and over again in other industries and other places. From their humble beginnings as traders, the Quaker families became the leading entrepreneurs in cotton, wool (Barclay, Gurney), coal, brass (Champion), brewing (Burton, Truman), iron (Darby, Lloyds), steel (Huntsman, Ransome), food (Cadbury, Fry, Huntley and Palmers, Rowntree), china (Cookeworthy, Champion), and chemicals (Allen and Hanbury, Crossfield, Reckitt). Through what they called their "Atlantic Community," the Quakers became active traders between England and America and played a significant part in the enterprises of the United States.[27] In the steel industry, for example, both Bethlehem Steel and Lukens Steel were founded by Quakers. Joseph Wharton, after making his fortune in steel, went on to endow the business school at the University of Pennsylvania. Several major innovations emerged from cross-industry fertilization as products and processes were transferred across industries via the Quaker network. For example, the bleaching and dyeing processes in the textile industries turned out to be the forerunners of the soap and chemical industries, and we have already seen how coke came to the iron industry.

From the primary industries, the Friends moved into manufacturing and tertiary industries such as banking, in which, in those unregulated times, their reputation for honesty and integrity gave them a natural competitive edge! Robert Barclay's descendants made a fortune in the wool trade before giving their name to Barclays Bank (which still has Quaker families represented on its board). Lloyds, another of Britain's major commercial banks, also began its life as a Quaker enterprise, as did dozens of the country's financial institutions. The Quakers were obsessive record keepers, and their precise accounts give us the most accurate pictures available of early businesses. It is thus not entirely surprising that Price Waterhouse & Company, the accountants, started as a Quaker business, as did the advertising agency J. Walter Thompson.

SOCIAL

The Quakers were social activists from the very beginning. Their egalitarianism and universalism ensured that they were the first religious group to denounce slavery and require their members to free their slaves.[28] They were untiring in their activities to reform prisons, asylums, and institutions of all kinds.

Of particular interest to managers are their pioneering efforts in industrial relations and the use of human resources. The Quakers were the first to develop many of the management practices employed today. The use of domestic travelers and sales agents first became common in the soap industry. Sick funds, pension schemes, and company outings and social activities were all developed and used in the nineteenth century in several Quaker enterprises. Quakers such as the Cadburys of Bournville and the Rowntrees of York were social activists. They formed social and religious charitable trusts and built libraries and schools, hospitals for the sick, asylums for the insane, and model living communities for their workers. All of this was done long before governments became involved in such activities in the form of the welfare state.

SCIENTIFIC

Everywhere, the Quakers were associated with invention and discovery. John Dalton, the discoverer of the atom, and Joseph Lister, the surgeon who researched and pioneered the use of antiseptics, were both Quakers. The Quaker emphasis on practice and experiment, coupled with the individual's search for truth, fitted perfectly with the new scientific temper of the times. Many had scientific hobbies in addition to their regular professions. Their representation as Fellows in the British Royal Societies has been over forty times what one would have expected from their presence in the general population.

QUAKERISM AFTER THE ENGLISH INDUSTRIAL REVOLUTION

As the reader might expect from the processes already discussed in this book, the vitality of the Quaker movement began to wane over time. It is not surprising that their transformation from "hunters" to "herders" seems to have been catalyzed by their phenomenal material success. In addition, as the movement aged, their gaze seemed to turn from the future back toward the past. They became more intellectual in their beliefs, and the emotional fervor started to decline.

For the first fifty years of their existence, during which time they had repudiated religious tradition as a guide to behavior, the Quakers were hugely productive writers, producing more writings per capita than any other denomination.[29] By 1700, their own traditions were starting to become decisive, and the meetings ensured that members knew their history. As a result, the volume of writings began to decline. "By 1725," according to Barbour and Frost, "virtually every part of Quaker procedures had been standardized and written down in books of 'Christian and Brotherly Advices,' and a Friend's life from birth until death took place under a maze of regulations. Exuberance gave way to steady habits."[30]

The emigration of so many Quakers to America had aggravated the problem. The continuity of the meetings in England allowed an oral and experiential tradition, with no compelling reason to write down what everybody knew. In America, when faced with unusual situations, Quakers could no longer consult this collective memory: they would need to refer to a book of policies. Thus, rather like the Bushmen in their herding mode, the Quakers began to lose their oral, experiential tradition. Policies, once written down, are subject to interpretation, and it is no coincidence that in the eighteenth and nineteenth centuries, the Quakers, both in England and in America, were wracked and split by a number of doctrinal and procedural disputes. During this time, many Quakers left to join the Methodist movement.

In addition, just as one might expect from the story of the Bushmen, the accumulation of wealth and possessions placed an increasing strain on the Quakers' ability to live their simple values. Many joined the Church of England and the Conservative Party, institutions whose values and traditions sanctioned the ownership (but perhaps not the accumulation) of possessions.

The Quaker enterprises grew into huge organizations, and the third and fourth generations of many of the families had problems financing, let alone managing, the complex, large-scale systems that their forebears had created. Many of the businesses either went public or were bought by public companies. As such, Quaker businesses formed the core operations of such giants as British Steel, I.C.I., and Unilever.

The Quakers' accomplishments peaked in the middle of the nineteenth century, and although their power has dwindled since, it is clear that they had contributed significantly to the transformation of an entire society.

REVISITING THE MODEL OF CHANGE

The complex story of the role played by the Quakers in the English industrial revolution is painted on a large canvas, but as is shown in Figure 4-1, it does help us see the full cycle of organizational change more clearly.

We begin (arbitrarily) with the constrained world of post-Elizabethan England in the 1620s and the stalemate between Parliament and the Crown (1). This situation is shattered by the Civil War (2) and the subsequent execution of Charles I. The aftermath of this is a fragmented society (3), whose members are, however, still constrained in their ability to act by the confusion of the destructive process.

Soon, though, individuals begin to take what one can call rational action (4). In the case of the Quakers, this action is taken by people like George Fox, Robert Barclay, and William Penn. Their actions are rational, not by virtue of their understanding of cause and effect (which is the kind of rationality that I have been talking about up till now), but by virtue of the values that those actions represent and express. These value-laden activities result in the attraction of a large number of followers and the development of the Quaker communities and

Figure 4-1 A Cycle of Crisis and Renewal

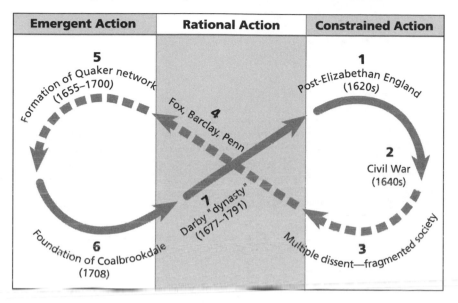

networks (5). Behavior in these contexts is unconstrained and full of novelty: it is emergent action.

Soon enterprises such as that at Coalbrookdale are started (6). In the beginning, they are small, haphazard activities, but soon (if they are to be successful) a means-end, instrumental rationality is developed by successive generations of managers, and the enterprises take off (7). As a result of these and other, similar activities, the society as a whole is renewed.

I have been highly selective in my choice of events to place on the infinity loop. Nevertheless, the infinity loop is a helpful way of organizing our thoughts about change and our thinking about the process as a whole.

In the next chapter, I will discuss the origins of the loop, what it reveals about the processes of organizational change, and how it applies to modern organizations and management action.

5

Growth and Renewal

THIS CHAPTER begins with a conceptual discussion of a helpful model of change and renewal developed from the study of natural ecosystems. The ecocycle, as the model is called, is then modified to apply to social organizations. The dynamics and dimensions of the model become clearer as we track the progress of several business organizations through the different phases of the cycle. Last, I begin to discuss the implications for managers of this model of organizational change and renewal.

THE ECOCYCLE

My colleague Brenda Zimmerman and I found the ecocycle model, with its distinctive "infinity loop" shape, in ecology, where it was derived

The ecocycle framework in this chapter and the description of the processes within it are partially based on the article "From Life Cycle to Ecocycle: A New Perspective on the Growth, Maturity, Destruction and Renewal of Complex Systems" (Hurst and Zimmerman 1994).

from the study of the evolution of complex ecosystems.[1] To understand how this model was developed, it is helpful to track a natural system through the ecocycle. A forest is an example of a complex natural system with which everyone is somewhat familiar (Figure 5-1).

THE ECOCYCLE OF A FOREST

A forest, like all complex organizations, is composed of many smaller organizational structures, all of which interact with each other and all of which also go through their own processes of change. Many of these subsystems—particular groups of trees, for example—will behave as "mini" forests, and their behavior will resemble that of the forest as a whole. The overall cycle of "the" forest is an emergent quality of the total system.[2] At any given moment, there will be some parts of the forest in every phase of the ecocycle.

Figure 5-1 The Birth, Growth, Destruction, and Renewal of a Forest

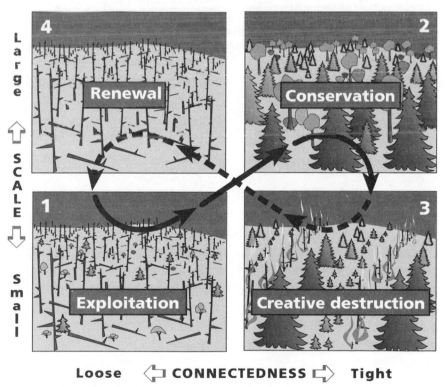

Source: Adapted from Holling 1987 (145). Reprinted by permission of Elsevier Science.

The phases of growth, conservation, destruction, and renewal described here, as well as the transitions between them, are widely observed tendencies of natural systems. Due to the many possibilities for variation in these complex systems, there is nothing inevitable about the timing of the changes, but it seems that most ecosystems will go through the phases in some form or another and in the order suggested here. Because the cycle is a continuous one, the numbering of the phases is arbitrary, and the numbers are used only for ease of reference. The discussion starts at the beginning of the conventional life cycle with the "birth" phase, or "exploitation" as it is called in ecology.

Exploitation (Phase 1)

The first phase of the ecosystem is characterized by a number of processes that lead to the rapid colonization of any available space. For example, when a gap appears in a forest due to, say, the fall of a large tree, a "microclimate" is created. The open patch offers many organisms equal access to energy and resources. It is the ecological equivalent of an immediate-return economy—the kind in which hunters thrive, for the resources are easily available and harvesting them requires little investment. Thus, the clearing will be colonized initially by a large variety of plants and other life.

Many of these organisms will be what some ecologists call r-strategists[3] ("hunters" as far as we are concerned)—that is, they will be species that are highly productive and mobile, producing large quantities of offspring. Available space allows the early inhabitants of the patch to grow without either running out of resources or bumping into each other. Such a system is loosely connected: there are many different ways for resources to flow through it.[4]

The r-strategists are the "pioneers," the opportunists who can take quick advantage of the open space that has appeared. As these "first movers" grow, some species will flourish better than others. Over a period of time, often quite a long one, what was once an open space starts to become crowded, and the plants begin to interfere with each other: the connections among the different species become stronger. Taller plants will shade shorter ones, those that have spreading root and branch systems may choke those that do not, and so on. The generalists—those that could survive under a variety of conditions—will start to give way to niche specialists in an environment that is becoming more stable and predictable. Slowly the open field becomes dominated by a few large systems and differentiated into a hierarchy of smaller niches, creating a relatively gradual transition to the next phase of the ecocycle.

The preceding description of this stage of the ecosystem has been vastly oversimplified. The so-called patch dynamics[5] of real forests are incredibly complex, and there are systematic differences, for example, between the structures of forests in the tropics and those in more temperate zones. Nevertheless, the presence of these exploitative processes in r-selection[6] environments seems to characterize all forests in this phase of the cycle.

Transition: From Exploitation (Phase 1) to Conservation (Phase 2)

As a forest ecospace becomes crowded, competitiveness grows and efficiency becomes increasingly important. Organisms that survive exhibit behavior very different from that of the opportunistic pioneers. These so-called K-strategy[7] organizations produce fewer progeny, invest their energy in protecting them for longer periods of time, and defend their territories. As far as we are concerned, they are the ecological equivalent of "herders," operating in what has become a delayed-return economy in which considerable investment is now needed to generate a return. It is the operation of these K-strategists that leads to the emergence of large-scale hierarchical organizations. The structure of the forest and the trees represents accumulated potential that now controls the usage of energy and materials in the ecospace. The system as a whole is now becoming tightly connected: there are relatively few ways in which resources can flow through the system.

In forests, the peak of this stage represents a cyclical climax. The system will be dominated by large hierarchical structures that control a set of niches beneath them, allowing a variety of specialists to flourish. Because of the great length of the growth cycle of trees, the trees and the niches they shield will appear to be relatively stable to human observers. So-called climax forests are characterized by their apparent steady state, and viewed at a distance, the forest will look impressive. Although many organisms in the system will be specialists, however, the total variety of the system will be lower than in the exploitation phase. In temperate zones in particular, there may be relatively little variety in the types of trees in the forest.

It is precisely the homogeneity of such systems in age, species type, and their specialized adaptation to protected niches that renders them brittle and vulnerable to catastrophe. Forests composed of only a few varieties of trees are especially susceptible to insect attack and disease. Mature forests contain huge amounts of burnable materials, and as they age, the conditions for disaster become more favorable as deadwood accumulates on the ground. This is why, in natural forests, efforts to preserve this stability too rigidly—by preventing forest fires, for example—have proved to be misguided. The U.S. National Park Service abandoned a policy of putting out all fires twenty years ago.[8] If all fires are extinguished, this will tend to reduce the variety of the forest further, as the mature trees choke other organisms. It will also build fuel on the ground and prevent the formation of natural firebreaks. This reduction of flexibility, variety, and resilience means that, when there is a fire, it may be catastrophic. Similar disasters, often caused by disease, occur in cultivated forests where monocultures are encouraged because of the ease with which the trees can be harvested mechanically.

Ideally, a healthy forest should consist of a mosaic of patches that developmentally are located all over the ecocycle. The optimal "spread" will depend upon a myriad of factors.

Transition: From Conservation (Phase 2) to Creative Destruction (Phase 3)

The third stage in the evolution of the ecosystem is the "forest fire." This phase is described as "creative destruction" because the system is not destroyed completely: it is partially destroyed in order to be renewed.[9] Nevertheless, in natural systems, this phase often sees much of the capital that has been accumulated in large-scale structures during the period of growth quickly destroyed as the system becomes disorganized.

The ecosystem is invaded by processes to which its age, specialization, low variety, and loss of resilience have made it peculiarly vulnerable. The highly developed structure is shattered, as the former strength of the system—its tight connectedness—is now seen to act as a pathway to destruction. The large, hierarchical components of the system (the old trees in the case of forests) are especially vulnerable. As they disintegrate, they are broken down into much smaller elements in a dramatic reduction in organizational scale. The elaborate hierarchy of niches that had developed under the umbrella of the larger, stronger structures is exposed to the full variability of the environment.[10] Strengths developed in other contexts and the stability that they conferred are of little help against the invading processes because those processes often "feed" on these strengths. The only ones that can survive are the mobile (forest animals, for instance), the lucky, and those prepared for the situation. (Examples of this kind of preparedness include several varieties of coniferous trees, such as lodgepole pine and jack pine, which grow special fire-resistant cones that open *only* when heated, thus allowing their seeds to survive.)

In contrast with its apparent steady state in phase 2, in phase 3, the ecosystem enters far-from-equilibrium conditions. The term *far-from-equilibrium* has a special meaning in the study of nonlinear systems, especially in chaos theory.[11] Nonlinear systems (like the earth's weather, for example) are loosely connected networks that have patterns and regularities unlike those of the more familiar linear systems (like those on a billiard table). When a nonlinear system is far from equilibrium, it is acutely sensitive to small changes in inputs to the system. Small inputs into such a system can eventually produce large changes in outcomes.[12]

Whereas linear systems have structures built up from stable components, nonlinear systems exhibit patterns that are shaped and sustained by processes operating in loosely connected networks. They are continually consuming energy, and because they require a significant throughput of energy to sustain their far-from-equilibrium condition, they are known as dissipative structures. This is to distinguish them from the more common conservative structures found in phase 2 of the ecocycle. To borrow William James's happy phrase that he used to describe consciousness, a dissipative system is like a "rainbow on the waterfall."[13] As long as the sun shines and the water flows, we can see it and it exists.

Transition: From Creative Destruction (Phase 3) to Mobilization and Renewal (Phase 4)

The fourth phase in the evolution of an ecosystem is the reconception of the system. This is the most ephemeral of the stages in the ecocycle, and the dynamics are hard to observe. One of the reasons for this is that, *after the structural disintegration of phase 3, it is often very difficult to distinguish the organization from "its" environment: the boundary that separates and defines them has disappeared.* In the forest, phase 3 has left the landscape flattened but fertile. Where is the forest? Without our memories, how do we differentiate the bare, scorched earth from open land? It is difficult to do this without identifiable, stable structures at which to point: we can't see the forest because there aren't any trees!

The trees of the climax forest can be thought of as just so many conservative, hierarchical systems that dominated the sources of energy and nutrients within the ecospace. In phase 2 of the ecocycle, their structures and their tightly connected interactions limited the variety of creative possibilities in the development of that space. With their reduction in phase 3 to small-scale structures, the creative potential of the ecospace has been vastly increased. Resources are no longer concentrated in specific structures, and they are widely scattered.

In phase 4 of the ecocycle, via numerous regenerative processes, these resources become loosely connected with each other into a large-scale network. Some of these processes break down the debris left behind by the destructive event; other processes start to metabolize the resources. Plants, insects, and animals seem to work in harmony as the entire system becomes mobilized via the processes of the loosely connected network. Nutrients are easily accessible, and sunlight and water are available to all. Little investment is required to harvest these resources. The forest is once again a hunter's environment with a high carrying capacity, and it favors fast growth. The stage is set for the ecospace to be recolonized by a large variety of small-scale r-strategy organisms. Within the constraints of the overall climate, anything is possible in this far-from-equilibrium system.

KEY FEATURES OF THE ECOCYCLE MODEL

Before moving on to apply a modified version of the ecocycle to human organizations, it is worth emphasizing the key features of the model:

- Change is continuous, although the pace and nature of it vary greatly. Sometimes it is smooth and almost linear (from phase 1 to phase 2, for example). At other times, it is rapid and nonlinear (from phase 3 to phase 4, for example).
- Renewal requires destruction. The only way to open up spaces in the forest is to creatively destroy the large-scale structures that hog the resources.
- The ecocycle resembles several other perspectives on change, but the dimensions and shape of the curve are unique.[14] The dimensions force one to think about the many components that make up complex

organizations and the relationships among them that allow us to infer the existence of an organization.

- The plants and trees that will make up the mature forest emerge from the open patches, grow, and are selected by the constraints imposed by the environment in which they find themselves. These are self-organizing processes. If they were human, we would call them learning organizations.

THE ECOCYCLE IN HUMAN ORGANIZATIONS

The major difference between a natural system such as a forest and a human organization is that the trees, plants, and other organisms that make up the forest are not self-conscious actors, capable of rational action (at least as far as we know). The behavior of these natural systems is determined by their natural growth rates and the constraints imposed upon them by their environment, including their interactions with each other. Hence the modified ecocycle applied to human organizations needs to have the capacity for conscious, rational action added to the emergent and constrained behaviors that characterize ecosystems like the forest. The resulting model is shown in Figure 5-2.

Figure 5-2 The Organizational Ecocycle

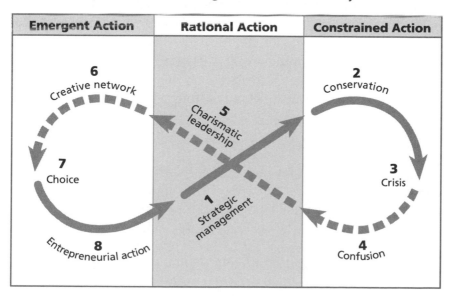

There are two important features of the modified model that should be pointed out immediately (all numbers refer to the diagram). First, the ecocycle splits the process of organizational change into two half-loops. The "front" (performance) loop is the conventional life cycle (solid line, 8 through 3). The "back" (learning) loop is a less familiar, renewal cycle of "death" and "reconception" (dotted line, 4 through 7).

The second feature of the model is that there are two types of rational action, because each of the half-loops traverses the area in which rational action is possible. As the model makes plain, each form of rationality takes the organization in quite different directions. Strategic management (1) is characterized by an instrumental, means-end rationality. (I have arbitrarily chosen to number it "1" because this is where conventional texts on management usually begin their discussion of management action.) This is the same logic that underpins the "rational model" with which every business school graduate is familiar. The fundamental purposes of the organization are seen as economic and hence calculable. All action is (or should be) a means to economic ends. It is the rationality captured in Milton Friedman's famous dictum that ". . . there is one and only one social responsibility in business—to use its resources and engage in activities designed to increase its profits so long as it stays within the rules of the game. . . ."[15]

Charismatic leadership (5), on the other hand, is a values-based rationality—action taken for its intrinsic worth in demonstrating deeply held beliefs about human relationships. Strategic management is the central management activity on the performance loop, which leads eventually toward organizations that become tightly connected and constrained. Charismatic leadership, on the other hand, develops loosely connected, creative networks from which new activities can emerge.

CONVENTIONAL LIFE CYCLE

The performance loop of the organizational ecocycle is identical to the conventional life cycle.[16] The heyday of the application of the life cycle to organizations was in the 1970s and the early 1980s.[17] For managers, the life cycle concept—whether applied to a product, a process, an organization, or an industry—has always had an enormous intuitive appeal.

I will now illustrate the life cycle portion of the ecocycle, starting with strategic management (1), the first of the phases of rational action.

Although the discussion will be linear, it is worth bearing the following points in mind:

- The infinity loop of the ecocycle is continuous: there are no beginnings and no endings. The choice of where one enters or quits the loop depends upon one's purposes. The boundaries between each phase are fuzzy, and one must continually refer to the previous phase in the ecocycle to supply context to the phase under discussion.
- It is very difficult to track the progress of a single organization around the full loop. The dimensions of the ecocycle cover processes of integration whereby unconnected elements *become* organizations as well as processes of disintegration whereby organizations are broken back down into "their" elements.
- Healthy human organizations should, like natural forests, consist of "patches" at different stages of development. One can use the ecocycle both to locate all the patches *at a moment in time* and to track the evolution of particular patches *over time.*

Instrumental Rational Action: Strategic Management (Phase 1)

As I have suggested in Chapter 2, instrumental rationality first becomes possible in young organizations when managers have learned cause-effect relationships. This learning is often a result of a series of trial-and-error experiments made in an earlier phase of the organization's existence. Of course, this does not preclude some organizations from imitating the apparently successful recipes of others and short-circuiting the trial-and-error process. Indeed, it has been suggested that much activity and change in organizations is driven by imitation.[18]

In its pure form, however, this phase of the cycle is characterized by the reduction of what was once a hunting strategy to a repeatable formula. This formula is then extended into multiple open "patches." The story of Nike's growth during the 1970s, for example, is a classic illustration of an r-strategy being extended in this way. Having established the company in high-performance track and field shoes, Nike managers developed products for a succession of other sports. With relatively little investment in plant and facilities and an informal organization, they were highly flexible as they moved from basketball to tennis, football, soccer, and a host of other activities.

Their progression was a combination of planning and opportunism in an unexploited field, with a formula that became steadily more rational. In the early days, for example, the endorsement of footwear by professional athletes and their coaches was in its infancy, and there were no published guidelines. The rules of sponsorship for athletes in events like the Olympic Games were in the process of being rewritten amid a morass of under-the-table deals. There were few precedents to be followed, and competing firms did more or less what they wanted. The unstructured environment was such that the results of actions were almost immediately apparent. This is typical of an immediate-return economy: product trials do not require large investments, and the rapid feedback encourages trial-and-error learning. Activities that pay off are extended; those that do not are stopped. During this phase of the cycle, strategies often emerge as a retrospective rationalization of what worked. Thus, many of Nike's strategies emerged over an extended period of time as the company exploited what was a huge, untapped market.

In contrast, in the 1980s, as the market for sports shoes grew, the niches became increasingly defined and specialized. Whereas the undifferentiated sneaker had performed a wide range of functions in 1950s, now each sport began to require its own specialized equipment. The application of research and the development of new materials and manufacturing techniques constituted an emerging technical system that allowed specialization to flourish. Nike began to be attacked by competitors such as Reebok also exhibiting r-strategies but targeting particular segments—the aerobics market, in the case of Reebok. The environment was becoming crowded, encouraging both specialization and efficiency.

From Hunters to Herders at Compaq   A critical period during this phase of rational action in the ecocycle is the organization's transition from a "hunting" r-strategy of growth to a "herding" K-strategy emphasizing efficiency. A new open patch in a market favors organizations that can grow fast, but as the market matures, the fast growers run the risk of being selected out if they cannot hold their own in a context that increasingly favors K-selection. From a product and technological perspective, the transition is marked by the emergence of what has been called a "dominant design."[19] This design embodies all the features that customers now regard as basic requirements. As such, its emergence often signals the end of radical product innovation in an industry (or organization) and a move toward improvement in the production process. It also marks the peak in the number of different firms involved in an industry.[20]

Although the transition from r-strategy to K-strategy is in the rational action portion of the ecocycle, this does not mean that it is an easy passage! This is illustrated by the recent, well-publicized, jolting transitions at Compaq.

The story of Compaq Computer Corporation[21] is well known. The company was founded in early 1982 by three former Texas Instruments (TI) employees. The design of their first machine was sketched on a place mat in a Houston pie shop. Led by Rod Canion, Compaq's emphasis was on introducing personal computers with leading-edge technology as soon as it became available. The manufacturing emphasis was on quality, flexibility in shifting products, and speed in bringing new products to market. Cost considerations were "way down the list." This is exactly what one would expect of an r-strategy organization.

Compaq reached the *Fortune* 500 after only four years of operation—the shortest time then on record. Sales topped one billion dollars by 1987 and were nearly three billion dollars by 1989. All this was accomplished in a culture that emphasized wide-open communication, teamwork, extensive consultation, and fact gathering and decision making by consensus. These are exactly the kind of social dynamics we would expect to find in a "hunting" organization.

By 1990, however, Compaq's growth rate had slowed dramatically to less than 4 percent in the United States. Competitors were undercutting its prices by as much as 35 percent on machines with comparable features. In 1991, sales fell for the first time—by 9 percent—and Compaq had its first-ever losses and layoffs. There were two competing rationales for the situation. The first was CEO Canion's belief that the worldwide recession was largely to blame, with the implication that no change in strategy was necessary. As would become apparent, this was another instance of the vagaries of the business cycle hampering a manager's ability to learn from experience.

The second argument was based on Chief Operating Officer Eckhard Pfeiffer's conviction that the market had changed and that Compaq would have to change its strategy. As a marketing executive in TI, Pfeiffer had seen a similar downward price spiral in the consumer electronics market. Where Canion saw a temporary interruption in Compaq's growth, Pfeiffer saw a more sinister pattern. He realized that what had once been a unique Compaq product configuration was now the dominant design being offered by many competitors. In his view, the firm now needed to focus on the efficient production of this established design.

The business world was shocked when, on October 25, 1991, the board of Compaq accepted Pfeiffer's view and fired Canion. Pfeiffer immediately set about to introduce what is easily recognizable as a K-strategy. The company was split into two divisions—one to take on the lower-cost clones, the other to sell the more complex systems for which a feature-based strategy would still be viable. At the same time, Pfeiffer launched a series of wide-ranging cost-cutting initiatives with the objective of still building high-quality computers, but at radically lower costs. In the first phase, the workforce was cut by 25 percent to nine thousand people. In a "herding" K-strategy, cost reductions and efficiency are at the top of the list.

Pfeiffer's view of the situation seems to have been a timely one. In the two years after he took over, the corporation quadrupled its output of PCs without adding any floor space to its core manufacturing facilities. Unit costs in some plants fell by over 75 percent.[22] Compaq's sales growth has returned, as have profits, although gross margins are down by a third due to savage cuts in selling prices. But the game has now changed. Although Pfeiffer has been putting in place a comprehensive long-range strategy, Compaq can expect to be increasingly constrained by the industry it helped to create.

Conservation (Phase 2)

Once the transition to a K-strategy has been made and the growth in overall demand slows, the competitive premise becomes "more of the same." As we saw in Chapter 2, when an organization becomes successful, the managers will naturally tend to restrict activities to those that have proved to work. Successful strategies will be elaborated upon and expanded. Considerable effort and capital will be invested in describing these activities and embedding them in technology and formal organizational procedures to perpetuate their performance. Activities within the system will become tightly connected with each other via technology of all kinds, and there will be limited variety in the ways in which procedures are performed. Often this is accompanied by an increase in the scale of operations. The organization will specialize, "stick to its knitting," and emphasize efficiency. This will make it even more successful than it might otherwise have been.

Immediately after World War II, the North American economy probably favored r-strategists in many industries. Through the late 1940s, 1950s, and early 1960s, there was a pent-up demand for consumer goods, together with the need to rebuild a war-shattered Europe and Japan. By the late 1960s and early 1970s, however, this growth began to slow. Major markets began to become saturated as demand for steel, autos, and housing peaked and then started to fall. By the 1980s, the majority of the Fortune 1000 were probably conservative structures pursuing K-strategies in their domestic markets. Even the conglomerates, like climax forests, were often made up of mature units. As such, these organizations represented the triumph of large-scale, complex technical systems. In the process of institutionalizing their successes and pursuing efficiency, however, conservative organizations sacrifice resilience and flexibility and become more vulnerable to catastrophe.

A particularly poignant instance of this is the U.S. integrated steel industry. The preservation of its production facilities from attack during the war gave the United States a tremendous production advantage in its aftermath, and in 1946, it accounted for 54.1 percent of the world's raw steel production. That success was accompanied, however, by a failure to innovate, and the U.S. steel industry stuck with the massive technology of the open hearth furnace long after it was obsolete. Its market share had fallen to 20.1 percent by 1970 and to 11.8 percent by 1984.[23] The industry is now under ferocious attack from a new, smaller-scale, more flexible technology—the scrap-fed, electric furnace minimill.

Indeed, the thought derived from the forest fire analogy—that our efforts to make large systems hyperstable actually make them brittle and vulnerable—is an intriguing one. There may be a systems logic that explains why the seeds of failure are often contained in the fruits of success.[24]

Crisis: Creative Destruction (Phase 3)

The description of the effects of a forest fire resonates with the carnage we see these days among what were once thought to be large, invulnerable organizations.

For practicing managers, the term *creative destruction* is a disturbing one. In human organizations, destruction is likely to seem creative only to those who are either at one level above the system being destroyed or entirely outside the situation! Observers can agree that trees must be burned to renew the forest, that organizations must be able to fail if an industry is to remain competitive, and so on. For those inside the system being destroyed, however, the implications are threatening because, as individuals, we are the elements of the system. This phase of an organization's life is characterized by crises, discontinuities, and wide fluctuations in variables such as sales and prices that have traditionally been stable. It is we inside the system who are the subjects of change, and the resulting feelings of fear and uncertainty contrast unfavorably with the feelings of control and even omnipotence that characterized the previous phase of the organizational ecocycle.

The forest fire reduces the forest to a smoking ruin, but it creates the necessary preconditions for new elements to enter the situation, for new connections to be made, for new processes to operate, and for new systems to emerge. Crisis seems to play the same role in human organizations.

This is what has happened in the case of Wang Laboratories.[25] The company's performance peaked in 1989 with over three billion dollars in revenues and a ranking of 146 in the *Fortune* 500. Wang had been a dominant player in dedicated word processors and its VS line of minicomputers. Three years later, it filed for Chapter 11 bankruptcy, with its common shareholders' equity all but wiped out. Wang had been blindsided by the very same small-scale technology that had made Compaq so successful. In some systemic sense, the rapid rise to success of Compaq and other personal computer manufacturers between 1982 and 1989 is the systemic counterpart to Wang's stunning fall.

Wang's hierarchical structure, under which the activities of 31,500 people had once been coordinated worldwide, was destroyed as the business shrank and divisions were either closed or sold. Capital of all kinds, from asset values to employee morale and the goodwill of customers and suppliers, evaporated. Customers turned to other suppliers, nourishing their businesses. Wang employees left to join other companies, form their own ventures, or retire. In these new roles, many of them made a significant contribution to society. Like the nutrients and seeds that were once bound up in a large tree, with its destruction and fall, they are returned to the soil to benefit the forest as a whole.

In September 1993, Wang emerged from bankruptcy shorn of its manufacturing operations and focused on document-imaging software and the service of its declining base of Wang minicomputers. It employed six thousand people. In contrast with the long period of growth and success from its founding in 1951 to its peak year in 1989, its destruction and reduction—the turnaround—had taken only thirteen months.

FROM LIFE CYCLE TO RENEWAL CYCLE

Wang's story is a familiar one in the business world. A once successful enterprise experiences a series of setbacks, and change is precipitated by a crisis of some kind. This is often accompanied by a change of control of the organization. A hectic period of "rationalization" follows, during which many parts of the business are shrunk, sold, or closed. After a while, a smaller version of the enterprise emerges. Often this organization is focused on the core businesses that led to the enterprise's original success.

Such turnarounds are often necessary in organizations that have become inefficient, usually during extended periods of prosperity. But the top-down, directive style that accompanies such activities frequently ensures that the business is reduced rather than renewed. Through the generation of cash and the reduction of liabilities, the organization's life cycle may have been prolonged, but in the absence of genius on the part of the turnaround manager, the core operations may not have been improved. There is destruction, but it may not be creative. To revert to the forest analogy, one might say that the forest has been logged but may not have been replanted: new organisms may not have been allowed to enter the ecospace.

This is where the familiar S-shaped curve of the life cycle is of little help to managers. In its usual application to products, it does not have to deal with what happens to products after they "die." They are simply replaced by new products emerging from some largely unspecified innovative process. As a result, the organization's progress has often been shown as a chain of discrete S curves, with the links between them undiscussed. It is the renewal portion of the organizational ecocycle, the second half of the infinity loop, that makes these creative links discussable.

RENEWAL CYCLE

Whereas the conventional organizational life cycle is the story of the evolution of a *technical* system, the renewal cycle is about the evolution of *social* systems. It is this emphasis on people and their interactions in the aftermath of crisis that allows one to explore the roots of innovation and the organizational contexts that nurture it.[26]

Confusion (Phase 4) and Charismatic Leadership (Phase 5)

As the story of the Quakers in the previous chapter suggested, renewal begins in the confused aftermath of crisis, which shatters the previous forms of hierarchical control. This is certainly what we experienced in Russelsteel during the early 1980s. Out of the confusion, there has to emerge one or more charismatic leaders: individuals who act in ways that express their values—their beliefs about how people ought to relate to each other. In the case of the Quakers George Fox, Robert Barclay, and William Penn, this took the form of a radical social vision for the whole of society. In our more modest situation at Russelsteel, it was a belief in democratic processes and open discussion about our predicament: the vision of our future would emerge later in the process. In both cases, however, the behavior of the charismatic individuals who led the process was rational. Their actions were rational, not in a means-end, instrumental sense, but in the sense that *their behavior consistently expressed a coherent belief system.*

Charismatic leadership is a controversial phenomenon toward which we should always feel ambivalent. Paradoxical by its very nature, it has been associated with both the most inspiring and the most terrible episodes in human history. There are examples of charismatic leaders who are egotistical, elitist, exploitative, and destructive. There are also examples of those who are humble, egalitarian, facilitative, and creative. For charismatic people exemplify, to an extreme degree, our human potential for the creation of both good and evil. As such, we need this paradoxical, contradictory concept to capture something of our paradoxical, contradictory nature: the phenomenon is all too real. I will return to this topic in more detail in Chapter 7. For the moment, we need to track an example of this kind of leadership in action.

Jack Welch at General Electric One of the best-documented examples of charismatic leadership as part of a planned effort to renew a major organization is that of Jack Welch's attempts to transform GE.[27] He was appointed CEO in 1981. Once he had created his own crisis by delayering the management hierarchy, reducing corporate staff, and slashing one hundred thousand employees to focus on what he believed to be the core elements of the business,[28] he set about to release the organization's emotional energy and creativity to capitalize on the opportunities offered by changes in GE's environment.[29] According to him, the jobs of middle managers had to be redefined: "They have to see their roles as a combination of teacher, cheerleader, and liberator, not controller."

His emphasis has been on the restoration of open communication: "Real communication takes countless hours of eyeball to eyeball, back and forth. It means more listening than talking. . . . It is human beings coming to see and accept things through a constant interactive process aimed at consensus."

Welch's emphasis on a values-based rationality rather than an instrumental rationality has been evident in his prescription for the decision-making process within GE. He has stressed the sharing of the facts and *assumptions behind decisions* rather than the *logic of the decisions* themselves: "Everyone in the same room, everyone with the same information. . . . The complications arise when people are cut off from the information they need." His view on what information is relevant for GE's managers has been astonishingly radical for a North American CEO. For example, the "Work-Out" program of in-depth communication was designed to "expose the business leaders to the vibrations of their businesses—opinions, feelings, emotions, resentments, not abstract theories of organization and management."

Welch's personal behavior and that of his senior managers has been consistent with the new egalitarian values he espouses. In the Work-Out sessions, managers met their people face-to-face to deal with pressing issues that had been raised in open dialogue. According to Tichy and Charan, commenting on one division's experience with the program, it represented

> an intense effort to unravel, evaluate, and reconsider the complex web of personal relationships, cross-functional interactions and formal work procedures through which the business of [GE] gets done. Cross-functional teams cooperated to address actual business problems. Each functional team developed a vision of where its operations are headed.

The Creative Network (Phase 6), Choice (Phase 7), and Entrepreneurial Action (Phase 8)

Welch's aim to transform the cognitive structures within GE, to explore new patterns of meaning within the organization, is explicit in the new organizational processes and the value statements that accompany them. Welch believes that this link is the essence of loyalty: "Loyalty is an affinity among people who want to grapple with the outside world and win. Their personal values, dreams, and ambitions cause them to gravitate toward each other and toward a company like GE that gives them the resources and opportunities to flourish."

The jury is still out on GE's transformation process, and I can track it no farther along the learning loop of the ecocycle. The logic of the renewal cycle suggests that, if it is to be successful, groups of individuals will begin to gel around a variety of opportunities and projects and start to take entrepreneurial action. The individuals will have interacted with each other in the "boundaryless" networks developed in the contexts created by Jack Welch and his senior managers. The opportunities will have been generated in the same way. In keeping with the emergent quality of activities in these phases of the ecocycle, the formation of the small work groups and the projects themselves will appear to be spontaneous and "lucky" rather than planned.

The cycle should progress in much the same way as it did at Blue Ribbon Sports (BRS) when Phil Knight and Bill Bowerman went through the creative process for the first time on their way to inventing Nike. This is the period during which, as we saw in Chapter 2, the organization had no permanent employees. It was a period during which a loosely connected network of athletes and suppliers was forming, anchored and sustained by the visions and passions of Phil Knight and Bill Bowerman. Knight and Bowerman were the nucleus of a new *social system* that would invent a new *technical system*.[30]

To an outside observer at that time, the organization would have been invisible or, at the very least, diaphanous. One would have looked right through it and seen only a social network. Yet this was the time when BRS was most acutely sensitive to its environment, when small, insignificant events had significant consequences. That is why, in retrospect, the so-called founding of the business often appears to consist of a series of unpredictable events and chance encounters with helpful people.

In the case of Nike, over time, the loosely connected network began to pulse in a pattern. If our hypothetical observer had attended the track meets where the athletes gathered to compete (and talk about their equipment), he or she might have noted how, after a brief period of bonding, the patterns in the loosely connected network began to change. Knight and Bowerman started selling their shoes to a wider market using new distribution channels and some of the contacts they had made. A more regular pattern of interactions began to emerge as the contacts and events became linked into coherent flows and better-articulated routines.

Soon a small, simple, but permanent structure would form and move into the next phase of the ecocycle. At about this time, the organization, although insignificant in size, would become clearly visible to outside observers and be ready to be named. Nike was on its way.

PERSPECTIVES ON MANAGEMENT ACTION

The organizational ecocycle is helpful as a conceptual model because, although it distinguishes among the three contexts of management action, it also integrates them into an uneven pattern of organizational change, showing *when* they are appropriate. It identifies a rhythm of renewal.

Once an organization is established, its conventional life cycle clearly lasts longer than any cycle of renewal. In addition, this front loop is dominated by a relatively lengthy period in which managers can behave "strategically"—that is, as instrumentally rational actors. During this phase of the process, organizational growth may be fairly smooth and linear. The emphasis is on economic performance, and the conventional rational actor perspective may work very well.

This perspective will not work well indefinitely, however. Over time, organizations become constrained by their own internal rigidities and the tightly connected web of relationships they have developed externally. Managerial discretion within the system becomes more and more constrained. Nevertheless, although managers may often be constrained and confused, *they are never powerless*. They can always do something. When they are constrained, they can jump out of the "box" by destroying the system "creatively": they can create crises to shatter those constraints. Indeed, the ecocycle suggests that, unless they do so, something else will. Even in the U.S. integrated steel industry, some firms (such as LTV) have succeeded in breaking many of the ties that bind them, usually by going through the "fire" of Chapter 11 bankruptcy proceedings. From the point of view of American society, that is Chapter 11's function—to encourage renewal sooner rather than later. It should be noted, however, that continuous "fires" in a business will not do the trick. Organizations must be of a certain scale to be effective as K-strategists, and scale takes time to build.

It is in the confused aftermath of this creative destruction that the stage is set for a values-based, charismatic leadership. Now managers have to live the values that they espouse—"walk the talk" in current management jargon. Their action is rational, not because it is a means to an end but because it is *intrinsically valuable*. Managers in this phase of the cycle model the behavior they expect from others.

This values-based rational action seems to be essential to the attraction of creative people and the creation of contexts that nurture innovation and entrepreneurship. It attracts followers to the charismatic leaders—followers who are self-selected and who themselves can learn to lead. This allows the formation of a network of relationships held together by shared values and an emerging vision of common purposes. With the emphasis on learning and the options so generated, the renewed organization now regains the ability to choose.

The organizational ecocycle is complex, and although the performance loop is familiar to most managers, the learning loop is not. It is obvious why the processes in this half of the ecocycle will not fit easily with North American management thought: there is no instrumental, means-end rationality to the renewal cycle. Indeed, I will show in Chapter 7 that if instrumental rationality is applied to the learning loop, it is easily detected as manipulation, and people will not "buy into" the change program.

In the last two chapters of the book, I deal in detail with the management action required on the renewal cycle, starting with the first and most controversial action—the need to create preemptive crises in mature organizations.

6

Crisis Creation

THE PREVIOUS chapter developed conceptually the ecocycle model of change and renewal and extended it to apply to human organizations. Some of the most important implications for management action were outlined, and these will be developed further in the last two chapters of the book.

As we have seen, the ecocycle splits the evolution of a sociotechnical system such as a business organization into two halves.[1] The first half of the ecocycle, the conventional life cycle, tracks the development of a performance-oriented organization from its entrepreneurial beginnings until it becomes dominated by its technical system and the institutions associated with it. It is toward the end of this loop that the total system starts to become negatively constrained, unable to adapt gradually to change and hence prone to crisis. The other half of the ecocycle, the learning loop, is the story of the evolution of a social system, which, after the constraints of the technical system are broken, leads to the emergence of choice, to freedom. Thus, for an organization to survive, it must continually traverse both loops at all scales—that is, on all levels of the organization.

In theory, the twin loops should be complementary—combining both discipline *and* freedom. If we are not disciplined, then freedom has no meaning. If the basic routines of an organization are absent, we are free only to fight fires. If, on the other hand, we are not free, then discipline has no real purpose: it cannot justify itself. Only value-based ends can justify instrumental means.[2]

In the practice of management in the Western world, however, the emphasis has been on the technical aspect of organizations, and there has been a preoccupation with the performance loop of the ecocycle. The implication has been that management can—or at least, should—be a rational, linear activity. Crises and surprises have usually been regarded as dysfunctional. In an effort to correct this imbalance, I will deal in these last two chapters with the management action required in the learning loop—the renewal portion of the ecocycle—and discuss the conventional, technical side only as the need to weave the two together becomes apparent.

The most controversial feature of the ecocycle is the need for crisis before an organization can make the transition from the end of the performance loop to the beginning of the renewal cycle. It implies that managers need to create crises if they are to avoid being overtaken by "natural" disasters. So before discussing the deliberate creation of crisis, it is worth reviewing some of the evidence that crisis itself can and does lead to innovation in organizations.

CRISIS AND CREATION

"I hate surprises," said the CEO of the conglomerate that acquired us in 1983. "Surprises are for birthdays." He simply meant that he hated bad financial news, but his management style and his public speeches said much more than that. The view that he promulgated to the investment analysts and business journalists was that the company as a whole was a smooth-working money machine. The implication was that his strategy of diversification, coupled with an ability to extract superior profits from apparently humdrum businesses, virtually guaranteed high rates of predictable, almost linear growth. Of course, this need to enhance credibility with external investors by representing an organization's strategy as a rational, linear process pervades Western financial markets. In Chapter 2, we saw the effect that it had on Nike, forcing it to become more formal and structured after it went public, but the effect has been noticed repeatedly.[3] It is a form of retrospective rationalization that is widely encouraged in our Western culture.

Although the CEO's claim of rationality referred to the financial aspects of the organization, any suggestion to him that innovation and discovery in the individual businesses might require discontinuity and crisis would have been met with outright shock and denial. In this attitude he would not be alone, for the view that technological change and innovation in business are a fundamentally rational affair is a popular one. One of the most influential proponents of this view is Peter Drucker, who has made a determined effort to interpret the history of innovation as a linear process.[4] As respected management researcher Donald Schon has shown, however, this view has been around for a long time:

> At each level of analysis, we will find, well embedded in the conventional wisdom, a rational . . . view whose function it is to place technological change within a stable state:
>
> - a rational view of invention as an orderly, plannable process;
> - a rational view of innovation as a manageable function of the firm;
> - a view of technological change as occurring within well-defined industrial boundaries;
> - a view of technological change in society as part of a Technological Program, extending from the eighteenth century to the present time.[5]

Despite the conventional wisdom, there is considerable evidence that crisis plays an important role in organizational innovation. For instance, it is hard to see how the radical changes in Russelsteel, recounted in Chapter 3, could have taken place without a crisis to precipitate them. We saw in Chapter 4 how the Quaker movement emerged from the chaos of the English Civil War to change the whole society, and there is evidence from other wars and political turmoil that they are accompanied by considerable innovation. The American Revolution, for example, created significant trading opportunities between America and Europe. This resulted in the emergence of many new entrepreneurs and contributed to the formation of a new aristocracy of wealth and power. It is thought also to have encouraged the development and spread of the joint-stock company and the rise in prominence of lawyers and law firms in American society (not all innovations are necessarily desirable!). The American Civil War, on the other hand, seems to have stimulated the transformation of the U.S. banking system and led to a good deal of innovation in the formation of federal government agencies.[6]

Even the physical destruction of war seems to offer opportunities for innovation. During World War II, there were times when Albert Speer, Hitler's minister of industry, actually welcomed the Allied bombing raids for their role in breaking the red tape of bureaucracy and destroying records.[7] Perhaps one of the most astounding stories of how the general destruction of war contributed to industrial innovation, however, is that of the revival of the automobile industry in post–World War II Japan. It is worth exploring this in some detail because the creation and rise of firms like Toyota and Honda in the 1950s and 1960s offer a neat contrast with the then concurrent maturation and decline of GM, Ford, and Chrysler.

THE REINVENTION OF THE JAPANESE AUTO INDUSTRY

As the learning loop of the ecocycle in Figure 6-1 shows, the renewal process began in crisis in the aftermath of Japan's shattering defeat in

Figure 6-1 The Reinvention of the Japanese Auto Industry

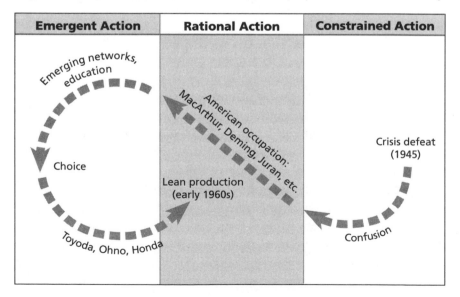

1945. Much of the physical economy had been, quite literally, burned to the ground, and the political structures had been reformed and made more open and democratic. The commercial institutions dominant before the war, the *zaibatsu*, were broken up. Many of the executives who had run them were purged and not allowed to hold senior positions in any corporation. The old class restrictions were eased under the egalitarian influence of the American occupation. In short, although there was tremendous confusion, a number of constraints on entrepreneurial activity were removed. A myriad of patches were opened in the economic and political "forest": small-scale experiments could now be conducted much more easily than in the past.[8]

Many of the numerous leaders and role models who emerged out of this chaos were American. They ranged from General Douglas MacArthur on the political front to experts like Edwards Deming and Joseph Juran, who taught the management of quality in manufacturing operations. The learning loop of the ecocycle makes it clear why teachers like Deming felt that they had such a receptive audience in the Japanese at that time. The status quo had been destroyed, and there were few tangible possessions left to defend, so the Japanese were eager learners. As we shall see, in contrast, the members of the American auto industry were on the performance loop of their ecocycle during the same period. They were approaching the peak of their power, and by any financial measure, their organizations were performing superbly. Even their customers seemed to be happy. Anyone who suggested that they had anything to learn was clearly a crank!

The Japanese culture is profoundly communal in its traditions,[9] so perhaps it is not surprising that the Japanese succeeded brilliantly in the next stage of the renewal cycle: the formation of creative networks providing nurturing contexts—containers for entrepreneurial activity. Like the Quakers long before them, the Japanese could not accept a business system that was based upon purely arm's length economic transactions. There had to be shared community feelings and mutual reciprocity among the players. The network organizations that emerged were the *keiretsu*, groups of companies held together by circular webs of cross-locking equity holdings.

Another important nurturing context was the educational system. The Japanese school system had always been excellent, but now, after the war, it was focused to fill the significant technology gap that had been made so painfully obvious by Japan's crushing defeat. All kinds of incentives were given to promising students to encourage them to become engineers. The firms that hired them sent their bright young graduates to study the state of the art in Western manufacturers. They returned to pursue their small-scale experimentation with renewed vigor. Soon Japanese industry was ready to move from the "learning" (back) loop of the ecocycle to the "performance" (front) loop.

In automobile manufacture, one of the most significant innovations during this time was the development of the system of so-called lean production.[10] The innovation, which took nearly twenty years to perfect, is attributed to Eiji Toyoda, a member of the family that founded Toyota, together with his production genius, Taiichi Ohno. Other entrepreneurs such as Soichiro Honda developed similar systems over the same extended period of time.

Upon his return from a visit to Ford's Rouge plant in 1950, Toyoda was faced with the problem of adapting the American production process to Japanese conditions. He realized that the Japanese market could not absorb the huge quantities of single models turned out by mass production. Furthermore, in 1949 at Toyota, a layoff followed by a bitter strike had underscored the fact that in Japanese society, workers could not be laid off the way they were in the United States. Neither were there "guest workers" or immigrants who would put up with this treatment. This meant that plants had to be able to switch models frequently if production levels were to remain steady.

In addition, the postwar Japanese economy was weak and could not afford either the huge capital outlays or the foreign exchange necessary to import the technology required for mass production. Fewer giant presses would have to produce a larger variety of parts. This placed a premium on fast die changes and setups. It made sense for the production workers, who were usually idle during these downtimes, to make these changes themselves.

As they tinkered with the system, Toyoda and Ohno found that the reduced scale of manufacture had unexpected benefits. First, there was a major reduction in inventories, but even more important, there was a *faster cycle time*. This enhanced their ability to improve the system on a continual basis because it reduced the time lag between the production of errors and their detection. Furthermore, it pushed the detection and correction of errors down to the lowest level in the organization—that of the factory worker. In the form of *kanban*, Toyota's famous just-in-time system, this set up "microclimates" for learning all over the lean production plants. The system was also extended to organizations traditionally considered to be outsiders, blurring the boundaries between Toyota and its suppliers. The search for errors could now be pursued further back in the overall supplier-assembler-customer system. Cooperative relationships resulted in cost reductions, which were shared between assembler and supplier.[11]

Because just-in-time systems had far fewer buffers than mass-production systems, glitches could have very serious consequences: whole plants could be shut down. Everyone had to respond to a problem. To be effective in these circumstances, workers had to be fully informed, multiskilled, and accustomed to working in teams.[12]

As North American consumers know, the products produced by the lean production plants reflected this continual process of learning and extension of control to smaller and smaller scales in the products they produced. For example, when it first came out, the Lexus luxury car produced by Toyota reflected an attention to fit, finish, and detail previously attained only in handcrafted vehicles and at considerable expense. The lean production process had given Toyota control of fine scales of detail as yet inaccessible to its mass-production–based rivals. The customers could tell the difference in scales and called it "quality."

This brief story of the invention of lean production and its role in the revival of the Japanese automobile industry underscores the interaction between social dynamics and innovation. Toyoda and Ohno did not invent a technology so much as they *invented a social process that changed the technical system.* Their subsequent success was the result not just of introducing new technology but of introducing a new sociotechnical system.[13]

CONSTRAINTS

Up until now, I have talked about constraints as if they were inherently bad. This is not technically correct. Constraints are an integral part of organization: to organize is to constrain. That is, in the process of specifying and promoting certain activities, we constrain, at least implicitly, the performance of others. In many cases, the constraints are explicit in the form of prohibitions. Of course, in the beginning, to the extent that the organizing is a deliberate action, we do this for the very best of reasons—to perpetuate a winning formula. The constraints play an important role in keeping the business on course. But over time, circumstances may change, until eventually the once beneficial influence of the constraints starts to inhibit learning and adaptive change. The most dysfunctional constraints are usually those that are tacit rather than explicit.[14] Elements of formal organization such as restrictive rules and policies are at least easily identified and can be changed. The more insidious constraints are the strictures imposed by the use of complex technology, the almost invisible influence of culture, and the pervasive effects of growth in organizational size. Over time, growth, in concert with technology and culture, can create powerful constraints on an organization's ability to change.

A classic example of this comes from the history of the U.S. auto industry, which, after reigning supreme for seventy years, found itself unable to react quickly enough to the threat from the Japanese industry in the 1970s and 1980s. It is worth tracking the story to understand how the constraints arose and how, in the case of GM, they emerged from the very strengths that had made that company the largest and most successful automobile manufacturer in the world.

THE EVOLUTION OF THE U.S. AUTO INDUSTRY

The twin loops of the ecocycle are a useful way of tracking the rise, fall, and subsequent attempts at renewal in the U.S. auto industry.[15] The front (performance) loop is shown in Figure 6-2.

Figure 6-2 The Rise and Fall of the U.S. Auto Industry

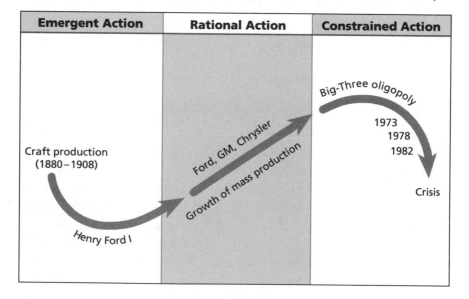

Craft Production

The era of small-scale craft production in the U.S. auto industry can be thought of as coinciding with the entrepreneurial action phase of the ecocycle. It extends from 1880 to 1908, the year in which Henry Ford I launched the Model T. In that same year, Bill Durant put together twenty-five automotive companies to found General Motors. This period of nearly thirty years saw hundreds of pioneering individuals and organizations enter the industry. As late as 1900, it is estimated that fifty companies a year were entering the business, mostly in Detroit.

In the early years, it was not at all clear that gasoline was going to be the fuel of choice: steam power was a proven technology, and electricity, as ever, showed great promise.[16] As a result, there was a huge variety of approaches, especially in engines and transmissions, and a high attrition rate as particular technologies fell by the wayside. Many of the entrants into the industry made only one prototype vehicle before going out of business. During this period, all vehicles were hand-assembled by skilled craftsmen, and it could take over twelve hours to put together the major preassembled components. Within six years of launching the Model T, Ford would reduce this time to an hour and a half.

Mass Production

The era of mass production in the auto industry corresponds with the instrumentally rational phase of the ecocycle, when managers have developed a logic for their success and extend the "recipe" to all parts of their operations. There were numerous elements to Ford's production system, and the most important of these was not the famous assembly line but the complete interchangeability of the parts that made up his automobile. This, in turn, was made possible by advances in metalworking that allowed him to hold fine tolerances consistently. Much production time in the craft system was spent tailoring unique components to fit together. With the standardization of parts, the use of fitters in assembly could be much reduced. In addition, the owners of the cars could make their own repairs—an essential feature for a mass-market vehicle.

Ford pioneered parts interchangeability, but this was soon extended to the industry via the creation of standards. The S.A.E. standards, for example, reduced the variety of lock washers from eight hundred to sixteen! All the while, the scale of the industry grew. Demand soared as Ford reduced prices and margins. The Model T had come out in 1908 selling for about $1,000, and nine years later, the price was down to $360. At that price, Ford sold over 730,000 cars during the year!

From Hunters to Herders

The Model T is an example of a classic r-strategy. The market was booming, and car manufacturers that could deliver an effective vehicle sold everything they could make. As a low-priced, general-purpose vehicle, the Model T dominated the early volume market. By 1922, however, volume was starting to peak.

At about this time, Alfred Sloan at GM began to express discomfort with his clutch of r-strategy products, which Durant had assembled in such higgledy-piggledy fashion:

> Not only were we not competitive with Ford in the low-price field—where the big volume and substantial future growth lay—but in the middle, where we were concentrated with duplication, we did not know what we were trying to do except to sell cars which, in a sense, took volume from each other. Some kind of rational policy was called for.[17]

The "rational policy" was the famous differentiation of the market and GM's products into the "full line" of six-tiered price/quality segments.

At the lower end, Chevrolet would take on the Model T by being a little bit more expensive but offering significantly better quality. It was a devastating move (and perhaps not dissimilar to that used by the Japanese against the Americans sixty years later). As a result, Ford's transition to a K-strategy in 1927 was marked by the closure of his plant for eighteen months while he retooled to produce the Model A.

In 1923, Dodge had introduced what would become the dominant design for cars—the all-steel closed body—and by 1925, 50 percent of cars produced in America conformed to it.[18] As all the major players adopted K-strategies, the familiar characteristics of mass production were extended throughout the industry:

- High scale, particularly in major mechanical components produced with single-purpose machines;
- Specialization of work tasks at every level from the shop floor to the design, engineering and financial staffs;

- Concentration of the industry at the assembler level into [in the United States] the familiar "Big Three";
- Vertical integration of the final assembly and components manufacturing with the objective of coordinating an extremely complex process with multiyear leadtimes and enormous capital investments.[19]

The Emergence of Oligopoly

The emergence of the "Big Three" as a shared monopoly in the 1960s marked the entrance of the U.S. auto industry into the constrained portion of the performance loop of the ecocycle. The system as a whole was now tightly connected. The individual companies were constrained both externally and internally by financial concerns and their huge scale. The first questions on every project were likely to be "What will the [Wall] Street [investors] think?," "What will this do to our triple-A bond rating?," and less obtrusively, "How will it affect this year's profit-sharing bonus?" It was, as Halberstam later wrote, as if the real customers of the companies were the stockholders, not those who bought the cars.[20] There was an obsession with high-volume, high-margin large vehicles and the need to keep the lines running at all costs. Improvements in quality were desirable in principle as long as they did not slow down the lines. Small cars were not important: they meant small margins and small profits.

Within each of the major producers, however, there was an even more insidious constraint in the form of the mind-set of the new breed of professional managers who now dominated the organizations. Hired into the businesses for the very best of reasons—to articulate and perpetuate a successful formula—they had by now taken over as conservators of the system they had perfected. A means-end, instrumental rationality now suppressed the old values. The "car people"—those close to production and design who used to run the organizations—had completely lost their ability to influence events. The two groups could no longer talk to each other. Hal Sperlich, a top production man at Ford, said of his relationship with Philip Caldwell, the cautious, conservative president (appointed by Henry Ford II in 1979):

> For a long time I thought we simply could not understand each other, that we were from such different backgrounds that we might as well use different languages. And then later when it was all over and I was gone, I realized it was more than that. It was a struggle between men for whom

a car was an end in itself, an object of passion, and someone for whom a car generated no excitement but was a means to success and power. It wasn't different languages, it was different businesses.[21]

The stifling effect of these constraints within the organizations and the feeling of the need to toe the corporate line were summed up perfectly in the explanation one senior Ford executive offered to another who had just been fired: "In this company, Bill, the people who do well wait until they hear their superiors express their views. Then they add something in support of those views."[22]

By the early 1970s, after thirty-five years of unbroken success, the American industry in the form of the Big Three was totally constrained by its huge achievements. It was almost impossible for any novelty to be introduced into its ponderous, monolithic structure in a timely fashion. Like a mature forest that had been protected for too long, it was ready for burning.

Crisis

There are three milestones on the industry's sharp downward curve into crisis:

1. 1973, when the first oil shock indicated that the oil industry had lost its ability to control the price and output of oil
2. 1978, when Lee Iacocca left Ford to join Chrysler, just before the fall of the Shah of Iran
3. 1982, when interest rates hit over 20 percent in North America, auto sales collapsed, and the scope of the crisis first became apparent to GM

Although, in retrospect, the fall seems sudden and inevitable, it did not seem that way at the time, especially from inside the industry. Between 1973 and 1982, the Big Three were rescued twice by general economic recoveries, which, as we saw in Chapter 2, make the interpretation of events difficult. Those who wanted to believe that things could stay the same could argue that the problems were temporary and that it was "only the business cycle." For the most part, they were the people in charge.

Nevertheless, to observers farther away from the epicenter, over a period of nine years, the richest, most powerful industry in the world seemed to disintegrate. Chrysler, the weakest member, was the first to get into trouble. It was followed by Ford, which sustained massive losses in 1980. GM, the richest and most powerful member of the industry, was the last to realize the extent of the catastrophe.

The American Response

The response of the U.S. auto industry to its financial troubles and the challenge of Japan's leading auto producers is captured in the renewal portion of its ecocycle, shown in Figure 6-3.

Initially, there was tremendous confusion and huge stress as companies feared for their survival. The pressure was most intense on the suppliers of components to the Big Three, especially on those whose financing was precarious. The assemblers tried desperately to cut unit costs by applying raw buyer power. Their goal was not to improve the total system but to unload costs onto other members of the supplier chain. The traditional bidding processes and cozy relationships that had flourished under the shelter of the oligopoly began to fragment.

Chrysler, whose lack of vertical integration had always weakened its margins during the good times, now found that this was a positive advantage in turbulent times! It could go to competitive tender on components quickly, without worrying about the effect on in-house

Figure 6-3 The Renewal of the U.S. Auto Industry

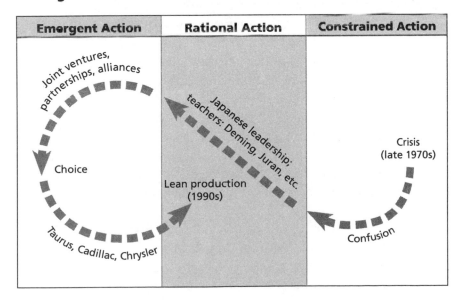

operations. GM's experience was exactly the opposite: the lower prices from outside suppliers had to be traded off against the reduction in the production volumes of its company-owned plants. This is an excellent illustration of how the tightly connected, large-scale organizations that do well in stable times become systemically vulnerable to turbulence. What were sources of strength in the first context often turn out to be the roots of weakness in the second.

After a time, the Big Three began to find role models whose lead they could follow and whose example they could no longer ignore. For a brief time, it had been possible to argue that lean production was a cultural phenomenon peculiar to Japan, but with the coming of the Japanese "transplants" to America, starting with Honda in 1982, this argument, too, was disproved. The role models for the U.S. auto industry were now the leading Japanese producers and those who had taught them the system. Now the industry turned to Deming and Juran, the same people whom it had ignored thirty years earlier. For now, in the renewal cycle, there was much less to defend, and American producers, too, were ready to learn.

The large-scale learning vehicles that emerged from this process were a number of joint ventures, strategic alliances, and other forms of cooperation between the Big Three and Japanese producers. GM's joint venture with Toyota in the NUMMI plant, Ford's acquisition of 25 percent of Mazda, and Chrysler's partnership with Mitsubishi are all examples of such learning vehicles.

In many cases, however, the American companies had trouble learning even in these situations, usually because they were looking for the wrong things. Most North Americans have learned in Economics 101 that labor and capital are substitutes for each other, and the complex relationships of a sociotechnical system are hard to grasp. GM's experience with the joint venture at NUMMI in Fremont, California, illustrates the point. This extraordinarily successful operation was low-tech, but the lessons learned from it, if any, did not stop GM from making a determined attempt to prove that technology could substitute for dedicated workers. It cost the company billions of dollars to find out that it could not.[23]

Many other similar, if less expensive, mistakes were made. Without a clear understanding of the social dimensions of lean production, the North American companies tended to seize upon the tangible techniques of the system—such as quality circles, cross-functional teams, and a variety of analytical methods—as if these were the "secrets." They then tried to use these techniques as inputs. That is, they tried to implement these techniques in an instrumentally rational way, as if they were on the performance loop of the ecocycle.

Usually, these attempts to shortcut the renewal process met with little success.[24] Another important issue was that the workers, quite understandably, would not participate in improving the processes if it was going to cost them their jobs. This, of course, had not been an issue in companies like Toyota and Honda with their policies of lifetime employment. Over time, however, and after a number of false starts, these attempts to learn began to pay off for the individual companies. Ford scored a major hit with the launch in 1985 of its Taurus/Sable line; Cadillac revitalized its range of luxury cars; and in the early 1990s, Chrysler came up with a new range of midsize vehicles. Although the gap between the American and Japanese manufacturers has not been closed completely, by the early 1990s, the Big Three had caught up significantly.

MORE CONSTRAINTS

The story of the American automotive industry's inability to change fast enough to avoid a "fire in the forest" is well known, and in retrospect, the flaws now appear obvious. Even so, it is easy to fancy that, had we but been there as managers at the time, we would have recognized what was happening and taken rapid remedial action. As the following three examples show, however, because the harmful effects of constraints can grow so slowly and insidiously, they can be very difficult to detect from the inside.

Case 1: Creeping Technological Constraint

After many years of considerable success as a supplier of sophisticated computer hardware and software to the telecommunications industry, this business found itself missing project deadlines, shipping bug-filled software, and dealing with a torrent of complaints from unhappy customers. Project deadlines were being set and agreed to, but no one seemed able to meet them in practice. In a highly egalitarian work culture with a flat formal structure, senior managers found themselves increasingly overworked, with a myriad of decisions coming up to them to be made, often in high-pressure situations with customers. Everyone agreed about the symptoms and complained bitterly about how things had changed over the years. "Ten years ago, we could work out these kinds of problems in an afternoon," was a typical comment. "Now we don't know where to begin." Apart from the growth in the size of the organization, its members were at a loss to explain why things had changed so drastically.

An organizational culture survey revealed a highly stressed workforce who had little sense of job satisfaction and felt that they had no control over their work lives. Most people expressed a sense of powerlessness and frustration. A review of the organization's history showed that over the years, the software component of the telecommunication systems had grown considerably. At the same time, the demand for the business's products had taken off. In the early days, when the software code was only a few hundred thousand lines in length, changes could be made fairly easily by pulling a dozen or so programmers into a room and agreeing on how to make them. Everyone could get his or her arms around the system: problems could be foreseen, and mistakes were easily corrected. Ten years later, the code had grown to several million lines in length and involved hundreds of programmers. The harmful constraint turned out to be in the structure of the system. Although, on the surface, the hardware and software appeared to be broken up into discrete pieces, the system was in fact functioning as a huge, monolithic structure, which was no longer well understood by anyone.

Programmers could not anticipate problems, and the consequences of making large changes to the system could be disastrous. Thus, every change had to be small and incremental and required extensive testing and debugging before release. This, in turn, led to the workforce's being given very small jobs to do with tight deadlines. Projects could be planned and budgeted individually, but the interactions among them could not be forecast accurately. Because of their potentially serious consequences, all decisions were handed up to the highest level. Senior managers, forced to choose between full testing and keeping customers happy, often allowed software to be released before it was quite ready. This, in turn, led to further problems, requiring further repair work and creating further delays in outstanding projects.

Thus, the system architecture, which had been the pride of the organization and one of its key competitive advantages, had become a harmful constraint.[25] This did not happen all at once but had emerged over time. To release the organization from this constraint, the system, like a mature forest, had to be "burned" to open up patches within it. That is, the monolithic software had to be broken down into real "chunks" of code of sensible size, each of which had clear interfaces with all the other chunks. Programmers could now get their arms around the code and make radical changes within a chunk, knowing that any disaster would not travel across the boundaries and crash the system. They could now take risks and behave as "hunters" in an open patch within the overall system. This "chunking" was not just a technical issue because, as one can imagine, during the rise of the monolithic system, conservative technocrats had flourished as managers. The organization had tracked the technical system and become a technocracy. Naturally, these technocrats were not pleased to see changes that placed a premium on experiment and innovation and changed the pecking order in the organization as a whole.

Case 2: The Softening Culture

In the 1950s and 1960s, this family-owned and -managed manufacturer of automotive parts had been a pioneer in profit sharing, teamwork, and employee participation. The philosophy behind the system had been developed by a brilliant, charismatic (sometimes autocratic) CEO, who had insisted on performance as a prerequisite for the system to function. The workings of the system itself were complex, requiring the operation of a number of interconnected committees and the participation of people throughout the organization. In the early years, under the leadership of the CEO, the system functioned well and was an integral part of the management process. The firm flourished, and the system attracted favorable journalistic comment, industry admiration, and the attention of business school case writers.

As the business grew, however, the workings of the system became harder to maintain and understand. Rapid growth meant that often people were hired without careful orientation and training in the operation of the system. The development of new facilities in places remote from the head office meant that fewer people had direct exposure to the philosophy embodied in the behavior of the charismatic leader. After a while, the system started to become peripheral to the management process. By the time the charismatic leader had withdrawn from active participation in the firm, the system had been thoroughly institutionalized in policy and procedures, although younger managers were scared of it. They did not feel the confidence of the founder to challenge his own creation, and few had ever seen how he had done it.

In an attempt to preserve the desirable human outcomes of the process, many tried simply being "nice" to each other. In the absence of any consistent demand for performance, the system started to spawn a culture of entitlement. The family had always taken pride in the fact that the company was nonunion, but now the company had a de facto union. In some ways, it was worse than a union because, in a union agreement, at least the constraints are explicit and renegotiable at regular intervals. In a culture, the constraints are tacit and impossible to negotiate in any formal way. Thus, instead of facilitating effective management, over a period of fifteen years, the system had become a constraint. Managers regarded it as a nuisance and did their best to work around it.

As the system, once the pride of the company and a distinct competitive advantage, became an unhelpful constraint, several other unhealthy dynamics arose. All the favorable publicity, which had once helped attract good people to the company, now had a dysfunctional impact internally. It created complacency in some—"There's no need to change: we're the best"—and feelings of cynicism in others, as reality diverged from the rhetoric. The absence of stress on performance meant that managers could fail without serious consequences, and good relationships rather than competence became the criterion for advancement. The climate within the organization became intensely political, as some managers started to use the organization's internal publicity media to promote their own careers.

In the previous case, the architecture of the technical system was monolithic; here the institutionalization of the participation system had rendered it monolithic. Crisis in this case had to take the form of a renewed focus on performance symbolized dramatically by the replacement of senior managers and a careful reform of the participation system to make it less intimidating. For example, making the system plant-specific rather than corporatewide helped reduce the scale and allow some interplant variability.

Case 3: Constraint through Acquisition

A highly successful North American steel distributor whose managers had always regarded themselves as "hunters"—the mavericks of the industry—was offered the opportunity to buy one of the premier companies in its business. The industry was mature and in need of downsizing, and the managers felt that they could play the role. The target company had once been the leading organization in the industry but had fallen on bad times. It was the same size as its potential acquirer but much less profitable, although its facilities and systems were impressive.

After a fierce internal debate about the merits of the acquisition and its potential effects on the "hunting" culture, the arguments for growth and the need to "rationalize" the industry won out and the acquisition was made. Because of the concerns about the hunting culture, the businesses were kept separate, with only selective rationalizations being made.

The acquired business started almost immediately to act as a harmful constraint on the acquirer. As independent competitors, the two companies had always clashed fiercely over customers, but now this conflict took on all the ferocity of a civil war! Arguments about sales territories and customers quickly became an internal preoccupation. With actual internal profit figures now available, charges that one's rival was "giving away the store" could be pursued to much greater lengths. Soon every point of difference between the two companies was a focus of savage argument: accounting policies, company cars, vacation policies, job titles, and compensation schemes all featured in the debate. While the two companies fought like groups of "herders" over territory and possessions, the external environment was collapsing as the economic boom of the late 1980s began to fade. The internal strife had distracted management and delayed the introduction of a much more comprehensive program of rationalization of the two operations. In addition, the best people in the acquired company were the first to leave, and many had done so. Everyone who remained was thoroughly disenchanted with the acquisition.

The rationalization that followed did not go well. With the loss of good people in the acquired company, it was the "hunters" from the acquiring company who found themselves struggling with the byzantine bureaucracy and cultural complexity of an "establishment" organization. The wholesale changes in personnel that followed against the worsening economic background did not help, and within a few years, the acquired company had been reduced to a shadow of its former self. The industry had been downsized, but at a terrible cost to the acquirer.

Lessons from the Cases

The first two cases show how the nature of constraints can change from beneficial to harmful. In these cases, the awareness of any problems crept up on the organizations very slowly, and there were no clear turning points in the process. The changes took place in the relationship between the environment and internal systems that had once been regarded as key competitive advantages. As the circumstances changed, strengths gradually became weaknesses. No doubt it was the unexpected direction from which the threat came that made it so difficult to recognize internally. By the time the harmful nature of the constraints became apparent, drastic action was required to break free of them.

In the third case, that of the "self-inflicted wound," the harmful consequences of the acquisition became clear very soon after the deal was closed, but by then, it was too late to undo the transaction. It might have been possible to turn around and sell the business, but it is unlikely that a buyer could have been found at the price that had been paid. And of course, the senior management was not yet convinced that the business could not be rescued. After all, the acquisition had been billed as a strategic masterstroke. How could one do a flip-flop and sell it at a discount? It seems that the need to appear rational can itself be a powerful constraint on the taking of sensible action!

The conclusion from these cases is that the sources of harmful constraints in an organization are so varied and their action is so subtle that insiders are unlikely to recognize them in time. Effective managers cannot wait for them to be diagnosed before taking action. The implication is that, almost as soon as an organization emerges from its infancy, its managers have to begin a systematic process of preemptive crisis creation. They must continually burn the firebreaks and open up patches in the organization if they are to avoid catastrophe.

MANAGEMENT ACTION IN THE RENEWAL CYCLE

From a systems[26] point of view, during the renewal cycle, managers are not managing change directly. They are managing *the organization's ability to change*—what my colleague Brenda Zimmerman calls the organization's *change-ability*[27]—rather than change itself. On the learning loop, a manager's position is analogous to that of a gardener: the gardener cannot make the plants grow; he or she can only create the optimum conditions under which the plants' natural self-organizing tendencies can function. The gardener has to *allow* them to grow.

This is why managers of the renewal process do not have to have any technical answers; they only have to understand the social contexts in which learning is possible. Thus, in the organizational renewal cycle, the emphasis is on *action that creates contexts for action.* On the performance loop of the ecocycle, in the strategic management phase, we can often think our way to a better mode of action. The use of logic is a prelude to action. On the learning loop, we have to *act our way into a better mode of thinking.*[28] Logic is an output—an induction from successful action. Having said that, managers don't stop thinking during the renewal process, but the thinking required is systems thinking. It is mindful[29] rather than instrumentally rational.

As Figure 6-4 shows, managerial action in the renewal cycle can be thought of as falling into three broad categories. These three categories bear a striking resemblance to Tichy and Sherman's description[30] of transformational leadership at GE as a "Three-Act Drama" consisting of "Awakening," "Envisioning," and "Rearchitecting." In the remainder of this chapter and in the following chapter, I will be discussing some of the parallels in the context of each action category.

Figure 6-4 Management Action in the Renewal Cycle

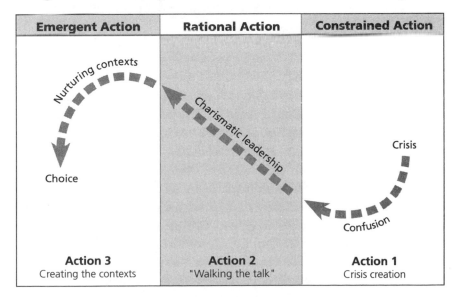

Emergent Action	Rational Action	Constrained Action
Choice		Crisis
Nurturing contexts	Charismatic leadership	Confusion
Action 3	**Action 2**	**Action 1**
Creating the contexts	"Walking the talk"	Crisis creation

ACTION 1: CRISIS CREATION

The objective of creating a crisis[31] is to break the harmful constraints that bind the organization in the final phase of the conventional life cycle. Toward the end of Chapter 2, we saw how all the elements of the successful performance organization can act as hindrances to the renewal process. This will be particularly true after a long period of financial success, as in the case of GM in the 1980s. The compensation system will likely be rewarding the wrong kind of behavior; the information systems will be supplying inappropriate data; and the dead hands of past administrators will continue to govern via policy manuals and standard operating procedures. Managers and stakeholders of all kinds will be totally committed to "the" strategy. As we saw in the case of the Big Three of the U.S. auto industry, a far more serious, insidious problem is that, during the lengthy period of success, people entering the organization and promoted within it will have almost certainly been selected for their abilities to preserve the status quo, not to challenge it.

In any event, the ecocycle suggests that if managers don't create their own preemptive crises, even in what appear to be successful operations, then something else will. It is the equivalent of burning a firebreak. One can't stop the forest from burning, but one can mitigate the destructive effects of the fires by keeping them small. Thus, an ongoing process of renewal would appear to demand continual, constructive damage to the status quo across all the scales—at all levels of the organization.[32]

External Sources of Crisis

The burning of the "firebreaks" within a conservative organization is perhaps the first and easiest stage of any renewal effort. Even so, it is often very difficult to accomplish and will usually demand help from external sources. As we have seen, mature, successful organizations usually change only after "midnight" has struck. That is, there has to be a manifest failure of the status quo before a concerted change effort will be undertaken. Thus, the manager of the renewal process is faced with a paradox: the change process cannot begin before the failure of the old order is manifest, but the process is likely to be more successful if it gets under way before too much damage has been done.

At GE, Jack Welch seems to have successfully resolved this paradox. As Tichy and Sherman have pointed out, in 1980, when Welch was appointed CEO, GE had some operating problems and the stock price was sluggish, but there was no generally perceived crisis.[33] In this case, the requisite crisis was precipitated by the appointment of Welch himself. A man with no stake in the status quo, Welch had spent most of his career on the fast-growing fringes of the giant organization, beyond the reach of the central bureaucracy. Yet he had been in an ideal position to observe the bureaucracy in action and what he perceived to be its stifling effect on the organization. When he became CEO, he was ready to conduct a frontal assault on the past, awakening all the members of the organization to the need for change. Some of the events during that "awakening" were discussed in Chapter 5.

In the case of Russelsteel, it was only during two crisis periods—the severe business recessions of 1982–1983 and 1990–1991—that the renewal cycle really seemed to get going. The onset of each of the crisis periods was signaled by the appearance of tensions and dilemmas that threatened the survival of the firm. Tensions came from outside in the form of fluctuations in the level of business activity and interest rates and sometimes from changing political arrangements. In the late 1980s, for example, the Free Trade Agreement between Canada and the United States affected many organizations and threatened to "burn" several industries. Additional stresses were created by changing ownership, particularly by the highly leveraged LBO in 1981.

Internal Sources of Crisis

External sources of crisis are helpful, but internal events can also provoke crises, although they may be unintentional by-products of other actions. Of more interest are deliberate actions taken internally that can open up "gaps" in the organization. In the case of GE, Welch's insistence that each business be number 1 or number 2 in its market, together with his passion for benchmarking performance against objective external standards, opened up perceived "gaps" in the organization. Paying attention to one's customers and working closely with successful but demanding ones can have a similar effect.

At 3M, the systematic "burning" of mature businesses using internal methods appears to have been institutionalized. The company now insists that all of its fifty or so divisions generate at least 30 percent of their sales from products introduced within the past four years. At the same time, the organization's culture clearly encourages "extracurricular" activities—for example, by allowing employees to spend up to 15 percent of their working time on personal projects.[34] The well-known story of the evolution of the Post-it note and its initial rejection by senior management suggests even more subtle cultural aspects of 3M that facilitate the mobilization of the talents of its people.[35]

Managers often talk about making their businesses "fireproof," a metaphor that conjures up notions of protection and insulation from external events. But although things that are insulated from the environment may be preserved, they are also unable to change. The approach used by 3M yields a different perspective. Far from making the company's businesses fire-resistant, its reliance on crisis seems to make them fire-dependent! The exposure of 3M's businesses to the environment allows them to be renewed. In the use of such a process, 3M bears a striking resemblance to the behavior in nature of the community of shrubland plants known in the American Southwest as chaparral. Chaparral is dependent on fire for its growth: as they age, plants within the community secrete volatile oils and esters that are highly flammable. When ignited by lightning or other sources, the plants burn fiercely. Fire destroys decadent growth and accumulated litter, recycles nutrients, and promotes vigorous growth in seeds and shoots, which are themselves protected from fire.[36] Just as is the case in 3M, it is the fire dependence of the chaparral that promotes growth and allows it to survive.

MEASUREMENT

As we found to our cost in Russelsteel, a heavy reliance on financial measurements tends to focus the organization on the past and discourage renewal, especially during the "good" times when everyone is making his or her numbers. Both GE and 3M have been able to develop measurements that *affect the future*. Often this involves the measurement of nonfinancial factors, particularly those related to customer satisfaction and employee morale and attitudes. Such measurements may serve as powerful aids to the perception of opportunities or gaps in the organization and may also raise the awareness of both internal and external constraints to change.

The best-known measurers of nonfinancial factors in business organizations are the Japanese. In their continuous improvement (CI) and total quality management (TQM) initiatives, they measure a host of variables that are directly connected to physical processes. The multiple goals pursued by these programs are often conflicting and paradoxical—high quality and low cost, for example. In addition, the goals often transcend current practice or even common sense, requiring perfection—"zero defects." These goals effectively ignore what has been achieved in the past in an attempt to create a clean slate and maximize potential improvement.[37]

Tichy and Sherman identify the conflict created by paradox as a key ingredient in GE's transformation: "Welch insists that GE managers learn to master paradox. In his view, an apparent conflict between two worthy goals is no excuse for not pursuing them both: He regards the simultaneous pursuit of long- and short-term objectives as a basic responsibility of management."[38]

We had direct experience of the power of creating paradox by pursuing conflicting goals when, after years of focus on financial returns, we set out to measure customer satisfaction. It was decided that "on-time delivery" would be an easily obtained proxy for this. Indeed, it was the ease of gathering this information that made it so attractive rather than the sophistication of the metric. In the process of making this measurement, each branch developed the reasons behind the late deliveries so that the causes could be addressed. These "reason codes," as they were called, were soon standardized so that comparisons could be made across the service centers:

Late Delivery Reason Codes
1. Sales lead time too short
2. Credit hold
3. Processing delay
4. Quality hold
5. Inventory location delay
6. Delivery truck delay
7. Third-party delivery delay
8. Outside processor delay
9. Interbranch delay

It was no surprise to anyone that overoptimistic sales promises were the primary cause of missed deliveries. But the fact that the dimensions of on-time delivery could be measured had the effect of fragmenting these dimensions, forcing the operating units to measure yet more variables. To improve performance, each unit set up still smaller teams composed of people closer to operations to investigate these subdimensions. Again, although both on-time performance and market share improved,[39] the units found themselves subdividing the reason codes in order to make finer distinctions. One unit subdivided the original nine reason codes into forty-three subcodes and had no reason to believe that it had reached the end of the process.

As the dimensions of on-time delivery became fragmented, the members of the organization effectively "zoomed in" on the processes behind the measures in finer and finer detail.[40] This was equivalent to discovering new open patches in the organizational "forest" on scales that had never before been explored. As each new patch was opened up, the hard analytical techniques and softer process skills that had been used at higher levels were replicated on the smaller scales in the effort to redesign the processes. As such, the "zoom" process is akin to using biofeedback to regain control over and modify habits that have long been subconscious. This requires the isolation of processes that are buried deep in the system and the use of sensitive measuring devices to detect changes in them. Trial and error can be used to return what were once unconscious processes to conscious control. I will discuss the organizational implications of this process further in Chapter 7.

REENGINEERING AND RENEWAL

By now, the reader may be wondering in what way the management implications of the ecocycle differ from the currently popular technique of reengineering.[41] After all, the classic definition of reengineering is: "the fundamental rethinking and radical redesign of business processes to achieve dramatic improvements in critical, contemporary measures of performance, such as cost, quality, service and speed."[42] In their emphasis on radical and dramatic change, the two appear to have much in common. The resemblance, however, is only superficial, for there is a profound difference between the two. Whereas reengineering is an avowedly instrumentally rational management technique, the learning loop of the ecocycle is explicitly nonrational in this instrumental sense.

The difference will be seen most clearly in the next chapter when the concept of leadership in the renewal cycle is discussed, but the fundamental distinction can be pointed out here. The two best-known proponents of reengineering define a leader as follows: "not as someone who makes other people *do* what he or she wants, but as someone who makes them *want* what he or she wants" (emphasis in the original).[43] This implies, however, that "the" leader knows what he or she wants. It will be argued in the next chapter that if this is indeed the case, then the process belongs firmly on the performance loop of the ecocycle. For on the learning loop, the assumption is that no one in the organization knows what he or she wants in any technical sense. After crisis has broken the most powerful constraints binding the organization and its people, selectively erasing parts of the organizational memory, there is no framework of logic to decide what is needed for the organization as a whole. The remaining two phases of management action in the renewal cycle are aimed at the creation of learning processes and contexts in which the question "What do we want?" can be answered.

7

Ethical Anarchy

THE PREVIOUS chapter dealt with the most controversial implication of the ecocycle model—the need for managers to create deliberate, preemptive crises in mature, successful organizations. By itself, however, creating crises is not enough. It is only the beginning and the easiest phase of management action in the renewal cycle. The phases that lie ahead are less controversial but much more difficult to execute. For they test to the utmost managers' integrity—their capacity not to stand outside the situation that they have created but to join with it, sharing the fate of their people. Managers must create crises, and then they must become part of the situation they have created. It is anarchy, but it is ethical anarchy.

ACTION 2: WALKING THE TALK

After the crises, the accompanying confusion, and the breaking of constraints, we have now reached that part of the renewal cycle in which rational action is again possible. This is the phase of the process that Tichy and Sherman call "Envisioning," although one must be careful not to interpret it as an individual, intellectual activity. It begins with values-based behavior that expresses the *social vision of the future*. It is a view—perhaps only an intuition—of a distant, over-the-horizon goal. It may be idealistic or even utopian in its scope—like the early Quakers' ambition to change all of society. It is the social aspect of the vision that is important, because *if managers have a comprehensive technical vision of the future, then they should be on the other side of the ecocycle*. If they already know the technical "answers," then there must be a logic that they can direct others to follow. Pretending that they want to empower their people in order to get them to "buy in" gets perilously close to manipulation. And in my experience, the people will tend to perceive it as such: they will feel that they are being used.[1] Instead of feeling empowered, they feel emotionally drained.[2]

If managers know the technical answers, there are still good reasons to communicate with people, but there is no need to go through the full, painful renewal cycle. The job can probably be accomplished by reengineering the process within the existing hierarchical structure. This saves a lot of time and doesn't try to fool anyone about who is in charge.

Compaq's switch from "hunting" to "herding" discussed in Chapter 5 is an excellent example of a radical change in an organization's performance being achieved in this way. Eckard Pfeiffer knew what he wanted, and he seems to have implemented his strategy with classic, instrumental rationality. The reengineers have been quick to claim this example as their own, but this may be a little ingenuous.[3] Pfeiffer's conviction that he was right and his realization that Compaq had to cut its costs dramatically did not come from any analytical technique. They came from his earlier experience at Texas Instruments with the collapsing prices for calculators and watches. He had seen products evolve that way before and knew what had to be done.

His action was successful because it was synchronous with the trends in the marketplace. The PC environment was changing rapidly from an r-selection climate favoring high-priced, features-based products to a much more competitive K-selection context in which high-volume, low-priced PCs would thrive. Like a surfer on a wave, Pfeiffer and Compaq put on a spectacular show, *but only because they were going with the power of the wave* and because they caught a particularly big one—a once-in-a-product-lifetime event.

The context was critical for success, yet rarely do the reengineers and other purveyors of instrumentally rational techniques acknowledge its existence, let alone its importance. Too often the impression is given that managers can take their organizations in any direction at any time. It is this neglect of context that makes it so easy to describe successful organizational change retrospectively *as if* managers had used a particular technique, even though it would have been impossible to go forward using that technique.

Thus, the change at Compaq qualifies as a transformation, perhaps a radical one, but not as renewal. For it all took place on the performance loop of the ecocycle. There was a modified logic but not a new logic: it was a technical vision, and the pathway to it had been trodden before. In the renewal cycle, however, a manager's behavior has to model the social vision—the behavior expected from all the members of the organization—because the technical logic remains to be discovered. The senior managers do not know what it is, and everyone's help is required. *And if we want everyone to contribute, it had better be an egalitarian vision.* This is the essence of the leadership required at this stage of the ecocycle.

Crisis creation, then, can be thought of as "ethical anarchy": the leader creates the crisis knowing only that it is necessary for the renewal of the organization. There is no hidden agenda, no instrumental rationality to the move, and *this is made clear by the leader's behavior.* Actions are taken not to get things done but to show the leader's total involvement in the situation with his or her people: the actions are a way of living. For unless everyone is seen to suffer a shared fate, the creation of crisis will come to be seen as a stratagem, a manipulation.[4] It will be viewed as a continual cry of "Wolf!" that gradually declines in its ability to rouse the members of the organization to action and replaces commitment with cynicism.

LEADERSHIP

Our notions of leadership in North America have been bedeviled by our individualistic psychology with its stress on rational-economic motivation and our post–World War II experience with what appeared to be smooth, manageable change. We have all too often confused leadership with hierarchical dominance, and it is very easy, at a distance, to mistake compliance with commands from the top of the organization with commitment to a cause. In recent years, however, the distinction has been made more clearly between "transactional" managers and "transformational" leaders.[5] It is clear that the generators of commitment in an organization are what we call charismatic leaders. As was mentioned in Chapter 5, however, the concept of charisma is fraught with problems. All I can do here is to highlight some of these and make clear what kind of charismatic leadership is required in this phase of the renewal cycle.

Although crisis is not a prerequisite for charismatic leadership to emerge, crisis often fuels its emergence, especially in its best-known version, that of the heroic leader:

> Heroic leaders—in contrast with leaders who are merely enjoying popular favor—usually arise in societies undergoing profound crisis. Existing mechanisms of conflict resolution have broken down; traditions, established authority, old legitimations, customary ways of doing things—all are under heavy strain. Mass alienation and social atomization are rising. Intense psychological and material needs go unfulfilled. Long-held values are ready to be replaced or transformed. A variety of secondary leaders come to the fore to raise expectations and sharpen demands. In short, a crisis in trust and legitimacy overwhelms the system's rulers, ideology and institutions. Then there appears a leader or leadership group, equipped with rare gifts of compassion and competence—dynamic, resourceful, responsive—that rebels against authority and tradition.[6]

Heroic leaders have featured prominently throughout our interpretations of history. Unfortunately, the heroes have all too often had a dark side. Perhaps it is this aspect of charisma, together with his experience in Germany in the 1930s, that has given Peter Drucker such an abiding distrust of individual leaders, particularly charismatic leaders: "Leadership is all hype. We've had three great leaders in this century—Hitler, Stalin, and Mao—and you see the devastation they left behind."[7] Whatever the reason, Drucker uses the word *leadership* sparingly throughout his writings, always emphasizing what he sees as its collective rather than individual nature.[8]

For creativity during the renewal cycle of an organization, the type of charismatic leadership required is egalitarian, collective, and nonexploitive. This is the form of charismatic leadership exemplified by the founders of the Quaker movement and, in modern times, by leaders like Mahatma Ghandi, Nelson Mandela, and Mother Teresa. It is true that this kind of charisma comes to mind less often than that exercised by Hitler, Stalin, and Mao, but it is just as real. Clearly, people in crisis are susceptible to both kinds of charisma, and although we may abhor the dark side, ignoring the phenomenon does not make it go away. Indeed, we need to understand the "light" manifestation of charisma if we are to avoid the dark.

A clue to this understanding is in one possible derivation of the word *lead* from the Latin *lira,* meaning a "furrow." This analogy evokes the image of a leader creating pathways that direct natural processes to flow along them. Leadership in this metaphor is *the creation of conditions under which self-organization or learning can occur.* That is, it is the creation of contexts in which people can organize themselves. One of the best descriptions that fits this interpretation of leadership is that by Mary Parker Follett (1868–1933), one of the first management thinkers to bring a process perspective to the subject:

> The leader guides the group and is at the same time guided by the group, is always part of the group. No one can truly lead except from within. . . . [T]he leader must interpret our experience to us, must see all the different points of view which underlie our daily activities. . . . He must give form to things vague, things latent, to mere tendencies. He must be able to lead us to wise decisions, not to impose his own wise decisions upon us. We need leaders, not masters or drivers. . . . The skillful leader then does not rely on personal force; he controls his group not by dominating but by expressing it. He stimulates what is best in us; he unifies and concentrates what we feel only gropingly and scatteringly, but he never gets away from the current of which we and he are both an integral part. He is a leader who gives form to the inchoate energy in every man. The person who influences me most is not he who does great deeds but he who makes me feel I can do great deeds.[9]

Welch puts it less poetically, but no less paradoxically. He calls it "leading while being led."[10]

Modeling and Framing

The objective of this leadership activity is to build a larger-scale, loosely connected network of talented individuals who are held together by common values, a shared vision of the future, and a unique sense of who they are as a people. The two most important outputs of these activities are commitment[11] and trust.[12] Individual efforts, previously self-centered and trivial, become connected with important values and take on new significance. Narrow self-interests are broadened to embrace collective and altruistic interests. Individual self-esteem as well as a sense of pride in belonging to the organization are increased. Thus, it is these leadership activities that are responsible for maintaining the dynamic balance between the individual and the team.

Charismatic leaders achieve this by modeling and framing[13] the behavior required to renew the organization. These activities are closely connected. In their day-to-day activities, leaders act out the kinds of behavior that they expect their people to exhibit. They must expect their followers *to walk their walk*. At the same time, they are framing that behavior—by telling the story of the past and articulating the vision of the future. It is a shared story and a shared vision.

These kinds of activities allow multiple leadership roles to be played all over the organization. For example, during the renewal of Russelsteel, recounted in Chapter 3, Wayne Mang articulated the vision, but after extensive interaction with many people over an extended period of time. My role was to tell the story of where we had been—to untangle the complex patterns of behavior and describe their significance. Between the two of us, between vision and history, together with the rest of the team, we created a sense of evolution and progress. Between past and future, there was a present that became full of meaning for the people in the organization, particularly those on the core teams. Events and activities took on a new significance for them. For meaning is not something that we possess; it is something we make. It is what we are—makers of meaning. Every time we told our story, we helped others make sense of who they were, and then *they knew how to behave*—in contexts with which they were intimately familiar. Their self-esteem and their need for self-expression became intimately tied to the behavior the senior managers modeled. All the members of the team became behavioral role models in the myriad of contexts in which members of organizations find themselves. The central "message"—the behavior—was spread like a contagious disease. This is the only way that it can be spread on the learning loop.

Values-based behavior cannot be reduced to a set of rules or instructions and issued to employees. In the words of Mary Parker Follett:

[M]orality is never static; it advances as life advances. You cannot hang your ideals up on pegs and take down no. 2 for certain emergencies and no. 4 for others. *The true test of our morality is not the rigidity with which we adhere to standard, but the loyalty we show to the life which constructs standards.* The test of our morality is whether we are living not to follow but to create ideals, whether we are pouring our life into our visions only to receive it back with its miraculous enhancement for new uses.[14]

A list of injunctions may help, but the actual behavior will always be a creative act and has to be acted out in the relevant contexts if people are to learn from it.

Symbols, Patterns, and Settings

There are a myriad of leadership behaviors and communication methods that promote openness, commitment, and trust (and even more that can kill those processes).[15] People in every organization scrutinize the behavior of their senior managers from the moment they arrive (or don't arrive) at their places of work. Their cars, their parking places, their clothes, their expressions, their offices, their language, where they sit, whom they do and don't talk to, where they eat, how they fly, what time they leave, and countless other facets of their existence are fed into a giant interpretive process that produces a continuous readout on the state of the organization.

It is a complex, multidimensional reality that people are scanning, with unlimited places for them to "zoom" in and out as they search for consistency between the "talk" and the "walk." Does the boss use "I" or "we"? When she has visitors, does she sit behind her desk or in front? Does she laugh? At what? What are his favorite images? These are often a dead giveaway to how people see the world. Shortly after acquiring our renewed steel business with its turned-on team, the CEO of the conglomerate (the one who "hated surprises") gave an interview to the press. I can still remember how depressed I felt when he described himself and his senior executives as "hired guns."

The implications of this for managers of the renewal process are profound: *values-based behavior cannot be faked* because people read the overall patterns and their consistency across all scales. They are looking to their leaders for a lived, communicative process with a multidimensional structure, not a monotonic press release or a canned vision statement.

In this phase of the renewal cycle, then, managers are role models, modeling desirable behavior. On the learning loop, *it takes behavior to change behavior.* In fact, this section should probably have been entitled "Talking the Walk." Behavior comes first, language second. Managers have to explain how their *behavior* is contributing to the social vision. They cannot stand outside the contexts in which their people work, like so many cooks making a meal for the shareholders. Managers are cooks, but they are also ingredients, and the last instruction in every renewal recipe or plan must be "Throw yourself into the mixture."

People's Response to the Renewal Effort

In any organization, the people most open to change are the young, who have little investment in the status quo, and the mavericks, if they have been able to survive in the organization during the prosperity of the conventional life cycle. Under the Watsons, IBM always espoused the need to keep its so-called wild ducks against the day when the company would need them, and this was at least part of the logic behind the IBM Fellows program.[16] It would seem to be a sensible way of maintaining greater cognitive variety within the organization than would otherwise be possible. Indeed, this is exactly what happened in the case of GE and Jack Welch. When the organization needed a maverick to lead it, he was groomed and ready to take over.

A more serious problem in the renewal of an established organization is how to handle the likely mismatch between the habits of the members of the "old" performance organization and the behaviors required for renewal. This is a particular problem for companies like GM that may have built their entire human resourcing function around the old recipe. Undoubtedly, some will not survive the process, but it seems that the appropriate social, psychological, and physical contexts can evoke the necessary behaviors in most people. An examination of Chrysler's renewal cycle from 1978 onward, for example, would show how Lee Iacocca, a constrained actor at Ford, played the role of charismatic leader in his new company. During Chrysler's turnaround and renewal, he was seen as the embodiment of everything for which the company stood. He became a spokesperson to external customers and a role model for the management team. Many members of this team had, like him, once been frustrated, constrained actors at other car companies. They flourished in their turn in the contexts that he and the crisis at Chrysler helped to create.

· · · · · · ·

ACTION 3: CREATING THE CONTEXTS

The ecocycle identifies three types of context, each of which promotes one kind of management action and restricts others. The relationship of effective managers to these contexts must change as they move around the ecocycle. On the performance loop, all managers in the rational phase work *within* the context. Indeed, instrumental rationality requires that they be able to appeal to a framework of logic to justify their actions. In the constrained part of the ecocycle, if the organization is to be renewed, managers have to get *outside* the context. As we saw in Chapter 6, they do this by creatively destroying the system, breaking the constraints that bind the organization. In the rational portion of the learning loop, managers are once again *inside* the context, although this time the framework appealed to is based on values rather than logic.

In the third phase of the renewal cycle, managers have to *maintain* a context—a context in which learning can take place across all levels of the organization. We are concerned with contexts that allow the emergence of new behaviors. That is, we are concerned with contexts that encourage learning. It has been my contention throughout this book that the characteristics of these contexts, these communities of learning, are to be found throughout human history—in organizations as diverse as those of the nomadic hunter-gatherers of the Kalahari, the Quakers, and as I shall now argue, the firms of Silicon Valley.[17]

FROM THE KALAHARI TO SILICON VALLEY

Observers have remarked that, in some ways, the entire community of Silicon Valley in northern California[18] seems to be a single organization consisting of a vast professional and social network of individuals.[19] The network includes institutions such as Stanford University and trade associations as well as a multitude of suppliers of technical, financial, and networking services.[20] The focus of individual commitment, the modern counterpart of the hunting band or Quaker meeting, is the project. Many individuals "sign up" for unspecified but finite periods of time to work with great intensity on project teams.[21] Once a project is over, they move to other projects, searching for the technological frontiers where the more immediate returns are to be had and the chances of success are greatest.

For many individuals, the notion of allegiance to a formal organizational structure, to the company within which the project takes place, is anathema. Continuity is provided by being plugged into the network, where the sense of community, professional respect, personal loyalties, and friendship transcend the ferment of innovation.[22] Survival depends on keeping individual skills honed, staying flexible, and finding the "hot" projects on which to work.

This dynamic could not work in "herder" structures with well-defined hierarchies and defended territories. Silicon Valley is an open meritocracy where what counts is the situation and the skills required to address it. Individuals are important, but the blending of their skills, the team, is preeminent. Like the nomadic Bushman hunters and the early Quakers, successful Silicon Valley firms achieve a dynamic balance of individuality and community. This is true even in firms like Intel, whose confrontational, "Spartan" culture can be contrasted with the much more friendly, "Athenian" culture of Hewlett-Packard.[23] Both firms are assertively egalitarian. HP appeals to family values, Intel to those of the team:

The image of a giant research team is important to understanding the corporate philosophy Intel developed for itself. On a research team, everyone is an equal, from the project director right down to the person who cleans the floors: each contributes his or her expertise toward achieving the final goal of a finished, successful project. In this schema, little else matters besides the final victory—not the bottom line per se, but the new chip, the new growth goal, the victory over a threatening opponent.[24]

The language sounds far too aggressive for either hunters or Quakers, but I contend that although the rhetoric may be different, the social dynamics are much the same. Indeed, the parallels between the social dynamics of Silicon Valley and those of the original nomadic hunters are striking. Both cultures are assertively egalitarian and reject hierarchical authority. They each find a dynamic balance between self-indulgent individualism and the deadening effects of collectivism. Individuals are self-directed within a context of mutual dependence: there is competition, but within a framework of cooperation. The dynamic flexing and flowing in the composition of the organization is also present in

. . . .

each society, whose organizational form, in the absence of hierarchy, can only be described as a system of dynamic networks.

CONTEXTS WITHIN ORGANIZATIONS

Within an individual organization, the creation of context is the stage that Tichy and Sherman call "Rearchitecting." Read casually, it carries unfortunate connotations. Although this word does not exist in the dictionary, the image it conjures up is of lone individuals working with computers and blueprints to design structures that make statements to outsiders. Nevertheless, Tichy and Sherman make it clear that it has to do with internal, social structures and the breaking of the barriers that separate people.

When Honda felt that its Civic and Accord models were losing their appeal to the youth market, it set up the City development project. The average age of the team members was only twenty-seven. They were told "to create a radically different concept of what a car should be like." For the team, it was "the kind of car that we, the young, would like to drive."

The metaphors used to describe the car contained opposing concepts. The car was to be "horizontally short and vertically long"! As Nonaka has put it: "Such visions can be regarded as metaphors in the sense that the metaphor provides novel and equivocal meanings (even contradictions) which depend on indefinite patterns of associated ideas or images. . . . [A] global vision as a metaphor encourages people to search for new meanings. . . ."[25]

Senior management gave the team complete autonomy and saw its own role as setting the environment with a certain tension in it:

> At times, management needs to do something drastic like setting objectives, giving the team full responsibility, and keeping its mouth shut. It's like putting the team members on the second floor, removing the ladder, and telling them to jump, or else. I believe creativity is born by pushing people against the wall and pressuring them almost to the extreme.[26]

On the surface, this example might still sound like any other North American management stratagem—set "stretch" objectives and apply pressure. But this is not the case, and the clue to this lies in the *social context:* Honda is working on the learning loop of the ecocycle. The objective is neither clear nor measurable, and the context of the pressure is one of lifetime employment. The challenge is not to perform but to transcend existing thinking: no one is going to get fired, but people's reputations and futures are on the line. The goal is visionary, and the pressure is contextual rather than pointed at individuals. The young, handpicked team has a minimal investment in the status quo. It is a miniature hunting system, and the "environment" of stress is designed to elicit r-strategies from them.

DIALOGUE

The central problem in unstable organizations in turbulent environments is that the situations in which managers find themselves are not just uncertain, they are equivocal. The difficulty is not in the distribution of probabilities across a range of outcomes but in the assignment of meaning to events. In the early days of the financial crisis at Russelsteel, for example, we could not make sense of all the contradictory information we were receiving. It wasn't a question of problem solving; it was a question of problem *finding*: we had to find the right questions before we could look for the answers.

It has been suggested that when problem finding, or the definition of problems, is an issue for an organization, then our conventional concepts of information processing are inadequate.[27] It is the *quality* rather than the *quantity* of information that counts in these situations, and information is richest in the small scale, face-to-face encounters in contexts like the hunters' campfire circles. It seems that we need the primary group to foster the use of our primary, creative cognitive processes.[28] I believe that this applies to us today as much as it did to our hunting-foraging ancestors.

The reason for the effectiveness of the campfire circle as physical context is the high quality of the face-to-face communication, or dialogue as it is being referred to in management writings.[29] Numerous benefits of face-to-face communication have been identified.[30] First, the participants in the process are always together in the same time and space, supplying rich contextual cues to supplement what they say to one another. The "bandwidth" of the channels being used is the widest possible, capturing all the possibilities of human interaction, covering all the senses and the complete range of emotional responses. It is this breadth of face-to-face communication that allows the Bushmen to raise the most delicate of subjects in a nonconfrontational way. It also gives the structure of their interaction an enormous capacity for interruption and repair, feedback and learning.

The reader may well be thinking that all this talk of "dialogue" is just a slightly more sophisticated way of making a plea for better communication. In a way, it is, but by looking at the contexts that constrain such communication, there may be a chance that something can be done about it. For the most serious constraint to such communication is the structure of the physical spaces in which we live and work.[31]

Physical Spaces

Research[32] on the habits of engineers in research facilities has found that:

- They get over 80 percent of their ideas through direct face-to-face contact with their colleagues. Comparatively few ideas come from attending conventions and reading technical journals.
- They will not travel more than 100 feet from their desks to exchange ideas.
- They hate to use the telephone to ask for information.
- The physical layout of the workplace influences interactions more than any other factor.
- Vertical separation between floors hinders communication more than horizontal separation between offices.
- Visual contact is critical to good communication and the generation of new ideas.

As a result of findings like these, firms such as Apple, Corning Glass, GE, and 3M design their research facilities to maximize the opportunities for interpersonal interaction. They keep the number of physical levels to a minimum, supplying multiple modes of moving between them—escalators and ramps as well as stairs and elevators. Their designs are "open," with glass walls in offices and meeting rooms, so that visual contact is possible at all times. Round tables in meeting rooms emphasize the egalitarian culture. Discussion areas, known as "blips," are placed in passageways along exterior walls. Each blip contains work chairs, tables, and writing surfaces, to encourage spontaneous creativity. Chance encounters are not left to chance: interactions are maximized.

As Figure 7-1 shows, the layout of the average executive office[33] in the Western world[34] could hardly be more opposed in design to that of these research facilities.

The traditional layout, "Mahogany Row," is designed to make symbolic statements that impress outsiders with the organization's success. At the same time, the countless nuances of design are carefully graded to show the rank and importance of the inhabitants. The overall layout is structured to restrict access to executives and to shape interactions into narrow channels. Coupled with a structured timetable ("We will send for you when we need you"), this layout ensures that little that is novel will enter the space. Spontaneity is inhibited.

An alternative layout, dubbed "Caves and Commons,"[35] reflects a quite different philosophy. It is designed to maximize interaction among insiders. It achieves this by placing a series of private, personal spaces ("caves") around an open, communal space (the "commons"). Two easily accessible, larger rooms are available—the one for larger meetings, the other for visual display of information. Everyone can see one another from the door of his or her "cave," maximizing the opportunities for spontaneous visual contact. The communal space is totally flexible in its use. It is literally an "open patch," which allows novel patterns of interaction to emerge and develop in an uncontrolled way.

Figure 7-1 Two Executive Layouts

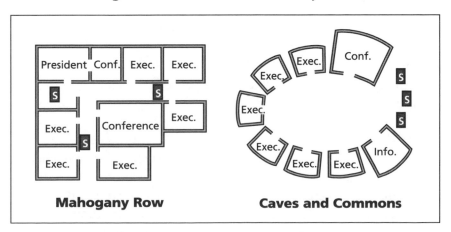

Mahogany Row   **Caves and Commons**

Source: Adapted from Steele 1983 (68, 74). Reprinted by permission of publisher, from *Organizational Dynamics,* Spring/1983 © 1983. American Management Association, New York. All rights reserved.

The reader should not have to turn back to the camp layouts in Chapter 1 to realize that these two designs are ten thousand years old. They are the modern equivalents of the living arrangements of the herders and the hunters.

At the same time, one is struck by a sobering thought: most of our general-purpose buildings are variations on the design of a box. The "Caves and Commons" layout needs circular spaces without utilities in the center. How difficult it is going to be to change the physical spaces in which executives interact! Worse than that, how difficult it is going to be to change workplaces where size[36] and technology mandate certain physical layouts that violate all the requirements for good communication!

Many people believe that electronic communications will solve these problems, but they are a long way from doing so. The bandwidth of E-mail, for example, is far too narrow to replicate the "social reality" of face-to-face contact. And such contacts will always be much more susceptible to fraud and deception than the real thing. Some researchers have suggested that the role of electronic communication is much more suited to use in markets and traditional hierarchies—in the cause of efficiency rather than creativity.[37]

A more optimistic example of what technology might allow us to accomplish in an administrative setting is that of Oticon, a Danish manufacturer of hearing aids, which has eliminated private offices altogether at its head office. Everyone has his or her personal possessions in a mobile filing cabinet and sits at whatever desk/terminal is available. This creates a highly mobile grouping of people that can flex and flow as required. Their permanent "locations" are their mailbox addresses on the computer network. Use of the system is encouraged by the practice of scanning all mail into the system and shredding everything except legal documents (80 percent of paperwork has been eliminated).[38]

EDUCATION

The physical contexts in which people work may be difficult to change, but the contexts in which they learn are relatively easy to construct. Unfortunately, this change in context is a double-edged sword: it makes learning easy yet renders it quite difficult to transfer knowledge and behavior back into the workplace. We found this out in our own in-house education program.

Tichy and Sherman describe the development of agents of change as demanding that people be put at intellectual, emotional, and even physical risk (the latter risk, which is of the "Outward Bound" training variety, is more perceived than real).[39] If the risk is seen as severe, people may "freeze," either locking in past behaviors or blindly following orders from above. If the risk is moderate, on the other hand, people may well try new behaviors. These behaviors usually emerge more easily if the learning context is radically different from that of the workplace.

We had direct experience of this phenomenon in our attempt to change the behavior of people within the steel business via the use of some seminars of radical design. Whereas GE has targeted managers for its initial change efforts, we focused on everyone within the organization. Groups of fifty people from all over the company—truck drivers, salespeople, switchboard operators, managers, and executives—went away for three days of communication and team building. Each seminar was a microcosm of the business, although, of necessity, it contained people from different branch operations. These were dubbed "core sample" seminars because their composition resembled that of a drill core taken from the earth.

The setting for the seminars was an old country home in the very best traditions of executive education, and the teaching vehicles were a series of team-building activities and facilitated discussions, including a Harvard case study![40] The aims of these seminars were very similar to those of GE's Work-Out program:

- Building trust
- Empowering employees
- Eliminating unnecessary work
- Developing a new paradigm

The seminars made excellent progress on the first two goals, although the dynamics often surprised us. Indeed, the best sessions were not the formal ones but the informal gatherings—breakfast, lunch, dinner, and the parties! The power of everyone's sitting down together for meals at long refectory tables astounded us. The intensity of the communication was palpable. The physical setting, together with the participation of senior executives, facilitated what might otherwise have been a high-risk venture.

We found it more difficult to deal with business processes in this initial phase. It was only later on—when the soft skills could be combined with the hard, analytical techniques and explicit measurement—that we could tackle the business processes. And it was this delay that created problems for the empowered people emerging from the seminars: their feelings of competence and empowerment, together with raised expectations of change, ran head on into the unchanged physical and psychological contexts of the workplace. We tried to prepare them for it intellectually, telling them that they were guerrilla fighters (a metaphor developed from the case), who would have to go "underground" and wait until the opportunities emerged. But intellectual explanations don't sway sentiments. The feelings of excitement and personal renewal, which the seminars had taken only a few hours to generate, were often extinguished even more quickly upon the attendees' return to the workplace.

This is the central problem with all educational programs within established organizations. If they are effective, they are subversive of the status quo, but as soon as the participants return to the performance context, their newly learned behaviors are suppressed. One can be successful in creating a learning environment in which desirable skills are learned and practiced—but how can these practices be transferred to a performance context? How can hunters live among herders? One answer is that they can do so only in an organization that has contexts for learning across all the scales.

IMPLICATIONS FOR ORGANIZATIONS: THINK DOUBLE

The requirement that organizations address both the performance and learning loops of the ecocycle simultaneously demands that managers "think double"[41] about structures and processes. One cannot go with either just the vertical performance structure or just the newly popular horizontal structure.[42] One has to think of both, weaving them together in space and time.[43]

In the periods of crisis in Russelsteel, there were two natural clusters into which the issues seemed to fall. These clusters became known as "horizontal" (or "learning") initiatives and "vertical" (or "performance") issues. The structure created by the overlaying of the "soft" learning initiatives on the "hard" performance structure resembled a woven fabric and was called a "soft" matrix.[44] Figure 7-2 shows the soft matrix at Fedmet[45] (as the steel distribution operations were then called) at the senior level in 1991.

The horizontal task forces and teams were temporary and self-managing, so individuals within the organization did not have two bosses in any hierarchical sense. They had a boss in the "permanent," vertical hierarchy and were part of a self-managing group in the learning system. The temporary horizontal task forces either produced changes that could be incorporated into the permanent vertical structure or went out of existence.

We found that it is extremely important to keep separate the two strands of the fabric of the soft matrix. As the biofeedback analogy suggests, the objective of the horizontal processes is learning. The clearer the association between action and result, the more effective that learning will be. The proliferation of measurements of different factors will often hamper the learning process, and the powerful mechanisms that enforce and sustain the performance organization are a continual threat to it. As the two processes are being woven together in space and time, it requires great vigilance to keep them apart. It is

Figure 7-2 The Fedmet Soft Matrix

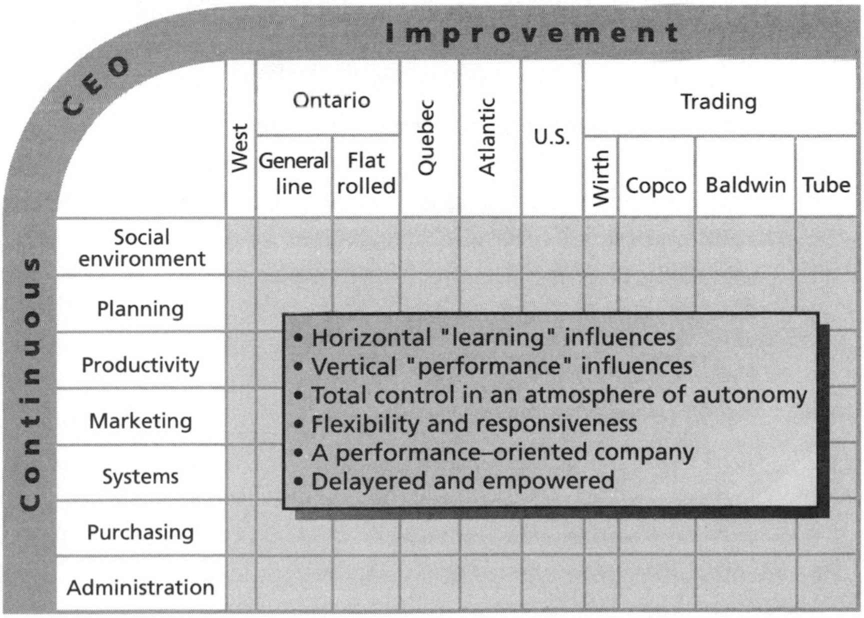

all too easy to "lock up" the matrix by making the horizontal initiatives rigid through premature application of performance-based incentives and sanctions. In our experience, the net effect of this was to turn the soft matrix into a hard matrix, with a performance structure running both horizontally and vertically. Caught in the resulting gridlock, torn between multiple objectives, dazed by the introduction of one "priority" after another, and intimidated by the resurgent hierarchical social system, people tended to "dig in," pay lip service to the initiatives, and develop myriad ways to beat the system. That is, they become masters at giving the appearance of change without actually changing.

REPLICATING THE HUNTING/RENEWAL PATTERN ACROSS ALL SCALES OF THE ORGANIZATION

Yet if one can keep the processes separate, the soft matrix can be an effective vehicle for renewal. The key is to replicate *across as many scales as possible* the social dynamics and physical contexts of a nomadic hunting band. Here flexibility existed at every level, reducing the chances that the whole organization might be constrained by factors operating at any one level:

- Individuals were self-directed and multiskilled.
- The relationship between pairs of individuals was one of mutual dependence: leaders and followers could switch their roles easily.
- Groups were open and unrestrictive: people could enter and leave them with a minimum of hassle.
- Territories were open and undefended so that neighboring groups could range over them.
- The social vision was of an egalitarian society, and this legitimated the dynamics at every level of the organization.
- All this took place in the context of "immediate-return" economies with short feedback loops between action and result.

IMMEDIATE-RETURN ECONOMIES

On the surface, creating immediate-return economies would seem to be the most difficult of tasks, especially in mature organizations dominated by their technologies. However, we found it to be relatively easy. The objective is to create "open patches" that demand minimum investment for their exploitation and provide fast feedback on the results of action.

The "zooming" process, discussed earlier, whereby members of Russelsteel tracked problems at finer and finer levels of detail, had the effect of opening up small niches in the organization. These usually functioned as miniature immediate-return economies because *they had never been measured at that scale before.* Some of the niches opened up by this process may in fact be very large, particularly when suppliers and customers become part of the expanded organization. Benchmarking may create similar open gaps by focusing attention on hitherto unexploited areas of performance.

Patches can always be opened up outside of the organization by funding, with either time or money, personal projects that may not seem to have much to do with the business one is currently in. At 3M, grants of up to fifty thousand dollars are awarded to individual researchers with no strings attached. The program, called Genesis, encourages people to pursue their own idiosyncratic projects and removes the need for financial justification of the investment (that is, the need to fabricate numbers to get over the corporate hurdle rate!).

At Johnsonville Foods, the workers (members, as they are called) on the production line are supplied with immediate feedback on quality, for which they are responsible. This locates the capacity to learn as close as possible to the action.[46]

As described in Chapter 6, the Japanese *kanban* system, in its essence, sets up a series of immediate-return situations in which the feedback lag between action and result is very short. Any buffers in a production process—inventories and delays—can be fruitful places to look for improvements.

Individual Self-direction

The organization needs to select people who have enough confidence in themselves to work openly with others and create an environment in which they are encouraged to develop their skills. Training can help, but only if the context is one that encourages learning. In our experience, the multiskilling produced by the horizontal cross-functional teams in combination with training in both hard and soft skills is a powerful builder of individual self-direction. The power comes from the fact that the learning is taking place within a small group with shared interests and the skills being taught are directly relevant to problems being faced by the group's members.[47]

Bootlegging, a term that has been popularized by Tom Peters, is a culturally sanctioned process at 3M that allows employees to spend up to 15 percent of their time working on their own projects. This has the effect of creating slack for learning to take place. It is essential that the formal incentive schemes reward behavior that favors learning. At Johnsonville Foods, the only way to get a raise is to learn a new skill. At Rosenbluth Travel, the pay-for-quality system rewards accuracy and professionalism first, and only after these does it reward productivity.[48]

Mutual Dependence

The requirement for mutual dependence involves sharing resources and emphasizing the interdependence of individuals as well as organizational units. Obviously, the experience of working on teams, where the team is held accountable for the work, is a profound builder of feelings of mutual dependence. Rotation of leadership enhances the process. But there are other, more subtle, ways of reinforcing this.

At Johnsonville Foods, teams handle the selection, hiring, and firing process. W. L. Gore & Associates uses a similar technique: every new employee, or "associate," has to have an internal sponsor before he or she is hired. Bottom-up performance appraisal, in which subordinates provide feedback to their hierarchical boss, is a powerful technique that underscores the reciprocal nature of authority: in the long run, leaders require willing followers. It has been used for many years by IBM, especially at the senior levels. In my experience, bottom-up appraisal is fiercely resisted by the vertical, performance organization!

Nevertheless, if activities like this can be implemented, apart from promoting mutual dependence, they send an enormously powerful message—the message that, within the mutual dependence system, people are *in charge of their own destinies.* I can still remember my excitement when, toward the end of a "core sample" seminar, one attendee suddenly spoke up excitedly and said, "I understand: there is no 'them'; there's only 'us'!" Exactly.

Open Territories

Territories or turfs in the formal hierarchy are defended. As one goes up the scales, the boundaries between divisions and functions become thicker and less permeable. Introducing the necessary dynamics here can be difficult. The boundaries between divisions and functions, for example, are often opened only under duress.

One of the secrets to Nike's ability to renew itself seems to have been through the formation of "hunting parties," which sweep across the formal organization, breaking the fences and trampling the crops, but introducing novelty into the enterprise. The "Launch Group" that took the fabulously successful Air Jordan to market had such a dynamic but proved incredibly disruptive to the formal system.

The intensity of turf wars at 3M is reduced by the company's insistence that all the technologies belong to 3M as a whole, not to the individual units that developed them: the units get to sell the products, but the knowledge resource is shared across all entities. With fewer possessions, people are more likely to share with each other.

In its research facilities, GE goes so far as to insist that researchers vary their table mates at meals to encourage casual contact between researchers from different disciplines. To ensure cross-pollination with operations, members of R&D are regularly sent out to work in manufacturing units. This makes it harder for the different divisions and functions to characterize their rivals as "them" versus "us."[49]

Assertive Egalitarianism

The objective of assertive egalitarianism is to reduce status differences between individuals, especially between individuals in the formal hierarchy and the rest of the organization. The integrative solution is best achieved by making authority dependent on what Mary Parker Follett long ago called the "law of the situation": "One person should not give orders to another person, but both should agree to take their orders from the situation."[50] The clearest examples of this are the outcomes of the Bushmen's campfire dialogues and the consensus emerging from the Quaker meetings.

As Tom Peters has been pointing out for a long time, there is plenty of scope for removing the innumerable distinctions that hierarchies award to their members. Executive dining rooms and washrooms, reserved parking spaces, private offices, access to perks of all kinds—the list goes on and on. At Russelsteel, we found that one of the major improvements to our communication process came from our insistence on *round* tables in *every* meeting room.[51] In the case of the boardroom, the table was 10 feet in diameter. The improvement in participation by changing from conventional rectangular or oval tables has to be experienced to be believed. Unfortunately, many meeting rooms are designed for these much more hierarchical shapes.

The dual-ladder career system at 3M allows technical people to advance to higher positions while continuing their research work. They do not have to cross over to the management hierarchy in order to be recognized. This asserts the importance of their skills against hierarchical position. The company uses a number of awards and other marks of recognition to preserve this equality.

One of the most interesting devices for deflating executive egos and asserting egalitarianism is from Nike. The meetings of the Nike senior management group are known as "buttfaces." The epithet was attached by employees of the early Nike to anyone who aspired to hierarchical power. There must be rather few large, successful organizations in which one can call a senior manager "buttface" and have it taken as a compliment!

IMPLEMENTING THE STRATEGY AT ALL LEVELS OF THE ORGANIZATION

It seems trite to suggest that for a strategy to be effective in an organization, not only must the strategy be appropriate, but it must also be present at all levels in the organization.[52] After all, customers are even less interested in reading strategic plans than restaurant diners are in reading menus. Customers want either to use the product or to receive the service. Customers are separated from the traditional corporate strategists by *a number of scales,* and the strategy has to be translated into many different media if it is to be made visible. The strategic pattern, in various embodiments (products, manufacturing operations, marketing plans, speeches, and behavior), has to pervade the entire organization at all scales if the strategy is to be coherent and robust.

This has implications for the role of "the" strategist, who has been seen as bearing the primary responsibility for "opportunistic surveillance"[53] of the environment and therefore for the creation of competitive advantage. A soft matrix organization is, however, clearly as complex at the "bottom" as it is at the "top." Thus, the idea of senior management's being capable of scanning "the" environment is critically flawed: there are many environments, depending on the level at which you operate.

Nevertheless, in a soft matrix organization, senior managers do have a privileged position. They are inherently less constrained than anyone else, and their mobility within the organization gives them the potential to identify and articulate the similarities that exist across the branches and levels of the fractal organization. That is, they can recognize the way in which the organization resembles itself at different levels and in different places and promote processes that develop these patterns on smaller scales.

PARADOXES

The renewal cycle itself is full of contradictions and paradoxes. But these contradictions become compounded when one juxtaposes the renewal cycle with the performance loop of the conventional life cycle. For during the renewal of established organizations, managers have to come to grips with both loops in real time. And the nexus of the conflict is where the two forms of rationality cross—where the demand to live our values clashes with the requirement for instrumental behavior. It is where the social vision of an egalitarian, participative community clashes with the need to run a technically rational, hierarchical organization.[54] Where community may clash with individuality, as ambition vies with obligation; where cooperation meets competition; where the long run often trips over the short term.

This is one dilemma that the managers of new organizations do not have to face. In Blue Ribbon Sports in the early 1960s, for example, there was no status quo that Phil Knight and Bill Bowerman needed to defend. In the early years, both men earned a living outside the athletic shoe business. The creative tension and consequent personal drive were generated by the perceived gap between the current situation and their vision of the future, but they had no investment in the current situation. In established organizations, in contrast, there is a status quo to be defended—parts of the existing conservative structures that had better be maintained if the organization as a whole is to be given the time required to reinvent the business. But this requires managers to stretch across the scales—to preserve something of the existing large-scale organization while nurturing the small-scale seeds of renewal.

RHYTHMS OF RENEWAL

In the physical world, there are two ways for an individual to navigate in unfamiliar territory—by using a map and by using a compass. Often the two methods are complementary—when one uses the compass to orient a map, for example, or to plot a course to a defined destination. At other times, the two methods may contradict each other—when the map suggests that, in order to avoid an obstacle, one has to go in a direction different from that indicated by the compass, or when the compass is affected by local magnetic fields.

When the territory is open, with clear landmarks and no dangers, either method may suffice. Sometimes only one method or the other may be used effectively: a compass is essential if you are lost at sea, but only a map will do in downtown Manhattan. Maps, by definition, can help only in known worlds—worlds that have been charted before. Compasses are helpful when you are not sure where you are and can get only a general sense of direction.

This variety of relationships between the use of a map and the use of a compass—complementary, oppositional, neutral, and exclusionary—mirrors those between the twin loops of the organizational ecocycle and thus the twin roles of the senior people involved in organizations.[55] The performance loop insists on the use of a map; successful navigation of the learning loop requires a compass.

On the conventional, performance, loop of the ecocycle, a manager is continually trying to fit a relatively well defined organization to "its" relatively objective environment. The territory will be well traveled and somewhat familiar. This will help him place the organization's reality into clear, conceptual categories—to map it—and to focus on the key outputs and success factors. His emphasis on planning and control, as well as the embedding of the basic routines deep in the organization, will help keep it smoothly on track toward objectives that are relatively clear and often quantified. There will be a good deal of consensus among the members of the organization as to what these goals are, and the rewards for achieving them are clearly visible.

The manager on the performance loop hates surprises. He values well-defined task assignments and structured accountabilities. By nature conservative and sensitive to the constituencies he represents, he prefers models of managed change that appeal to an instrumental rationality and concepts of adaptability, congruence, and fit.

In the renewal portion of the ecocycle, the manager's role is very different. She is deliberately out of sync, trying to disrupt the organization's maddening predictability. She distrusts the neat categories into which the elements of the business have been divided and understands the wealth of detail that has been lost in that process of abstraction. For the business's tight focus ignores what she sees as multiple perspectives of reality.

Her focus is not on concepts, but on process and on action based on experience. Her goal is continually to provoke the organization to move into the next phase of the renewal process. If people are complacent or constrained, she "throws grenades," breaking the frameworks of interpretation and constructively damaging the status quo. When people are confused, she models the desired social relationships, tells the story of where they have been, and articulates the vision of goals that lie beyond the organization's horizon.

When the situation appears hopeless, she never fails to see the humor of their predicament, helping people to "jump out" of the mental boxes in which they have become trapped. She is continually on the lookout to make rather than meet the next situation, changing the contexts to create a climate favorable for collective action. She values novelty and surprise and uses them to promote the agenda, celebrating success wherever it is found. In real time, she never quite knows what she is doing, but she has a deep, tacit feeling for how human systems function.

Lost in uncharted territory, she has no maps to guide her. Never before has anyone been in quite such a situation. There is little time to think, and anyway she often has to act without thinking. Her egalitarian values serve as a compass needle: they are all she has to keep her pointing in roughly the right direction. These values—evoked, released, and shared with others—act for the overall organization as a sea anchor in the storms of change.

The creative integration of all these activities demands a manager who is sometimes rational, sometimes constrained, often confused, but never powerless—a manager who has a profound sense of the natural cycles of creation and destruction that all living systems must undergo. It demands a feel for the timing of when to act and when to wait, of when to go with the flow and when to oppose it, of when to stay on the beaten track and when to strike out for the distant hills. In short, it demands a deep understanding of the recurrent patterns in organizational change—an intuition of the rhythms of renewal.

Notes

Introduction

1. For this definition, I am indebted to the thoughts of Karl Weick (1990) on renewal.
2. Frye 1988 (15).
3. Chester Barnard said something similar: "It seems to me extremely unlikely that human beings can control the evolution of their society. This does not mean that what men do will not affect that evolution, but that the effects will be different than desired and many effects will be completely unforeseen. Is it not evident that we have very little understanding of complex social phenomena even after occurrence?" (written in a letter to William F. Whyte in August 1946 and quoted in Wolf 1974 [53]).
4. Tom Peters' book *Liberation Management* (1992) is indicative of what happens when one tries to avoid theory. In the words of one reviewer, "In such a thicket the reader quickly gets lost, so entangled in the undergrowth that each fresh anecdote detracts from others rather than adding to them" (*The Economist*, 5 December 1992, 96).
5. These are the perspectives developed by Pfeffer (1982).

6. It has been modified by notions of limits to our ability to understand complex systems that place limits or bounds on our rationality (Simon 1957).

7. For example, see Hannan and Freeman 1977.

8. In management academia, this third perspective is associated most closely with the work of Karl Weick (1969) and the "garbage can" model of Cohen, March, and Olsen (1972). In the field of strategy, the concept of emergent strategy has been developed most extensively by Mintzberg and Waters (1985).

9. Although I did not know it at the time I graduated from business school, the academic business community was then just starting to address the limitations of the rational actor model and to propose alternative frameworks. In the political field, for example, Graham Allison's (1971) well-known triple perspective on the Cuban missile crisis not only showed the pervasiveness of the rational model but demonstrated that equally valuable explanations could be generated using alternative perspectives.

10. Schon comments as follows:

> [O]ur present attitude toward change is essentially the view of Parmenides. We conceive of our institutions—nations, religions, business organizations, industries—as enduring. Change of values is seen as deviance, undependability, flightiness. Values are presumed to be firm and constant. To the extent that we admit historical change, we see it according to the model of progress—steady change occurring within a stable framework of value. (Schon 1967, xii)

11. Lewin 1947. A good example of the modern equivalent of Lewin's model is contained in Nadler's description of the process: "In its most general terms, then, the effective management of change involves developing an understanding of the current state (A), developing an image of a desired future state (B), and moving the organization from A through a transition period to B (Beckhard & Harris, 1977)" (Tushman and Moore 1988, 722).

   Some change experts have expressed surprise that the Lewinian model has survived for so long, attributing its longevity to the fact that "[i]t offers managers a very straightforward way of planning their actions, by simplifying an extraordinarily complex process into a child's formula." Nevertheless, many academics do not like change models that constrain actors—the change equivalents of the constrained action model. These have been described as "passive, pessimistic models of long-term evolution," to be contrasted unfavorably with "activist, optimistic models of strategy making." Quotes are from Kanter, Stein, and Jick (1992, 10, 24).

12. This distinction between the two kinds of rationality is attributable to Weber, who contrasted *zweckrational,* or formal rationality, with *wertrational,* or substantive rationality. The former is based on calculability and is value-neutral; the latter is value-laden.

   Brubaker summarizes Weber's views as follows:

First, rationality does not inhere in things, but is ascribed to them. Secondly, rationality is a relational concept: a thing can be rational (or irrational) only from a particular point of view, never in and of itself. . . .

Weber applies this relational conception of rationality to the analysis of social structure by distinguishing between formal *rationality and* substantive *rationality. Formal rationality is a matter of fact, substantive rationality is a matter of value. Formal rationality refers primarily to the* calculability *of means and procedures, substantive rationality primarily to the* value *(from some explicitly defined standpoint) of ends and results. From the point of view of the purely formal objective of maximizing the calculability of action—purely formal because maximally calculable action can be oriented to any of an infinite variety of possible substantive ends—capitalism, science, technology, and the modern legal and administrative system are highly rational. Such purely formal rationality, however, is in perpetual tension with what Weber calls substantive rationality, meaning rationality from the point of view of some particular substantive end, belief, or value commitment. . . .*

The antagonism between formal and substantive rationality may thus be interpreted as a tension between conflicting values: between calculability, efficiency and impersonality on the one hand and fraternity, equality and caritas on the other.
(Brubaker 1984, 35–41)

This distinction was picked up by the Frankfurt school, where it has formed the basis of its critique of positivist science. Marcuse's attack on modern technological society and Habermas's distinction between work and interaction seem to be based on the double dimensions of rationality. Values-based action would seem to have much in common with Habermas's concept of "communicative action" (Burrell and Morgan 1979, 291–296).

13. The primacy of perception in cognition has been forcefully argued by Rudolph Arnheim (1969, 244).
14. For a brief overview of the role of metaphor in management, see Zimmerman and Hurst 1993 (335).
15. Weick 1990.

Chapter 1: The Wisdom of the Hunters

1. *San* means "aborigines" in the Cape Hottentot dialect. It has been suggested among anthropologists that the term *Bushmen* carries racist overtones, although there is no consensus on the matter. I do not believe this to be the case in the readership toward which this book is directed. I think that *Bushmen* reads more easily than *San* or *!Kung* and take my lead from Sir Laurens Van der Post (1988).
2. The word *hunter* is highly evocative, arousing both positive and negative feelings in people. To some, it sounds glamorous; to others, excessively "macho." Some

experts (Margaret Power, personal communication) prefer to talk of male and female foragers rather than hunter-foragers. Indeed, there is evidence that primitive people were better scavengers than they were hunters (Blumenschine and Cavallo 1992). Nevertheless, *hunters* is in common usage and can be contrasted easily with *herders*. Also one must take pity on publishers faced with the problem of selling a management book with a chapter entitled "The Wisdom of the Scavengers"!

3. The distinction between immediate- and delayed-return societies is made most clearly by Woodburn (1982).

4. This so-called fission-fusion dynamic (Power 1991) is facilitated by three levels of flexibility in the society:

1. Individuals are multiskilled; they can contribute in many important ways to any group they join. Considerable knowledge and skill are required to live in the environment, but they are freely available. Members learn by participation, modeling their behavior on that of individuals who have the skills.

2. Groups are open, and the criteria for access to them are unrestrictive. An individual can leave one group knowing that he or she will not be denied entry to another.

3. The territories are open and undefended—permeable to outsiders.

5. As anthropologist Colin Turnbull has put it, "[T]he major function of flux is not ecological adaptation, but political adaptation" (Turnbull in Lee and DeVore 1968, 137).

6. Lee 1979 (345).

7. Lee and DeVore (1968) estimate that the Bushmen devote only about twelve to nineteen hours a week to getting food.

8. An observer describes it this way:

> It is difficult to convey a sense of the closeness, intimacy, and isolation of these bush camps. We Westerners combine intensely private domestic life (shared with five or fewer individuals) with daily exposure to hundreds or thousands of total strangers. The !Kung conduct their daily domestic life in full view of 30–40 relatives and friends and rarely see a stranger. (Draper in Lee and DeVore 1976, 200).

9. This quote as well as those in the following text paragraph are from Marshall 1976 (289–290).

10. If social "fission" was necessary for the preservation of egalitarianism in the hunter-forager society, social "fusion" seems to have been just as necessary to create a sense of common cause and shared purpose among groups of people who were often physically remote from each other. In the absence of opportunities to get together and take joint action, their sense of who they were as a people would soon be eroded. The literal meaning of *religion* is to "rebind" or "retie,"

and perhaps this is why trance dances and other religious activities were such a feature of the occasions on which the Bushman hunter-foragers "fused" with each other.

11. Silberbauer 1981 (120–121).

12. Anthropologists have remarked on how closely this cognitive framework resembles systems thinking. For the Bushmen in their hunter-forager mode of life did not see linear chains of cause and effect. Rather, they saw complex webs of interaction in their relationships with their environment. The system in which they lived was extremely "open" in a systems sense—that is, it was in a state of constant spontaneous exchange with the environment. These exchanges were unmediated by any technology or processes of abstraction, and the Bushmen were not blinkered by any functional specialism in their working roles:

> The structure of causal explanation is not linear, with each event being ascribed to a single cause, which, in turn is the effect of a chain of one-to-one relationships. There is a web of causation. Factors combine in multiple causation and the strands merge where different events have in common one or more causal factors. . . . Structuralists and system theorists have a common concern with the interrelationships of the parts of the whole and with processes of self-regulation and transformation. The concepts of the systems theory of development and of entropy-negating processes in open systems have their counterpart in the [Bushman] account of the dynamics of their world. (Silberbauer 1981, 116)

13. Frye explains:

> In early societies [myths] also develop a social function. . . . They play a leading role in defining a society, in giving it a shared possession of knowledge, or what is assumed to be knowledge, peculiar to it. Its proclamation is not so much "This is true" as "This is what you must know." Such a mythology is close to what is meant by the Biblical term torah, essential instruction, including the laws, which no one can be excused from learning. So a mythology creates in the midst of its society the verbal equivalent of a temenos or sacred ground, a limited and sacrosanct area. (Frye 1990, 31).

14. The change induced in a Bushman society by a possession formed the plot of the popular movie The Gods Must Be Crazy (James Uys 1984).

15. From O Pioneers, Part II, Chapter 4, quoted in Partnow 1993 (250).

16. In hunter-forager societies, individuals have considerable self-directive ability and autonomy. This self-direction seems to be learned early as children grow up. None of their relationships supply models for authority or dependency, and they are very rarely exposed to aggressive behavior. Although they may receive food and resources from their parents and elders, they are not dependent on them specifically for access to these things. In a highly positive social climate of

gentle affection from all, they learn early to fend for themselves by observation and imitation.

One of the reasons for this appears to be the unusual environment in which the children grow up—unusual, that is, from a Western perspective. The children spend an enormous amount of their time with adults. Given the smallness of the camps, they do not grow up with peer groups the way we do in North America, but with multiaged groups. This has several important effects:

1. The older children learn to look after the young ones early in life, which develops their ability to look after themselves early.
2. The transition of the infant from interactions with parents to interactions with children is easy because the relationship is similar.
3. Cultural transmission is child-to-child rather than parent-to-child. It is a model of a mentor relationship.
4. The absence of a peer group also contributes to a lack of competitiveness among the children, and there are no team sports. In the games that are played, each individual concentrates on perfecting his or her own skill.

In this process, individuals become adept at all the skills necessary for survival. Not only does this make them self-sufficient, but it lays the foundation for the relationships of mutual dependence that will characterize the adult society. As has already been pointed out, within a relationship of mutual dependence, the roles can reverse, and multiskilling is a prerequisite for this to happen. For similar reasons, multiskilling also creates the conditions for the reaching of group consensus on general strategies and the emergence of leadership based upon situational requirements rather than hierarchical dominance (Lee and DeVore 1976, 220).

Chapter 2: Learning and Performance

1. Some people have argued that the term *learning organization* is an oxymoron. For an organization to exist, something must have already been learned. Perhaps *organization* is the past tense of *learn.*
2. My principal sources for information on Nike are Strasser and Becklund 1991; Christensen and Rikert 1985a, 1985b; Christensen, Rikert, and Roberts 1985; Katz 1993 and 1994; and other published information. I also had some limited exposure to senior Nike personnel during 1992.
3. Bill Bowerman and two colleagues had published a book on jogging in 1967. Entitled *Run for Your Life,* it sold a million copies.
4. Katz 1993 (61).
5. Phil Knight, quoted in Christensen and Rikert 1985b (5), emphasis in the original.
6. Quoted in Strasser and Becklund 1991 (126).

7. "Wicked" problems have been identified as a feature of social organizations by Rittel and Webber (1973).

8. This kind of behavior has been observed in the aftermath of emergencies of all kinds, especially natural disasters such as earthquakes (Lanzara 1983).

9. Bob Woodell, quoted in Christensen and Rikert 1985a (6). From the same source, Del Hayes, also one of the early Nike employees, is quoted as saying, "We like people who aren't afraid to strap on a tin bill and pick shit with the chickens."

10. In sociology, these are known technically as "weakly connected" networks (Granovetter 1973). I have used the word *loosely* to avoid the pejorative connotations of *weak*.

11. In contrast with uncertainty,

> *Equivocality means ambiguity, the existence of multiple and conflicting interpretations about an organizational situation. . . . High equivocality means confusion and lack of understanding . . . that asking a yes–no question is not feasible. Participants are not certain about what questions to ask, and if questions are posed, the situation is ill-defined to the point where clear answers are not forthcoming.* (Daft and Lengel 1986, 556–557)

12. David Chang and Rich Werschkul, quoted in Christensen and Rikert 1985a (22–23).

13. Katz 1994 (307).

14. Christensen and Rikert 1985b (1). This attribution of entrepreneurial success to rational thinking processes pervades management literature. Peter Drucker (1955) has been a highly influential offender in this respect. He did it nearly forty years ago in his analysis of Sears' entry into the retail business, when he attributed "the" decision to General Robert E. Wood's analysis of America's changing demographics. Undoubtedly, Wood's passion for reading issues of the *Statistical Abstract of the United States* (and the opportunity to do so in Panama in 1910–1911) helped rationalize "the" decision, but there is evidence that Sears (and Wards, where Wood was working at the time) went retail initially in cash crises experienced during the economic panic associated with the sharp 1920–1921 recession. With their warehouses bulging, they set up counters on the streets in a desperate attempt to reduce the inventory. It worked (Worthy 1984).

15. The emergent nature of strategy, together with the preeminent role of the informal organization at this stage in the evolution of an organization, are the major points of difference between my framework and that developed by prominent change experts such as Nadler and Tushman (1988). Their model clearly regards strategy as existing prior to organization and the informal organization as emerging from the resulting organizing process. As a result, their model emphasizes the role of the rational actor in change and stresses congruency and equilibrium.

16. The phrase "retrospective sensemaking" is from Weick. The process is a good deal more complex than I have suggested it to be. Weick describes it as follows:

> Think of any enacted equivocal display as a potential figure-ground arrangement. The activity of selection involves both the differentiation of alternative figures from the ground (equivocal displays by definition can be read in a variety of ways) and stabilization of that figure-ground arrangement or that limited set of arrangements that provides reasonable clarity and allows the continuation of living. . . . [S]ome cause maps repeatedly prove helpful in reducing the equivocality of displays, whereas other maps add to the equivocality. Those maps that are helpful tend to be selected, and those that aren't helpful tend to be eliminated. (Weick 1979, 131)

17. Argyris and Schon (1978) have suggested this notion of "encoding."
18. Quoted in Christensen and Rikert 1985a (3).
19. This is where I part company with Tom Peters on the need for hierarchy. As I understand him, he tends to equate hierarchy with bureaucracy, whereas I see it from a systems perspective. From that perspective, complex systems cannot exist without hierarchy (Simon 1969).
20. Del Hayes, interviewed in 1983 and quoted in Christensen, Rikert, and Roberts 1985 (3).
21. In North America, our notions of information in management have been dominated by concepts from information theory and their applications to the computer. The result is that we tend not to distinguish clearly between information and meaning. A useful distinction is made by Nonaka, who distinguishes between syntactic and semantic information:

> Syntactic information is a quantitative type in which no attention is given to the inherent meaning of the information. Shannon's communication theory conceptualizes the basic nature of this type of information as symbolic information measured in bits. A telephone bill is not computed based on the content of conversation (meaning), but on the length of time the communication takes. The information-processing paradigm mainly deals with this quantitative type of information. . . . In contrast semantic information examines the actual meaning of information. Although actual measurement is difficult, it is this qualitative type of information that somehow changes our perception and meaning association. . . . The new meanings provide a new standpoint for interpreting events . . . a new dimension for organizing and interpreting information. . . . One cannot . . . create a total distinction between syntactic information and semantic information. Most syntactic information . . . can be perceived within normal routine information, but when it is integrated above a certain level, clues regarding new dimensions of information can be discovered. Once formed and made into routine, semantic information, or meaning, becomes syntactic information. In this way syntactic information is

gradually mechanized, and humans are able to devote more of their efforts to non-routine information. (Nonaka 1990a, 78, my emphasis)

22. Kelly puts it this way in the context of individuals:

> Man looks at his world through transparent patterns or templates which he creates and then attempts to fit over the realities of which the world is composed. The fit is not always very good. Yet without such patterns the world appears to be such an undifferentiated homogeneity that man is unable to make any sense out of it. Even a poor fit is more helpful to him than nothing at all. (Kelly 1963, 8–9)

23. Katz 1994 (106).
24. This process has been well described in Berger and Luckmann 1980.
25. Strasser and Becklund 1991 (491).
26. The performance model is from Galbraith 1977. The learning model was derived by searching for a contrast with each of the elements of this model.
27. The "From Tents to Palaces" portion of the preceding heading is derived from an article by Hedberg, Nystrom, and Starbuck (1976).
28. Katz 1994 (307).
29. "One of the great traps of focusing on financial measures alone is that it gives people the ammunition to argue that their actions are undiscussable as long as they are meeting their numbers" (Eccles and Nohria 1992, 160).

Chapter 3: Boxes and Bubbles

1. From Russelsteel company records.
2. It is interesting to note that our reaction was very similar to that of the researchers in the Hawthorne experiments fifty years earlier. In the words of Fritz Roethlisberger:

> My first startling Eureka-kind of experience with natural phenomena in the social realm was probably with what has come to be called the "Hawthorne effect." In the Relay Assembly Test Room when the supervisor was replaced by an observer—that is, when one of the customary constraints in the work situation was removed—by golly, the five employees began to speak for themselves. Output rose and continued to rise, even when the better physical conditions they had been given were taken away. This so baffled management, it will be remembered, that they brought in [Elton] Mayo to explain what had happened. They were so accustomed to thinking they controlled the phenomena that it was unthinkable for them to believe that if they took their man-made and God-damned controls away, the phenomena might speak for themselves and even control themselves. It was even more surprising that the phenomena might move in the direction that management wanted them to move! (Roethlisberger 1977, 366)

Chapter 4: Hunters of the Spirit

1. This is associated with the work of McClelland (1961).
2. For example, in trying to explain the success of Dissenters during the industrial revolution, Ashton argues as follows:

    > Many explanations have been offered of this close association between industry and Dissent. It has been suggested that those who sought out new forms of worship would also naturally strike out in secular fields. It has been argued that there is an intimate connection between the tenets peculiar to Nonconformity and the rules of conduct that lead to success in business. And it has been asserted that the exclusion of Dissenters from the universities, and from office in government and administration, forced many to seek an outlet for their abilities in industry and trade. There may be something in each of these contentions, but a simpler explanation lies in the fact that, broadly speaking, the Nonconformists constituted the better educated section of the middle class. (Ashton 1960, 18–19)

    Ashton goes on to talk about "Scottish vigour of mind and character" almost as if it might be an explanatory principle.
3. Ashton 1960 (1–2).
4. Weber 1976. Although Weber never claimed that the Protestant ethic was a sufficient explanation, the other factors are all "macro"—the separation of the productive enterprise from the household, the development of the city, the inheritance of legal frameworks, and so on.
5. Emery and Trist summarize the conventional view of the impact of the Protestant ethic as a pattern:

    > (a) The doctrine of personal responsibility (for salvation) became associated with either that of redemption through good works (rather than by being in a state of grace attainable through the church); or, in the Calvanist [sic] version, that of proving one was among the elect because one's works turned out to be good. . . .
    >
    > (b) Material prosperity, because it symbolized spiritual prosperity, could not remain an ancestral right—simply through the inheritance of land. It had to be acquired or demonstrated. . . .
    >
    > (c) Not to prosper became a sign of wickedness. The poor could therefore come to symbolize the sinful rather than the innocent and those who remained poor could be perceived as the unrepentant rather than the unfortunate. . . .
    >
    > (d) These attitudes warranted an ostracism of the poor, their sanctioned shaming, while the poor were expected to internalize these values and feel ashamed of themselves. . . .
    >
    > (e) Poverty could be construed as one's own fault. . . .
    >
    > Though held intensely and more explicitly only by the core members belonging to the more extreme of the non-conformist sects, themselves in any case a minority,

in a vague and attenuated form these beliefs coloured the ethos in terms of which the 19th century was to develop. Such values lent support to the developing entrepreneurial part of the society whose welfare (prosperity) had become pivotal. (Emery and Trist 1975, 142–143)

Although space does not permit me to make this argument at any length, I suspect that this intellectual abstraction of Protestantism was used to *rationalize* the industrial revolution in nineteenth-century England, much as strategy is used to rationalize the structure and activities of the firm. There is a hint of this intellectual use in the story of Josiah Wedgwood, a nonconformist who nevertheless made good use of John Wesley (1703–1791) and the Methodist evangelical movement to reform the slack working habits of his workers (Langton 1984).

6. See Hampden-Turner and Trompenaars 1993.

7. McClelland 1961 (147).

8. Burke 1985 (185).

9. Space does not permit me to deal with the Quaker involvement in American history. After a grant of land from Charles II in 1681, William Penn sailed to America to found Pennsylvania. Here the Quakers made a significant contribution to the political, economic, and social structure of the country. The reader is referred to Barbour and Frost 1988 for a comprehensive history of the leading Quakers.

10. Brinton 1973 (53).

My principal sources for information on the Quakers are Barbour and Frost 1988; Brinton 1973; Emden 1940; Nevaskar 1971; Punshon 1991; Raistrick 1968; Rowlinson and Hassard 1993; and Windsor 1980.

11. According to George Fox: "The Lord showed me, so that I did see clearly, that he did not dwell in these temples which men had commanded and set up, but in people's hearts. . . . [H]is people were his temple and he dwelt in them" (*Journal* [1694], quoted in Bartlett 1955, 273).

12. Brinton 1973 (ix).

13. According to George Fox: "The Lord opened unto me that being bred at Oxford or Cambridge was not enough to fit and qualify men to be Ministers of Christ" (*Journal* [1694], quoted in Bartlett 1955, 273).

14. Brinton explains:

The West seeks to understand by analysis—that is, by taking a thing apart and then putting it together. The East attempts to grasp something synthetically—that is, by seeing it as a whole, by mystical intuition rather than intellectual rationalization. For example, in the West a word is understood by using different letters for its parts, while in the East it is grasped by a single symbol as in the case of Chinese characters. Each character does not indicate the parts but indicates the whole, around which the related parts are grouped. Thus the West finds it difficult to grasp Zen Buddhism or Quakerism because these religions represent, not the result of intellectual analysis, but intuitional feelings. (Brinton 1973, 20)

15. According to George Fox; "He [Oliver Cromwell] said: 'I see there is a people risen, that I cannot win either with gifts, honours, offices or places; but all other sects and people I can' " (*Journal* [1694], quoted in Bartlett 1955, 273).

16. According to George Fox: "When the Lord sent me forth into the world, He forbade me to put off my hat to any, high or low" (*Journal* [1694], quoted in Bartlett, 1955 273).

17. There were some interesting side effects:

> *One result of this [in America] was that the Puritans of New England admitted to their theocracy at first only Christians like themselves, while in Pennsylvania everyone was welcomed—Jews, Catholics, Anglicans, Mennonites, Moravians, and later on (1763) Methodists, and adherents from many other sects. As a result Philadelphia, although founded about forty years later than Boston, outstripped it as a center of colonial culture.* (Brinton 1973, 28)

18. If there is a lesson here about the role of women in modern management, perhaps it is that the problems do not lie in the "glass ceilings" but in the foundations—the nonegalitarian values—that underpin most of our organizations.

19. As Kanter has pointed out:

> *Persecution serves several functions for communion and cohesiveness. Facing a common enemy binds people together, such integration being one of a number of functions of social conflict. Blumer has proposed that the development of an ingroup-outgroup relation is one of the mechanisms creating an esprit de corp in social movements, and that persecution clarifies this relation. . . . According to Turner and Killian, persecution "heightens the symbolic intensity of a group's values."* (Kanter 1972, 102).

20. Brinton 1973 (50).

21. "The basic word I-You can be spoken only with one's whole being. The concentration and fusion into a whole being can never be accomplished by me, can never be accomplished without me. I require a You to become; becoming I, I say You. All actual life is encounter" (Buber 1970, 62).

22. In the view of Tom Chappell, this is the problem in modern business: "Business is all about 'I-It' relationships. Making objects out of people. Making objects out of perceptions and turning them into some kind of useful means-end activity" (Chappell 1993, 13).

23. Ouchi describes an almost identical financing system among Asian-American immigrants:

> *. . . Asian-Americans brought with them from their homelands the tradition of informal revolving-credit societies, the Tanomoshi for the Japanese-Americans and the Hui for the Chinese-Americans. A Tanomoshi or Hui typically consists of about one dozen individuals, each wanting to own his own service station, a one-*

truck hauling service or other such small businesses. Once each month, the group gathers at one member's home for dinner, and each person brings with him a prespecified amount of money, perhaps $1000. The host of the evening keeps the whole sum—say, $12,000—which he then uses to buy a second truck or open his service station. The group meets in this fashion for twelve successive months until each person has put in $12,000 and taken out $12,000. In this manner, people who would have great difficulty saving the whole sum of $12,000 are able to raise capital. . . . [O]ne can only be born into a Tanomoshi or a Hui, and one can never escape from the network of familiar, communal, social, religious, and economic ties that bind those groups together. If a member should fail to make good on his obligations, members of his family would certainly take up his obligation or else pay the very high price of having all branches of the family shut out of the economic and social network of the community. . . . [E]ach adult in these ethnic communities typically participates in a large number of Huis or Tanomoshis over his lifetime, at times participating in two more. Many opportunities arise to repay past debts by taking a later position in the chain. In addition, a debt incurred to one person can be repaid to that person's son or brother, who in turn has the capacity to repay the initial creditor through one of a thousand favors. (Ouchi 1981, 86–87)

24. Barbour and Frost 1988 (115–116).
25. My material on Coalbrookdale is based on Raistrick 1989; Trinder 1981; and Windsor 1980.
26. The material on the canals is based on Gladwin 1988 and Hadfield and Boughey 1994.
27. The Boston Tea Party was "held" on a pair of Quaker ships!
28. In response to earlier petitions, the Philadelphia yearly meeting issued its first official statement on slavery in 1696, discouraging the importation of slaves, although the same meeting did not declare it to be "unrighteous" until 1754.
29. Barbour and Frost 1988 (61).
30. Barbour and Frost 1988 (95).

Chapter 5: Growth and Renewal

1. The ecocycle is adapted from Holling 1986 and 1987.
2. The self-organizing behavior of a complex system like a forest is based upon the repeated application of relatively simple rules at many levels. For a discussion of the dynamics of self-organization in social systems, see Drazin and Sandelands 1992.
3. A more detailed description is helpful:

    Pure r-strategists, on the one hand, are organizations that move quickly to exploit resources as they first become available. Their structure makes them relatively inexpensive to set up; that is, they concentrate on activities that require low levels of capital investment and simple structures. They are called r-strategists because they trade on speed of expansion. Their success depends heavily on first-mover advantages, which makes them high-risk and high payoff organizations which gain maximally from temporarily rich environments. Such organizations persist only where the pattern of resource availability is highly uncertain and resources are dispersed over time and space. Where critical resources are available with any certainty, exploitive strategies will usually fail when faced with organizations emphasizing competitive efficiency. Thus industries that are unchanging should not have r-strategists. (Brittain and Freeman 1980, 311–312)

4. *Connectedness* refers in a general sense to properties of networks such as density, connectivity, and hierarchy (Ibarra 1992). A loosely connected system has much in common with a loosely coupled system (Weick 1976; Orton and Weick 1990). A loosely coupled system is one in which elements affect each other "suddenly (rather than continuously), occasionally (rather than constantly), indirectly (rather than directly), and eventually (rather than immediately)" (Orton and Weick 1990, 203–204).

5. The information on patch dynamics is from Terborgh 1992 (90). The complexities of species succession in forests is discussed by Loucks (1970).

6. The terms *r-strategy organization* and *r-selection environment* are complementary— opposite sides of the same coin—with their usage depending on whether one sees the attribute as a function of the organization or the environment. The prefixes r and K are derived from the Pearl-Verhulst logistics equation, where the rate of growth of a population (X) over time (t) is a function of both the natural reproductive rate (r) in the population and the carrying capacity (K) of the environment. The equation for the change in the population over time is $dx/dt = rX(K - X)/K$. Initially, when K is very large compared with X, the growth rate in the population is very close to r, its natural growth rate. As X grows, the carrying capacity of the environment becomes more and more of a factor until, when $X = K$, no further growth in the population is possible. The equation generates the familiar S-shaped curve of the life cycle. The terms *r-selection* and *K-selection* were coined by MacArthur and Wilson (1967).

7. A more detailed description is helpful:

K-strategists, on the other hand, are organizations that are structured to compete successfully in densely settled environments. . . . [They] generally expand more slowly into new resource spaces than r-strategists because the structures generating competitive efficiency frequently preclude the rapid adjustments necessary to capture first-mover advantages. Competition on the basis of efficiency generally involves higher levels of investment in plant and equipment and more elaborate organizational structures. (Brittain and Freeman 1980, 311–312)

8. Information on the U.S. National Park Service and the ecological role of fire is from Jeffery 1989 and Wright and Bailey 1982.

9. The term *creative destruction* used to describe this stage of the forest ecocycle is borrowed from economist Joseph Schumpeter's well-known description of the process of capitalism as a "perennial gale of creative destruction" (Schumpeter 1950, 83).

10. There has recently been a striking example of the effects on business organizations of the removal of an economic "umbrella" with the closure of Sears' catalog operations. For years, many businesses, both small and large, had flourished in the protected environment created by the continuing success of the Sears catalog business. Overnight they were exposed to a much more hostile environment. See Valente and Duff 1993.

11. Chaos theory is the best-known example of several theories of nonequilibrium:

> *As most natural scientists are aware, there is actually not one, but rather there are many kinds of nonequilibrium theory, of which "chaos" is only one of several names. One form is a precise, reasonably well-developed aspect of the mathematical study of dynamics. With its comprehension limited to specialists, this theory acts as a main tributary into the other form, which . . . is today being advanced throughout natural science. . . . This broader kind of theory—also called "nonlinear dynamics," "bifurcation" or "self-organizing" theory, but to which the term "chaos" theory is sometimes applied . . . is still at an early stage of development.* (Loye and Eisler 1987, 54)

12. An example of this phenomenon is the "butterfly effect," named by Edward Lorenz from his work on weather systems. It comes from the notion that a butterfly, by flapping its wings in Beijing today, can affect the storm systems in New York next month (Gleick 1987, 11–31).

13. Wilshire 1971 (126).

14. A number of life cycle models are discussed in Quinn and Cameron 1983, although their overall summarizing framework is a linear one. There appears to be a cultural reluctance to discuss "death" and "conception" as they apply to organizations of any kind!

    This formulation resembles that in Greiner's seminal paper (1972), but there are some key differences between his concept of process and the organizational ecocycle. As one might expect from the time at which it was published, Greiner's model is implicitly rational throughout, and although he uses scale on the vertical axis, organizational progress is represented as being linear (Greiner did subsequently state, however, that dialectics were central to his view of the process and that the process is without end [Van de Ven 1992]).

    The organizational ecocycle would appear to address a number of the issues raised by Van de Ven (1992) in his discussion of the requirements for studying strategy process. With its reflexive infinity loop, perspectives on management action, and base in ecology, the ecocycle appears to cover all four "families" of theories on development and change identified by Van de Ven—life cycle, teleology, dialectic, and evolution. Although it was not explicitly designed as such, the dynamics of the ecocycle are very similar to those captured in the Chinese Taoist yang-yin symbol of process and transformation.

15. Friedman 1971 (133).
16. The life cycle and its applications are covered extensively in Kimberly, Miles, and Associates 1980.
17. Hayes and Wheelwright 1988 (417–433).
18. Kanter, Stein, and Jick 1992 (29).
19. Abernathy and Utterback 1978.
20. Utterback 1994.
21. My sources on Compaq are: Eccles and Love 1990; Forest and Arnst 1992; Francis 1992; Ivey and Levine 1991; Ivey, Depke, and Peterson 1991; Therrien 1992; and Webber 1990.
22. Buxton 1994 (14).
23. The figures for the integrated steel industry are from Hoerr 1988 (94).
24. Danny Miller has described this as the Icarus paradox: "One of the most seductive traps that face outstanding companies is that the focus and simplicity that ultimately got them into trouble may once have been responsible for their initial successes. . . . Icarus's wings did indeed contribute to his downfall, but they also allowed him to soar to unprecedented heights. And therein lay their danger. Paradoxically, the ultimate cause of failure had once been the source of success" (Miller 1993, 130).
25. Information on Wang was gathered from a variety of articles: Bulkeley and Wilke 1992; Kenney 1992; McWilliams 1989; and Nash 1992. The decline of Wang has been attributed to factors ranging from personal traits ("arrogance," "nepotism," "shortsightedness") to hard technical issues such as lack of emphasis on R&D. My thesis is not that these elements are irrelevant to Wang's decline but that they were aided and abetted by systemic processes.
26. The distinction between social and technical systems and the concept of a sociotechnical system are attributable to Emery and Trist (1965 and 1975).
27. Portions of this subsection on GE appeared in Hurst 1991.
28. Petre 1986.
29. The quotes in this subsection and the following one are from Tichy and Charan 1989 (112–120).
30. In this position, Knight and Bowerman seem to meet Kanter's definition of change masters:

> Change masters are—literally—the right people in the right place at the right time. The right people are the ones with the ideas that move beyond the organization's established practice, ideas they can form into visions. The right places are the

integrative environments that support innovation, encourage the building of coalitions and teams to support and implement visions. The right times are those moments in the flow of organizational history when it is possible to reconstruct reality on the basis of accumulated innovations to shape a more productive and successful future. (Kanter 1983, 306, emphasis in the original)

Chapter 6: Crisis Creation

1. Kochan and Useem (1992, Chapter 1) use a similar split cycle, but the emphasis is on "using" both halves for "strategic advantage." This has the effect of placing the "strong, intelligent, visionary" leaders outside of the process. As such, it is another version of the rational actor model.
2. It is the confusion between instrumental rationality and values-based rationality that leads to the statement that "the end does not justify the means." Instrumental ends cannot justify instrumental means: value-based ends are the only justification for them.
3. For example, see Henry Mintzberg's comments (1994, 214) on the experience of entrepreneur Sam Steinberg.
4. Drucker rejects evidence that other processes might be at work, dismissing cases of nonlinear innovation as unique accidents:

   > [T]here are innovations . . . that are not developed in any organized, purposeful, systematic manner. There are innovators who are "kissed by the Muses," and whose innovations are the result of a "flash of genius" rather than hard, organized, purposeful work. But such innovations cannot be replicated. They cannot be taught and they cannot be learned. There is no known way to teach someone how to be a genius. . . . [P]urposeful innovation resulting from analysis, system, and hard work is all that can be discussed and presented as the practice of innovation. But this is all that need be presented since it surely covers at least 90% of all effective innovation. (Drucker 1986, 133–134)

   If the concepts and evidence I have presented in this book are even partially right, Drucker is quite wrong on this. We may not be able to "teach someone how to be a genius," but that is the wrong question. We should be asking, "In what social contexts are individual talents best developed?" The evidence is that we can create social learning contexts that "grow" genius. It is not solely a question of education so much as it is a problem of evocation, the challenge of "calling out" and realizing individual potential in communities of trust.

5. Schon 1967 (xviii). One of the major stages on which the argument between the linear and nonlinear view is being fought is that of biological evolution. Here the debate is between Darwinian gradualism and so-called punctuated

equilibrium (Gould and Eldredge 1977). This debate has been brought to the management field by Greiner (1972); Tushman and Romanelli (1985); and Gersick (1991).

6. These examples are cited in Carroll, Delacroix, and Goodstein 1990. Once government agencies are formed, however, they may prove much more difficult to get rid of. Precipitating a crisis may be relatively simple in for-profit, private-sector organizations, but it is much more difficult in the public sector. Here outputs are hard to measure, and the access to public funds prevents outright failure and reduces the credibility of any threats to organizations. Deregulation and privatization may be the only ways to create any real innovation in the public sector.

   In the renewal of whole societies, the collapse of the Soviet Union is supplying some real, live cases. The evidence is casual, but the extent of renewal seems to depend upon the degree of the precipitating crisis and the speed with which the old "herding" boundaries are broken. If the reforms take too long, the old elite may be able to entrench itself in the new system and abort the renewal process. This seems to be happening in the Ukraine, in contrast with the rapid renewal taking place in Poland. See "Counter-Revolution" 1994.

7. Speer wrote:

   > The idea that bureaucratic methods were now taking root in our work depressed me. Again and again I called upon my associates to cut down on record keeping. . . .
   > [T]he bombing raids on German cities forced us to constant ingenuities. There were times when I actually regarded these raids as helpful—witness my ironic reaction to the destruction of the Ministry in the air raid of November 22, 1943: "Although we have been fortunate in that large parts of the current files of the Ministry have burned and so relieved us for a time of useless ballast, we cannot expect that such events will continually introduce the necessary fresh air into our work." (Speer 1970, 213)

8. It is interesting to note that the metaphor of the forest seems to have deep significance in Japanese culture. Hampden-Turner and Trompenaars (1993, 138) cite Japanese philosopher Takeshi Umehara, who talks of Japan's ancient culture as "The Civilization of the Forest."

9. As Yoshino (1968) points out, the idea of the collectivity is deeply rooted in the Japanese culture, with the concept of the "house" transcending that of the family and serving as a model for all types of secondary groups. Any adversity would be shared by the group rather than inflicted on particular individuals. Similarly, prosperity would be shared equally among the three stakeholders in a corporation—the shareholders, management, and labor.

10. The term *lean* production was coined in 1990 by researcher John Krafcik, a member of the International Motor Vehicle Program (IMVP) at MIT, because the

system uses less of everything than conventional mass production (Womack, Jones, and Roos 1991).

11. Once again, this cooperative relationship between supplier and assembler fits in very well with the concept of collectivity expressed in the form of the "house." For a more detailed discussion of the relationships between Toyota and its suppliers, see Kamath and Liker 1994.

12. The emphasis on teams ties in naturally with Japan's cultural bias toward the collectivity:

> To the Japanese, a task is performed by a group, not by individuals, and responsibilities are consequently shared by the entire group. True, each group has a formal leader with appropriate status and title, but the task is assigned not to him but to the group of which he happens to be head. It is the group's performance that matters, rather than that of the individual or the formal leader. The basic unit of organization is a collectivity, not an individual. (Yoshino 1968, 202–203)

As a direct consequence of this, the key requirements for effective leadership in Japanese organizations are social rather than technical. Leaders must be able to evoke and sustain harmonious group relationships.

13. Emery has made the same point about the industrial revolution: "The first phase of industrialization did not emerge on the back of any particular technological revolution and certainly not on the back of the steam engine. . . . The industrial system emerged on the basis of the 'factory system,' a form of work organization, *not* a new technology" (Emery 1982, 1099).

14. A useful way of thinking about these systems comes from Kenneth Boulding (1978) and his concept of three social systems: threat, integration, and exchange. This triad pervades management literature. Etzioni (1961) suggested that there were three methods of organizational control: coercive, normative, and utilitarian. There is a similar troika of ideas in McClelland's (1961) concepts of power, affiliation, and achievement. Ouchi (1981) and Lawrence and Dyer (1983) have also used the triple classification of bureaucracies, clans, and markets as lenses to look at organizational phenomena.

15. The account of the evolution of the auto industry is largely based on Halberstam 1986; Lamming 1993; Sloan 1967; and Womack, Jones, and Roos 1991.

16. I cannot resist quoting the 1911 *Encyclopaedia Britannica* comment on electric-powered vehicles: "The electric car is still the luxury to be employed in towns and in covering short distances, for the weight of the accumulators has not been greatly reduced, despite sensational announcements made from time to time" (vol. 18, 919).

17. Sloan 1967 (84).

18. Utterback 1994 (36).

19. This list is quoted in Lamming 1993 (12).

20. Halberstam 1986 (545).

21. Halberstam 1986 (588).
22. Halberstam 1986 (610).
23. See Hampton and Norman 1987. GM's decision to manufacture the Saturn model in Springhill, Tennessee, represents a dramatic attempt to break with the social traditions of the past as represented by Detroit and to create a new sociotechnical system on a smaller scale.
24. See, for example, "The Cracks in Quality" 1992, in which it is estimated that only 20 percent to 30 percent of programs in England and America have had a significant impact.
25. The architecture itself was not necessarily at fault directly. One could have a well-designed system with poorly maintained and disciplined interfaces that would function as if it were monolithic in design.
26. Systems thinking is a powerful antidote to the fragmentation produced by rational, linear thought. Once one sees reality as process, as a system of systems, it is difficult to sustain belief in linear chains of cause and effect. Systems thinking allows one to embrace both instrumental and values-based rationality, as well as the concepts of constraint and emergence (Senge 1990).
27. Zimmerman 1992a.
28. See Thompson in Quinn and Cameron 1988 (134). Mary Parker Follett made the same point many years ago in a slightly different context: "The theory of consent rests on the wholly intellectualist fallacy that thought and action can be separated. . . . that we think with our 'minds' and we don't. . . . [H]ow often we see cases where we have not been able to persuade people, by our most careful reasoning, to think differently, but later, by giving them an opportunity to enter on a certain course of action, their 'minds' are thereby changed" (Follett 1951, 198).
29. The concept of mindfulness is developed in Langer 1989.
30. Tichy and Sherman 1993 (305).
31. The word *crisis* is derived from the Greek *krinein*, meaning to "sift," and I think that by going back to its original meaning, we can come up with a better understanding of the kind of process required. Many managers do operate by creating crises—emotional crises for other people. Usually, through a combination of fear and intimidation, they can get compliance with almost any action they want. Any improvements in performance, however, are likely to be temporary. For by taking this route, managers are actually reinforcing the status quo. Excessive emotional stress freezes a system because it locks in the hierarchical performance structure, effectively precluding learning.
32. The theory has been advanced that systems "poised" on the edge between order and chaos have an optimal capacity for evolution:

> Networks on the boundary between order and chaos may have the flexibility to adapt rapidly and successfully through the accumulation of useful variations. In

such poised systems, most mutations have small consequences because of the system's homeostatic nature. A few mutations, however, cause large cascades of change. Poised systems will therefore typically adapt to a changing environment gradually, but if necessary they can occasionally change rapidly. These properties are observed in organisms. (Kauffman 1991, 82)

33. Tichy and Sherman 1993 (Chapter 3).
34. The information on 3M is from Mitchell 1989 and Mitsch 1992.
35. The story of the Post-it note is told in Nayak and Ketteringham 1986.
36. The tough, durable chaparral-type shrub growth flourishes all over the world in Mediterranean climates. For five years after a burn, the output of the plants has been estimated to be between twenty-five and sixty times their preburn levels. After five years, the output slows, leveling off after twenty to thirty years, depending on the species of plant. Fire at roughly the same frequency keeps the chaparral healthy (Wright and Bailey 1982, 179).

    It is the chaparral in southern California that promotes the devastating wildfires in that region. See "The Arsonist's Match" 1993.
37. Eisenhardt and Westcott (in Quinn and Cameron 1988) have suggested that it is the three elements of just-in-time philosophy—the paradox of multiple, seemingly conflicting goals; the pursuit of perfection; and the dynamic view of the environment—that are responsible for the generation of creative tension in Japanese organizations.
38. Tichy and Sherman 1993 (21).
39. On-time delivery improved from 66 percent to 90 percent in a period of nine months. Although market share is more difficult to measure, it is estimated to have risen from 5 percent to 6 percent over the same period (Zimmerman and Hurst 1993).
40. The metaphor of "zooming" comes originally from photography, but its usage here is derived from using the zoom function in computer graphics to study the complexity of structures known as fractals (Zimmerman and Hurst 1993).
41. Hammer and Champy 1993.
42. Hammer and Champy 1993 (32). The authors go on to emphasize "fundamental," "radical," "dramatic," and "processes."
43. Hammer and Champy 1993 (105).

Chapter 7: Ethical Anarchy

1. There is evidence to support this view in a study that examined the performance of two pairs of similar organizations—one run by Japanese managers, the other by Americans. The two pairs of companies were NUMMI, GM's joint venture with Toyota, compared with GM's Van Nuys operation and Bridgestone compared

with Firestone. Both pairs of companies used similar management techniques, but the performance of the Japanese-run operations has been markedly superior. The researchers attribute the difference to the faith of the Japanese-run companies' managers in the effectiveness of their system and the abilities of their workers, which was communicated in their high expectations of them. The workers were able to tell the difference (Mahoney and Deckop 1993).

2. William Dill's comment is helpful here: "Organizational life is some kind of alternation between initiative and adaptation, between proclaiming and listening, between leading and following. Strategy pertains to initiative, proclaiming and leading; and pretending that it stretches to cover activities that involve adaptation, listening and following simply gets in the way of having your motives accepted as honest ones" (in Schendel and Hofer 1979, 50).

3. See Furey and Diorio 1994.

4. The line between management and manipulation is razor-thin. See the cheerfully instrumental use of crisis reported on in Dumaine 1993.

5. The distinction between transactional and transformational leadership is attributable to Burns (1978). Zaleznick (1977) is best known for making this distinction between managers and leaders, but he does so without placing them in a cyclical context of any kind. He does, however, make the connection between managers and leaders and what William James described as "once-born" and "twice-born" souls. Here is what James had to say:

> In the religion of the once-born the world is a sort of rectilinear or one-storied affair, whose accounts are kept in one denomination, whose parts have just the values which naturally they appear to have, and of which a simple algebraic sum of pluses and minuses will give the total worth. Happiness and religious peace consist in living on the plus side of the account. In the religion of the twice-born, on the other hand, the world is a double-storied mystery. Peace cannot be reached by the simple addition of pluses and the elimination of minuses of life. (James in Wilshire 1971, 236–237)

It is an intriguing thought that the renewal cycle in organizations may be best handled by the twice-born—those who have been through the process of renewal in their personal lives.

6. Burns 1978 (244).

7. Quoted in Huey 1994 (54).

8. In the 811 pages of *Management*, Drucker (1974) makes only three references to leadership. It is interesting, however, that, like Plato, he offers the opinion that the system he describes is the only alternative to tyranny.

9. Follett was one of the early writers on management, but she had the misfortune to write at the same time as scientific management was sweeping North America. The quote is from Follett 1918 (229–230). See also my appreciation of her work (Hurst 1992).

10. Tichy and Sherman 1993 (62).

11. Kanter (1972, 69) has suggested that organizations achieve their cohesion by generating three kinds of individual commitment—instrumental, moral, and affective. The first, as the name suggests, is the result of a rational cost-benefit calculation. It is the kind of commitment induced by our compensation and incentive schemes and, as such, belongs on the conventional loop of the ecocycle.

   The second, moral commitment, is based on the degree to which the demands of the organization coincide with an individual's values. Selection, on the part of both the organization and the individuals who join it, would seem to be the most important factor in determing whether this is present.

   Affective commitment has to do with commitment to interpersonal relationships and group solidarity. As such, it is most relevant to this part of the renewal cycle.

12. Trust is an elusive concept at the best of times. We know it when we see it but are often hard put to understand why it is absent from a situation. One of the problems is that we tend to think of it as a noun rather than a verb. That is, we think of it as a substance, a "thing," rather than as a process. Trust is evoked and cannot be stored: it has to be recreated every moment. To capture this process nature of trust, it is perhaps better to think of it as trusting rather than trust. Smith and Berg have identified the problem of trust as one of the central paradoxes of group dynamics:

    > Group life is filled with dilemmas in which one needs to trust others but where the development of trust depends on trust already existing. Before we are willing to trust others, we want to know how they will respond to us, not just at the level of acceptance or rejection but with respect to our weak parts as well as our strong ones, our fears as well as our hopes, our ugliness as well as our beauty. In order to discover how others will respond, someone in a group must be willing to expose his or her weak, fearful, and ugly sides. (Smith and Berg 1987, 115)

    The "someone" who must first expose his or her shortcomings is, of course, a leader.

13. This subsection makes use of the framework suggested by Shamir, House, and Arthur (1993).

14. Follett 1918 (55), emphasis in the original.

15. The preceding subheading is from Peters 1978. This subsection is based on this article together with McCaskey 1979.

16. It does not appear to have saved IBM from a major business crisis, but Benoit Mandelbrot, the discoverer of fractals, did much of his work at the Thomas J. Watson Research Center!

17. There is other evidence from history to suggest that such contexts do nurture entrepreneurship and innovation. Whether it is the Jains (Nevaskar 1971) and Parsees of India, the Jews of Europe, the Huguenots of France, the Puritans of

England and America, the Basques of Spain (Whyte and Whyte 1988), the overseas Chinese (Kraar 1994), or more recently, the Indochinese refugees, these network-type communities make creative contributions to society out of all proportion to their numbers. The Jewish diaspora is the quintessential example of such a community (Sombart 1969). The magnum opus in the field is, of course, Toynbee's *A Study of History* (1947), which discusses the unique contributions of many different groups to their respective societies.

18. For my information on Silicon Valley, I have relied on Gregory 1984; Malone 1985; and Rogers and Larsen 1984.

19. Gregory (1984) points out that many Silicon Valley "job hoppers" lead more stable lives than the "organization men" of the 1950s, who, although employed by the same firm, were constantly on the move from place to place. In this sense, "it is as if the entire Valley were a single organization" (220).

20. Saxenian 1990 (96).

21. This phenomenon is described extensively by Gregory (1984).

22. Saxenian 1990 (97).

23. This contrast is made by Gregory (1984, 405).

24. Malone 1985 (147).

25. Nonaka 1990a (82). The material on the Honda City project is from Imai, Nonaka, and Takeuchi 1985 and Nonaka 1988 and 1991. Nonaka describes the role of metaphor in management:

> The story of the Honda City project suggests how Japanese companies use figurative language at all levels of the company and in all phases of the product development process. . . . One kind of figurative language that is especially important is metaphor. . . . [It] is a distinctive method of perception . . . a way for individuals grounded in different contexts and with different experiences to understand something intuitively through the use of imagination and symbols without the need for analysis or generalization. Through metaphors, people put together what they know in new ways and begin to express what they know but cannot yet say. As such, the metaphor is highly effective in fostering direct commitment to the creative process in the early stages of knowledge creation. (Nonaka 1991, 100)

26. Mr. Kawamoto, vice president of Honda, quoted in Imai, Nonaka, and Takeuchi 1985 (345).

27. This suggestion was made by Weick and Van Orden (1991), following Daft and Lengel (1986).

28. Students of individual creativity have, following Freud, distinguished between *primary*, or unconscious, mental processes and *secondary*, conscious, processes. See Rothenberg 1979 and Arieti 1976. Although these processes can be evoked in all cultures, it is interesting to speculate on why the Japanese culture might evoke primary processes so effectively. The Japanese culture is assertively egalitarian ("The nail that stands up will be hammered down") and, as we have seen,

highly collective in its culture. But there may be other, more subtle, factors. In Japanese, there are two writing systems, *kana* and *kanji*. The former is phonetic, sound-based, whereas the latter is meaning-based (Springer and Deutsch 1989, 89). In English, the two systems are combined. Perhaps the requirement for the Japanese to learn both systems separately, or the sequence in which they are handled, sets up a creative tension between two modes of cognition, giving them greater aesthetic sensitivity.

Yoshino cites Nakamura when he writes:

> We should note here that the heavy reliance on the intuitive approach in decision-making is also consistent with the aspect of Japanese culture that emphasizes intuitive judgement over the analytical problem-solving approach. . . . [T]he Japanese language is not very well suited for logically precise expression, though it is well adapted for the expression of intuition and of individual emotion. . . . [T]he Japanese have valued intuitive perception (kan) more than scientific inferences based on postulational thinking. (Yoshino 1968, 259)

As an aside, the power of the Japanese culture to maintain community contexts may also explain its alleged failure to produce the frame-breaking geniuses that our culture claims have featured so prominently in the history of Western intellectual progress.

Bateson has an excellent discussion on the nature of primary processes and throws some light on our own cultural problems with them:

> Anglo-Saxons who are uncomfortable with the idea that feelings and emotions are the outward signs of precise and complex algorithms usually have to be told that these matters, the relationship between self and others, and the relationship between self and environment, are, in fact, the subject matter of what are called "feelings"— love, hate, fear, confidence, anxiety, hostility, etc. It is unfortunate that these abstractions referring to patterns of relationships have received names, which are usually handled in ways that assume that the "feelings" are mainly characterized by quantity rather than by precise pattern. This is one of the nonsensical contributions of psychology to a distorted epistemology. (Bateson 1972, 140)

29. See, for example, the entire autumn 1993 issue of *Organizational Dynamics*.
30. The following list is from Nohria and Eccles 1992 (293). They developed these characteristics to make the argument that electronic data networks cannot substitute for face-to-face communication.
31. The examples that follow deal with physical spaces within organizations. Physical spaces within industries also seem to be important. See, for example, Dyer 1994 for a discussion of the importance of physical proximity and face-to-face communication between automobile manufacturers and their suppliers.
32. Based on studies made at MIT's Sloan School of Management (Leibson 1981).

This subsection is based on this article, together with Davis 1984 and Sommer 1969.

33. The material on executive office layouts is based on Steele 1983.

34. Japanese executive offices, on the other hand, tend to express the values of collectivity. Pascale describes the situation at Honda:

> [T]he top forty directors and managing directors of Honda are housed in a single open area with only six individual desks and five large circular conference tables. While the room has forty chairs, they are arranged around the conference tables where one's work gets done alongside others. Each person has one file drawer, and there are only eleven secretaries. . . . [T]he intent is to prevent top executives from getting too settled at headquarters. Equally important, the proximity imposed by the conference tables causes the seniors to interact." (Pascale 1990, 258)

35. See Markoff 1993.

36. There are various views on the maximum number of people who can work together effectively in one location. Kanter's (1972) work on utopian communities suggests that they have a modal number of two hundred people, although that is not necessarily optimal. The Hutterites, a successful community, live in villages of about a hundred. She cites kibbutz planners in Israel who believe that problems are encountered if more than a thousand people are in one location.

Magna, a successful Canadian auto parts manufacturer, tries to restrict its plant size to one hundred and fifty people. Hewlett-Packard, on the other hand, has an upper limit of two thousand.

The fission-fusion dynamic of the Bushman hunting-foraging band makes it very difficult to define "the" organization. It seems that a band might have comprised anything up to one hundred and fifty people but was subdivided for living purposes into three or more camps (Lee and DeVore 1976).

37. Nohria and Eccles 1992 (Chapter 11).

38. The information on Oticon is from "Eliminating Paper and the Organizational Structure" 1992.

39. Tichy and Sherman 1993 (132).

40. The Harvard Business School case study, "Evans Carlson and the Carlson Raiders" (Zak 1981), is accessible to people who have very little formal understanding of how business organizations work.

41. "Think double" is just the opposite of Orwellian "doublethink." Doublethink is (or was) the process that denies the existence of mental processes other than the use of logic and deals with the resulting paradoxes by holding the contradictory ideas simultaneously, but walled up in different compartments, so that they need not be considered at the same time (Orwell 1949).

42. Although it is called a "horizontal" organization (Ostroff and Smith 1992), it is in fact a matrix with a much-reduced vertical component. Sometimes, however,

the need for the vertical, the requirement for hierarchy, is overlooked. The metaphor of "weaving" is a helpful antidote to this tendency.

43. The metaphor of weaving features most strongly in the work of Mary Parker Follett: "What then is the essence of the group process by which are evolved the collective thought and the collective will? It is an acting and reacting, a single and identical process which brings out differences and integrates them into a unity. The complex reciprocal action, the intricate interweavings of the members of the group, is the social process" (Follett 1918, 32).

44. According to Koestler (1964), the word *matrix* is derived from the Latin word for *womb* and is figuratively used for any pattern or mold in which things are shaped or developed. Koestler sees a matrix as being halfway between a framework and a field in its definiteness, which is why, together with its feminine associations, I like the word.

The idea of a matrix organization is not new to the literature (Galbraith 1977), but Fedmet's management team articulated its concept of a "soft" matrix to distinguish it from the traditional "hard" matrix (Goggin 1974).

The soft matrix is very similar in concept to what W. L. Gore & Associates call a "lattice" organization. Based on the experiences of Bill Gore on teams at Du Pont, the name probably reflects his scientific background. Features of the lattice are described by Shipper and Manz:

1. *Lines of communication are direct—person to person—with no intermediary.*
2. *There is no fixed or assigned authority.*
3. *There are sponsors not bosses.*
4. *Natural leadership is defined by followership.*
5. *Objectives are set by those who must "make them happen."*
6. *Tasks and functions are organized through commitments.*

The structure within the lattice is complex and evolves from interpersonal interactions, self-commitment to responsibilities known within the group, natural leadership, and group-imposed discipline. . . . Another phenomenon within the lattice is the constant formation of temporary cross-area groups. . . . The cross-level and cross-functional interpersonal accessibility created by this structure enables all kinds of teams to self-develop, as specific needs arise. Associates can team up with other associates, regardless of area, to get the job done. (Shipper and Manz 1992, 53–54)

45. The story of FedMet is from "Breaking the Boundaries: The Fractal Organization" (Zimmerman and Hurst 1993).

46. The information on Johnsonville Foods is from Stayer 1990.

47. Such groups have been described as "communities of practice" (Seely Brown and Duguid 1991).

48. Rosenbluth 1991.

49. See Naj 1990.

50. Follett 1965 (59).
51. The symbolism of round meeting places where all can contribute equally is well established in the symbols of our culture, perhaps as a distant echo of the circle round the campfire. I understand that interior designers work hard to create internal "bubbles"—circular spaces where people can sit and talk among themselves. Of course, the round table also features prominently in the Arthurian legend—the story of a team of equals who used their diverse talents to perform great deeds and pursue impossible quests.
52. My colleague Brenda Zimmerman and I have suggested that effective strategy can be thought of as a fractal pattern at many levels in the organization (Zimmerman and Hurst 1993).
53. Thompson 1967.
54. Kanter (1972) has shown that this paradox is not restricted to business organizations but is also encountered in utopian communities.

   The tension between the two rationalities may explain why many corporations run successfully with a team of two or more at the top. Often the responsibilities for technical decisions and social decisions are split between a "hard" operator and a "soft" charismatic.
55. For a discussion of these twin roles, but within an instrumentally rational framework, see Nadler and Tushman 1990.

Bibliography

Abernathy, W. J., and J. M. Utterback. 1978. Patterns of industrial innovation. *Technology Review* 80, no. 7:40–47.

Abraham, F. D. 1991. *A visual introduction to dynamical systems theory for psychology.* Santa Cruz, Calif.: Aerial Press.

Abraham, R. H., and C. D. Shaw. 1987. *Dynamics—The geometry of behavior.* Santa Cruz, Calif.: Aerial Press.

Allison, G. T. 1971. *Essence of decision.* Boston: Little, Brown.

Amabile, T. M. 1983. *The social psychology of creativity.* Berlin: Springer-Verlag.

Andrew, A. M. 1989. *Self-organizing systems.* New York: Gordon and Breach.

Ardrey, R. 1970. *The social contract.* New York: Atheneum.

Argyris, C., and D. A. Schon. 1978. *Organizational learning: A theory of action perspective.* Reading, Mass.: Addison-Wesley.

Arieti, S. 1976. *Creativity.* New York: Basic Books.

Arnheim, R. 1969. *Visual thinking.* Berkeley: University of California Press.

Arnst, C., et al. 1992. Compaq: How it made its impressive move out of the doldrums. *Business Week,* 2 November, 146–151.

The arsonist's match. 1993. *The Economist,* 6 November, 26.

Ashton, T. S. 1960. *The industrial revolution.* London: Oxford University Press.

Barbour, H., and J. W. Frost. 1988. *The Quakers*. New York: Greenwood Press.

Barnard, C. I. 1968. *The functions of the executive*. Cambridge, Mass.: Harvard University Press.

―――. 1948. *Organization and management*. Cambridge, Mass.: Harvard University Press.

Bartlett, C., and S. Ghoshal. 1990. Matrix management: Not a structure, a frame of mind. *Harvard Business Review*, July–August, 139–145.

Bartlett, J. 1955. *Familiar Quotations*. Boston: Little, Brown (13th edition).

Bateson, G. 1972. *Steps to an ecology of mind*. New York: Ballantine Books.

―――. 1980. *Mind and nature*. New York: Bantam Books.

Bateson, M. 1972. *Our own metaphor*. New York: Knopf.

Bavelas, A. 1948. Some problems of organization change. *Journal of Social Issues* 4:48–52.

Beer, S. 1984. The viable system model: Its provenance, development, methodology and pathology. *Journal of the Operational Research Society* 35, no. 1:7–25.

Berger, P. L., and T. Luckmann 1980. *The social construction of reality*. New York: Irvington Publishers.

Blumenschine, R. J., and J. A. Cavallo. 1992. Scavenging and human evolution. *Scientific American*, October, 90–96.

Boulding, K. E. 1978. *Ecodynamics*. Beverly Hills, Calif.: Sage.

―――. 1981. *Evolutionary economics*. Beverly Hills, Calif.: Sage.

Bourgeois, W. V., and C. C. Pinder. 1983. Contrasting philosophical perspectives in administrative science: A reply to Morgan. *Administrative Science Quarterly* 28:608–613.

Bowlby, J. 1973. Self-reliance and some conditions that promote it. In *Support, innovation, and autonomy*, edited by R. Gosling. 23–48. London: Tavistock Publications.

Briggs, J., and F. D. Peat. 1989. *Turbulent mirror*. New York: Harper & Row.

Brinton, H. H. 1973. *The religious philosophy of Quakerism*. Wallingford, Pa.: Pendle Hill.

Brittain, J. W., and J. H. Freeman. 1980. Organizational proliferation and density dependent selection. In *The organizational life cycle*, edited by J. R. Kimberly, R. H. Miles, and associates, 311–312. San Francisco: Jossey-Bass.

Brubaker, R. 1984. *The limits of rationality*. London: George Allen & Unwin.

Buber, M. 1970. *I and Thou*. New York: Scribner.

Buckley, Walter. 1967. *Sociology and modern systems theory*. Englewood Cliffs, N.J.: Prentice-Hall.

Bulkeley, W. M., and J. R. Wilke. 1992. Filing in Chapter 11, Wang sends warning to high-tech circles. *Wall Street Journal*, 19 August, 1.

Burke, J. 1985. *The day the universe changed*. Boston: Little, Brown.

Burns, J. M. 1978. *Leadership*. New York: Harper Colophon Books.

Burns, T., and G. M. Stalker. 1961. *The management of innovation*. London: Tavistock Publications.

Burrell, G., and G. Morgan. 1979. *Sociological paradigms and organisational analysis.* London: Heinemann.

Buxton, J. 1994. On time and to order. *Financial Times,* 18 October, 14.

Caplan, N., M. H. Choy, and J. K. Whitmore. 1992. Indochinese refugee families and academic achievement. *Scientific American,* February, 36–42.

Carr, E. H. 1988. *What is history?* London: Penguin Books.

Carroll, G. R., J. Delacroix, and J. Goodstein. 1990. The political environments of organizations: An ecological view. In *The evolution and adaptation of organizations,* edited by L. L. Cummings and B. M. Staw, 67–100. Greenwich, Conn.: JAI Press.

Chance, M. R. A., ed. 1988. *Social fabrics of the mind.* Hillsdale, N.J.: Lawrence Erlbaum Associates.

Chappell, T. 1993. *The soul of a business.* New York: Bantam Books.

Christensen, C. 1973. *The "contingency theory" of organization: A methodological analysis.* Research paper HBS 73-36. Boston: Harvard Business School.

Christensen, C. R., and D. C. Rikert, 1985a. *Nike (B).* Case 9-385-027. Boston: Harvard Business School.

———. 1985b. *Nike (C): Phil Knight.* Case 9-385-029. Boston: Harvard Business School.

Christensen, C. R., D. C. Rikert, and M. J. Roberts. 1985. *Nike (E).* Case 9-385-033. Boston: Harvard Business School.

Churchman, C. W. 1968. *Challenge to reason.* New York: McGraw-Hill.

———. 1971. *The design of inquiring systems.* New York: Basic Books.

Cohen, M. D., J. G. March, and J. P. Olsen. 1972. A garbage can model of organizational choice. *Administrative Science Quarterly* 17 (March):1–25.

Counter-revolution. 1994. *The Economist,* 3 December, 23–27.

The cracks in quality. 1992. *The Economist,* 18 April, 67.

Daft, R. L., and R. H. Lengel. 1986. Organizing information requirements, media richness and structural design. *Management Science* 32, no. 5:554–571.

Daft, R. L., and J. C. Wiginton. 1979. Language and organization. *Academy of Management Review* 4, no. 2:179–191.

Davis, S. M., and P. R. Lawrence. 1978. Problems of matrix organizations. *Harvard Business Review,* May–June, 131–142.

Davis, T. R. V. 1984. The influence of the physical environment in offices. *Academy of Management Review* 9, no. 2:271–283.

Dill, W. R. 1979. Commentary. In *Strategic management,* edited by D. E. Schendel and C. W. Hofer, 47–52. Boston: Little, Brown.

Doz, Y. L., and C. K. Prahalad. 1991. Managing DMNCs: A search for a new paradigm. *Strategic Management Journal* 12:145–164.

Drazin, R., and L. Sandelands. 1992. Autogenesis: A perspective on the process of organizing. *Organization Science* 3, no. 2 (May):230–249.

Drucker, P. F. 1955. *The practice of management.* London: Heinemann.

————. 1968. *The age of discontinuity.* New York: Harper & Row.

————. 1974. *Management.* New York: Harper & Row.

————. 1980. *Managing in turbulent times.* London: Heinemann.

————. 1986. *Innovation and entrepreneurship.* New York: Harper & Row, Perennial Library Edition.

Dumaine, B. 1993. Times are good? Create a crisis. *Fortune,* 28 June, 123–128.

Dyer, J. H. 1994. Dedicated assets: Japan's manufacturing edge. *Harvard Business Review,* November–December, 174–178.

Eccles, R. G., and E. G. Love. 1990. *Compaq Computer Corporation.* Case 9-491-011, revised 6 February 1991. Boston: Harvard Business School.

Eccles, R. G., and N. Nohria. 1992. *Beyond the hype.* Boston: Harvard Business School Press.

Eldredge, N. 1985. *Time frames.* New York: Simon & Schuster.

Eliminating paper and the organizational structure. 1992. *Denmark Review* (January): 2–4.

Eliot, T. S. 1963. *Collected poems, 1909–1962.* London: Faber and Faber.

————. 1979. *Four quartets.* Orlando, Fla.: Harcourt Brace.

Emden, P. H. 1940. *Quakers in commerce.* London: Sampson Low, Marston.

Emery, F. 1967. The next thirty years: Concepts, methods and anticipations. *Human Relations* 20:199–237.

————. 1982. New perspectives on the world of work. *Human Relations* 35, no. 12:1095–1122.

Emery, F., and E. L. Trist. 1965. The causal texture of organizational environments. *Human Relations* 18:21–32.

————. 1975. *Towards a social ecology.* New York: Plenum (paperback edition).

Etzioni, A. 1961. *A comparative analysis of complex organizations.* Glencoe, Ill.: Free Press.

Feyerabend, P. 1988. *Against method.* London: Verso.

Follett, M. P. 1918. *The new state.* New York: Longmans, Green & Company.

————. 1951. *Creative experience.* New York: Peter Smith.

————. 1965. *Dynamic administration.* London: Pitman.

————. 1987. *Freedom & co-ordination: Lectures in business organization.* New York: Garland Publishers.

Forest, S. A., and C. Arnst. 1992. Compaq declares war on the clones. *Business Week,* 15 June, 40.

Francis, B. 1992. Compaq's new CEO: A focus on price. *Datamation,* 1 January, 37–38.

Friedman, M. 1971. 11th printing. *Capitalism and freedom.* Chicago: University of Chicago Press. Original edition, Chicago: University of Chicago Press, 1962. (Page references are to reprint edition.)

Frye, N. 1982. *The great code.* Toronto: Academic Press Canada.

————. 1988. Reprint. *Creation and recreation.* Toronto: University of Toronto Press. Original edition, Toronto: University of Toronto Press, 1980. (Page references are to reprint edition.)

————. 1990. *Words with power.* Markham, Ontario: Viking Penguin Books Canada.

Fuller, B. R. 1982. *Synergetics.* 2 vols. New York: Macmillan.

Furey, T. R., and S. G. Diorio. 1994. Making reengineering strategic. *Planning Review* 22, no. 4 (July–August):6.

Galbraith, J. R. 1977. *Organization design.* Reading, Mass.: Addison-Wesley.

Gersick, C. J. G. 1991. Revolutionary change theories: A multilevel exploration of the punctuated equilibrium paradigm. *Academy of Management Review* 16, no. 1:10–36.

Gladwin, D. 1988. *Building Britain's canals.* Studely, Warwickshire, England: K. A. F. Brewin Books.

Gleick, J. 1987. *Chaos.* New York: Viking Penguin.

Goggin, W. C. 1974. How the multi-dimensional structure works at Dow Corning. *Harvard Business Review,* January–February, 76–87.

Goldberger, A. L., D. R. Rigney, and B. J. West. 1990. Chaos and fractals in human physiology. *Scientific American,* February, 43–49.

Goldstein, J. 1988. A far-from-equilibrium systems approach to resistance to change. *Organization Dynamics,* autumn, 16–26.

Gould, S. J., and N. Eldredge. 1977. Punctuated equilibria: The tempo and mode of evolution reconsidered. *Paleobiology* 3:115–151.

Granovetter, M. S. 1973. The strength of weak ties. *American Journal of Sociology* 78, no. 6:1360–1380.

Gregory, K. L. 1984. *Signing-up: The culture and careers of Silicon Valley computer people.* Ann Arbor, Mich.: University Microfilms International.

Greiner, L. E. 1972. Evolution and revolution as organizations grow. *Harvard Business Review,* July–August, 37–46.

Hadfield, C., and J. Boughey. 1994. *Hadfield's English canals.* Rev. ed. Phoenix Mill, Gloucestershire, England: Alan Sutton Publishing.

Halberstam, D. 1986. *The reckoning.* New York: Morrow.

Hammer, M., and J. Champy. 1993. *Reengineering the corporation.* New York: HarperCollins.

Hampden-Turner, C. 1981. *Maps of the mind.* New York: Collier Books, Macmillan.

————. 1990. *Charting the corporate mind.* New York: Free Press.

Hampden-Turner, C., and Trompenaars, F. 1993. *The seven cultures of capitalism.* New York: Doubleday.

Hampton, W. J., and J. R. Norman. 1987. General Motors: What went wrong. *Business Week,* 16 March, 102–110.

Hannan, M., and J. Freeman. 1977. The population ecology of organizations. *American Journal of Sociology* 82, no. 5:929–964.

Haskell, R. E. 1987. *Cognition and symbolic structures: The psychology of metaphoric transformation.* Norwood, N.J.: Ablex.

Hayes, R. H., and S. C. Wheelwright. 1979a. The dynamics of process-product life cycles. *Harvard Business Review,* March–April, 127–136.

————. 1979b. Link manufacturing process and product life cycles. *Harvard Business Review,* January–February, 133–140.

————. 1988. Matching process technology with product/market requirements. In *Readings in the management of innovation.* 2d ed. Edited by M. L. Tushman and W. L. Moore, 417–443. Cambridge, Mass.: Ballinger. Originally published in *Restoring our competitive advantage.* New York: Wiley, 1984.

Hedberg, B. L. T., P. C. Nystrom, and W. H. Starbuck. 1976. Camping on seesaws: Prescription for a self-designing organization. *Administrative Science Quarterly* 21 (March):41–65.

Hesse, M. B. 1966. *Models and analogies in science.* Notre Dame, Ind.: University of Notre Dame Press.

Hoerr, J. P. 1988. *And the wolf finally came.* Pittsburgh: University of Pittsburgh Press.

Hofstadter, D. R. 1979. *Godel, Escher, Bach.* New York: Vintage Books.

Holling, C. S. 1986. The resilience of terrestrial ecosystems: Local surprise and global change. In *Sustainable development of the biosphere,* edited by W. C. Clark and R. E. Munn, 292–317. Cambridge, England: Cambridge University Press.

————. 1987. Simplifying the complex: The paradigms of ecological function and structure. *European Journal of Operational Research* 30:139–146.

Homans, G. C. 1950. *The human group.* New York: Harcourt, Brace & World.

Huey, J. 1994. The leadership industry. *Fortune,* 21 February, 54–56.

Hurst, D. K. 1984. Of boxes, bubbles and effective management. *Harvard Business Review* 62, no. 3:78–88.

————. 1986. Why strategic management is bankrupt. *Organizational Dynamics,* autumn, 5–27.

————. 1989. Creating competitive advantage: Welding imagination to experience. *Academy of Management Executive* 3, no. 1:29–36.

————. 1991. Cautionary tales from the Kalahari: How hunters become herders (and may have trouble changing back again). *Academy of Management Executive* 5, no. 3:74–86.

————. 1992. Thoroughly modern—Mary Parker Follett. *Business Quarterly* 56, no. 4 (spring):55–58.

Hurst, D. K., James C. Rush, and Roderick E. White. 1989. Top management teams and organizational renewal. *Strategic Management Journal* 10:87–105.

Hurst, D. K., and B. J. Zimmerman. 1994. From life cycle to ecocycle: A new perspective on the growth, maturity, destruction and renewal of complex systems. *Journal of Management Inquiry* 3, no. 4 (December):339–354.

Ibarra, H. 1992. Structural alignments, individual strategies, and managerial action: Elements toward a network theory of getting things done. In *Networks and organizations,* edited by N. Nohria and R. G. Eccles, 165–188. Boston: Harvard Business School Press.

Imai, K., I. Nonaka, and H. Takeuchi. 1985. Managing the new product development process: How Japanese companies learn and unlearn. In *The uneasy alliance,* edited by K. B. Clark, R. H. Hayes, and C. Lorenz, 337–375. Boston: Harvard Business School Press.

Itami, H. 1987. *Mobilizing invisible assets*. Cambridge, Mass.: Harvard University Press.

Ivey, M., D. A. Depke, and T. Peterson. 1991. Compaq's new boss doesn't even have time to wince. *Business Week*, 11 November, 41.

Ivey, M., and J. B. Levine. 1991. Coming to America: Compaq's European star. *Business Week*, 4 February, 86.

Jantsch, E. 1980. *The self-organizing universe*. Oxford, England: Pergamon.

———, ed. 1981. *The evolutionary vision*. Boulder, Colo.: Westview Press.

Jaques, E. 1982. *The form of time*. New York: Crane, Russak.

Jaynes, J. 1982. *The origin of consciousness in the breakdown of the bicameral mind*. Boston: Houghton Mifflin.

Jeffery, D. 1989. Yellowstone: The fires of 1988. *National Geographic* 175, no. 2 (February):255–273.

Jewkes, J., D. Sawers, and R. Stillerman. 1969. *The sources of invention*. 2d ed. London: Macmillan.

Jung, C. G. 1976. *Psychological types*. Princeton, N.J.: Princeton/Bollingen Paperbacks.

Kagono, T., I. Nonaka, K. Sakakibara, and A. Okumara. 1985. *Strategic versus evolutionary management: A U.S.-Japan comparison of strategy and organization*. Amsterdam: North-Holland.

Kamath, R. R., and J. K. Liker. 1994. A second look at Japanese product development *Harvard Business Review*, November–December, 154–170.

Kanter, R. M. 1972. *Commitment and community*. Cambridge, Mass.: Harvard University Press.

———. 1983. *The change masters*. New York: Simon & Schuster.

Kanter, R. M., B. A. Stein, and T. D. Jick. 1992. *The challenge of organizational change*. New York: Free Press, Macmillan.

Katz, D. 1993. Triumph of the swoosh. *Sports Illustrated*, 16 August, 54–73.

———. 1994. *Just do it*. New York: Random House.

Kauffman, S. A. 1991. Antichaos and adaptation. *Scientific American*, August, 78–84.

Kelly, G. A. 1963. *A theory of personality*. New York: Norton.

Kelman, H. 1969. *Kairos:* The auspicious moment. *The American Journal of Psychoanalysis* 29, no. 1:59–83.

Kenney, C. C. 1992. Fall of the house of Wang. *Computerworld*, 17 February, 67.

Kermode, F. 1967. *The sense of an ending*. Oxford, England: Oxford University Press.

Kimberly, J. R., R. H. Miles, and Associates. 1980. *The organizational life cycle*. San Francisco: Jossey-Bass.

Kochan, T. A., and M. Useem. 1992. *Transforming organizations*. New York: Oxford University Press.

Koestler, A. 1964. *The act of creation*. London: Hutchison.

———. 1979. *The sleepwalkers*. New York: Pelican Books, Penguin Books.

Koontz, H., and C. O'Donnel. 1968. *Principles of management*. 4th ed. New York: McGraw-Hill.

Korzybski, A. 1980. *Science and sanity.* 4th ed. Lakeville, Connecticut: International Non-Aristotelian Publishing Company.

Kraar, L. 1994. The overseas Chinese. *Fortune,* 31 October, 91–114.

Kuhn, T. S. 1970. *The structure of scientific revolutions.* 2nd ed. Chicago: University of Chicago Press.

Lakoff, G., and M. Johnson. 1980. *Metaphors we live by.* Chicago: University of Chicago Press.

Lamming, R. 1993. *Beyond partnership: Strategies for innovation and lean supply.* Hertfordshire, England: Prentice Hall International.

Langer, E. J. 1989. *Mindfulness.* Reading, Mass.: Addison-Wesley.

Langton, J. 1984. The ecological theory of bureaucracy. *Administrative Science Quarterly* 29:330–354.

Lanzara, G. F. 1983. Ephemeral organizations in extreme environments: Emergence, strategy, extinction. *Journal of Management Studies* 20, no. 1:71–95.

Lawrence, P. R., and D. Dyer. 1983. *Renewing American industry.* New York: Free Press, Macmillan.

Lee, R. B. 1979. *The Dobe !Kung.* New York: Holt, Rhinehart and Winston.

Lee, R. B., and I. DeVore, eds. 1968. *Man the hunter.* New York: Aldine.

———. 1976. *Kalahari hunter-gatherers.* Cambridge, Mass.: Harvard University Press.

Leibson, D. E. 1981. How Corning designed a "talking" building to spur productivity. *Management Review,* September, 8–13.

Leifer, R. 1989. Understanding organizational transformation using a dissipative structure model. *Human Relations* 42, no. 10:899–916.

Lewin, K. 1947. Frontiers in group dynamics. *Human Relations* 1:5–41.

Lewis-Williams, J. D., and T. A. Dowson. 1989. *Images of power.* Cape, South Africa: National Book Printers.

Lincoln, Y. S., and E. G. Guba. 1985. *Naturalistic inquiry.* Beverly Hills, Calif.: Sage.

Loucks, O. I. 1970. Evolution of diversity, efficiency, and community stability. *American Zoologist* 10:17–25.

Loye, D., and R. Eisler. 1987. Chaos and transformation: Implications of nonequilibrium theory for social science and society. *Behavioral Science* 32:53–65.

MacArthur, R. H., and E. O. Wilson. 1967. *The theory of island biogeography.* Princeton, N.J.: Princeton University Press.

Mackenzie, K. D. 1989. The process approach to organizational design. *Human Systems Management,* no. 8:31–43.

Mahoney, T. A., and J. R. Deckop. 1993. Y'gotta believe: Lessons from American- vs. Japanese-run U.S. factories. *Organizational Dynamics,* spring, 27–38.

Malone, M. S. 1985. *The big score.* New York: Doubleday.

Mandelbrot, B. 1983. *The fractal geometry of nature.* San Francisco: Freeman.

Manning, P. K. 1979. Metaphors of the field: Varieties of organizational discourse. *Administrative Science Quarterly* 24 (December):660–670.

Margolis, N., and M. Johnson. 1991. Industry challenge: Survival. *Computerworld,* 1 July, 1, 8.

Markoff, J. 1993. Where the cubicle is dead. *New York Times,* 25 April, B6.

Marshall, L. J. 1976. *The !Kung of the Nyae.* Cambridge, Mass.: Harvard University Press.

Martindale, D. 1960. *The nature and types of sociological theory.* Boston: Houghton Mifflin.

Maslow, A. H. 1954. *Motivation and personality.* New York: Harper & Row.

Maturana, H. R., and F. J. Varela. 1972. *Autopoiesis and cognition.* Dordrecht, Holland: D. Reidel.

McCaskey, M. B. 1979. The hidden messages managers send. *Harvard Business Review,* November–December, 135–148.

McClelland, D. C. 1961. *The achieving society.* Princeton, N.J.: D. Van Nostrand.

McKim, R. H. 1980. *Experiences in visual thinking.* 2nd ed. Belmont, Calif.: Wadsworth.

McLuhan, M. 1962. *The Gutenberg galaxy.* Toronto: University of Toronto Press.

McWhinney, W. 1990. Fractals cast no shadows. *IS Journal* 9:9–20.

McWilliams, G. 1989. Wang's turnaround specialist prepares for surgery. *Business Week,* 11 December, 108–109.

Miller, D. 1993. The architecture of simplicity. *Academy of Management Review* 18, no. 1:116–138.

Mintzberg, H. 1990. The design school: Reconsidering the basic premises of strategic management. *Strategic Management Journal* 11, no. 3 (March–April):171–195.

———. 1994. *The rise and fall of strategic planning.* New York: Free Press.

Mintzberg, H., and J. A. Waters. 1982. Tracking strategy in an entrepreneurial firm. *Academy of Management Journal* 25, no. 3:465–499.

———. 1985. Of strategies, deliberate and emergent. *Strategic Management Journal* 6:257–272.

Mitchell, R. 1989. Masters of innovation: How 3M keeps its new products coming. *Business Week,* 10 April, 58–63.

Mitsch, R. A. 1992. R&D at 3M: Continuing to play a big role. *Research Technology Management,* September–October, 22–26.

Morgan, G. 1980. Paradigms, metaphors and puzzle solving in organization theory. *Administrative Science Quarterly* 25:605–622.

———. 1983. More on metaphor: Why we cannot control tropes in administrative science. *Administrative Science Quarterly* 28:601–607.

———. 1986. *Images of organization.* Beverly Hills, Calif.: Sage.

Morris, D. 1969. *The human zoo.* Toronto: Clarke, Irwin.

Murray, F., and T. Stengos. 1988. Chaotic dynamics in economic time-series. *Journal of Economic Surveys* 2, no. 2:103–133.

Nadler, D. A., and M. L. Tushman. 1988. A model for diagnosing organizational behavior. In *Readings in the management of innovation,* edited by M. L. Tushman and W. L. Moore, 148–163. Cambridge, Mass.: Ballinger. Originally published in *Organizational Dynamics* (autumn 1980).

———. 1989. Organizational frame bending: Principles for managing reorientation. *The Academy of Management Executive* 3, no. 3:194–204.

———. 1990. Beyond charismatic leaders: Leadership and organizational change. *California Management Review,* winter, 77–97.

Naj, A. K. 1990. GE's latest invention: A way to move ideas from lab to market. *Wall Street Journal,* 14 June, A9.

Nash, K. S. 1992. Worried VS users seek an open path. *Computerworld,* 9 March, 1.

Nayak, P. R., and J. M. Ketteringham. 1986. *Breakthroughs.* New York: Arthur D. Little.

Nelson, R. R., and S. G. Winter. 1982. *An evolutionary theory of economic change.* Cambridge, Mass.: Belknap Press.

Nevaskar, B. 1971. *Capitalists without capitalism.* Westport, Conn.: Greenwood.

Nicolis, G. 1989. Physics of far-from-equilibrium systems and self-organisation. In *The new physics,* edited by Paul Davies, 316–347. Cambridge, England: Press Syndicate of the University of Cambridge.

Nicolis, G., and I. Prigogine. 1977. *Self-organization in nonequilibrium systems: From dissipative structures to order through fluctuations.* New York: Wiley Interscience.

Nisbet, R. 1972. *Social change.* New York: Harper & Row.

Nohria, N., and R. G. Eccles, eds. 1992. *Networks and organizations.* Boston: Harvard Business School Press.

Nonaka, I. 1988a. Creating organizational order out of chaos: Self-renewal in Japanese firms. *California Management Review,* spring, 57–93.

———. 1988b. Toward middle-up-down management: Accelerating information creation. *Sloan Management Review,* spring, 9–18.

———. 1990a. Managing globalization as a self-renewing process. In *Managing the global firm,* edited by C. A. Bartlett, Y. Doz, and G. Hedlund, 69–94. London, England: Routledge.

———. 1990b. Redundant, overlapping organization: A Japanese approach to innovation. *California Management Review* 32, no. 3:27–38.

———. 1991. The knowledge-creating company. *Harvard Business Review,* November–December, 96–104.

Orton, J. D., and K. E. Weick. 1990. Loosely coupled systems: A reconceptualization. *Academy of Management Review* 15, no. 2:203–223.

Ortony, A., ed. 1979. *Metaphor and thought.* Cambridge, England: Cambridge University Press.

Orwell, G. 1949. *Nineteen eighty-four.* London: Secker & Warburg.

Ostroff, F., and D. Smith. 1992. The horizontal organization. *The McKinsey Quarterly,* no. 1:148–168.

Ouchi, W. G. 1981. *Theory Z.* Reading, Mass.: Addison-Wesley.

Partnow, E., ed. 1993. *The new quotable woman.* New York: Meridian, Penguin Books.

Partridge, E. 1983. *Origins: A short etymological dictionary of modern English.* New York: Greenwhich House.

Pascale, R. T. 1982. Our curious addiction to corporate grand strategy. *Fortune,* 25 January, 115–116.

———. 1983. *Honda "A"* and *Honda "B."* Cases 384-049 and 384-050. Teaching note 386-034. Boston: Harvard Business School.

———. 1990. *Managing on the edge.* New York: Touchstone.

Pepper, S. C. 1942. *World hypotheses.* Berkeley: University of California Press.

Peters, T. J. 1978. Symbols, patterns, and settings: An optimistic case for getting things done. *Organizational Dynamics,* autumn, 3–23.

———. 1992. *Liberation management.* New York: Knopf.

Peters, T. J., and R. H. Waterman. 1982. *In search of excellence.* New York: Harper & Row.

Petre, P. 1986. What Welch has wrought at GE. *Fortune,* 7 July, 43–47.

Pfeffer, J. 1982. *Organizations and organization theory.* Marshfield, Mass.: Pitman Publishing Inc.

Pianka, E. R. 1970. On r- and K-selection. *The American Naturalist* 104, 592–597.

———. 1974. *Evolutionary ecology.* New York: Harper & Row.

Pinder, G. C., and V. W. Bourgeois. 1982. Controlling tropes in administrative science. *Administrative Science Quarterly* 25:605–622.

Polanyi, M. 1962. *Personal knowledge.* Chicago: University of Chicago Press.

Polanyi, M., and H. Prosch. 1975. *Meaning.* Chicago: University of Chicago Press.

Poole, M. S., and A. H. Van de Ven. 1989. Using paradox to build management and organization theories. *Academy of Management Review* 14, no. 4:562–578.

Popper, K. R. 1965. *Conjectures and refutations.* New York: Harper & Row.

———. 1966. *The open society and its enemies.* Vol. 1. Princeton, N.J.: Princeton University Press.

———. 1979. *Objective knowledge.* Oxford, England: Oxford University Press.

Porter, M. E. 1985. *Competitive advantage.* New York: Free Press.

Poundstone, W. 1985. *The recursive universe.* New York: Morrow.

Power, M. 1991. *The egalitarians—human and chimpanzee.* Cambridge, England: Cambridge University Press.

Prahalad, C. K., and G. Hamel. 1990. The core competence of the corporation. *Harvard Business Review,* May–June, 79–91.

Prigogine, I. 1980. *From being to becoming.* San Francisco: Freeman.

Prigogine, I., and Isabelle Stengers. 1984. *Order out of chaos: Man's new dialogue with nature.* Toronto: Bantam Books.

Punshon, J. 1991. *Portrait in grey.* London: Quaker Home Service.

Quinn, R. E. 1988. *Beyond rational management.* San Francisco: Jossey-Bass.

Quinn, R. E., and K. Cameron. 1983. Organizational life cycles and shifting criteria of effectiveness: Some preliminary evidence. *Management Science* 29, no. 1 (January):33–51.

———, eds. 1988. *Paradox and transformation.* Cambridge, Mass.: Ballinger.

Quinn, R. E., and M. R. McGrath. 1985. The transformation of organizational cultures. In *Organizational culture*, edited by P. Frost, L. Moore, M. Louis, C. Lundberg, and J. Martin, 315–334. Beverly Hills, Calif.: Sage.

Raistrick, A. 1968. *Quakers in science and industry.* Newton Abbot, England: David & Charles (Holdings).

———. 1989. *Dynasty of iron founders.* 2nd ed., rev. York, England: William Sessions, Ebor Press.

Rittel, H. W. R., and M. M. Webber. 1973. Dilemmas in a general theory of planning. *Policy Sciences* 4:155–169.

Roethlisberger, F. J. 1977. *The elusive phenomena.* Boston: Harvard University Press.

Rogers, E. M., and J. K. Larsen. 1984. *Silicon Valley fever.* New York: Basic Books.

Rosenbluth, H. 1991. Tales from a nonconformist company. *Harvard Business Review,* July–August, 26–36.

Rothenberg, A. 1979. *The emerging goddess.* Chicago: University of Chicago Press.

Rowlinson, M., and J. Hassard. 1993. The invention of corporate culture: A history of the histories of Cadbury. *Human Relations* 46, no. 3:299–326.

Sahal, D. 1976. Homeorhetic regulation and structural stability. *Cybernetica* 19:305–315.

———. 1979. A unified theory of self-organization. *Journal of Cybernetics* 9:127–142.

———. 1981. *Patterns of technological innovation.* Reading, Mass.: Addison-Wesley.

Sandelands, L. E., and G. C. Buckner. 1990. Of art and work: Aesthetic experience and the psychology of work feelings. In *Work in organizations*, edited by B. M. Staw and L. L. Cummings, 123–149. Greenwich, Conn.: JAI Press.

Saxenian, A. 1990. Regional networks and the resurgence of Silicon Valley. *California Management Review,* fall, 89–112.

Schendel, D. E., and C. W. Hofer, eds. 1979. *Strategic management.* Boston: Little, Brown.

Schilpp, P. A., ed. 1974. *The philosophy of Karl Popper.* 2 vols. La Salle, Ill.: Open Court.

Schon, D. A. 1963. *Displacement of concepts.* London: Tavistock Publications.

———. 1967. *Technology and change.* Oxford, England: Pergamon Press.

———. 1979. Generative metaphor: A perspective on problem-setting in social policy. In *Metaphor and thought*, edited by A. Ortony, 254–283. Cambridge, England: Cambridge University Press.

Schumpeter, J. A. 1950. *Capitalism, socialism and democracy.* New York: Harper & Row.

Scott, W. G. 1992. *Chester I. Barnard and the guardians of the managerial state.* Lawrence: University Press of Kansas.

Seely Brown, J., and P. Duguid. 1991. Organizational learning and communities-of-practice: Toward a unified view of working, learning, and innovation. *Organization Science* 2, no. 1 (February):40–57.

Senge, P. M. 1990. *The fifth discipline.* New York: Doubleday.

Shamir, B., R. J. House, and M. B. Arthur. 1993. The motivational effects of charismatic leadership. *Organization Science* 4, no. 4 (November):577–594.

Shaw, M. E. 1981. *Group dynamics: The psychology of small group behavior.* 3d ed. New York: McGraw-Hill.

Shipper, F., and C. C. Manz. 1992. An alternative road to empowerment. *Organizational Dynamics,* winter, 48–61.

Shrivastava, P. 1983. A typology of organizational learning systems. *Journal of Management Studies* 20, no. 1:7–28.

Silberbauer, G. B. 1981. *Hunter and habitat in the central Kalahari Desert.* Cambridge, England: Cambridge University Press.

Simon, H. A. 1957. *Administrative behavior.* New York: Macmillan.

———. 1960. *The new science of management decision.* New York: Harper & Row.

———. 1969. *The sciences of the artificial.* Cambridge, Mass.: MIT Press.

Sloan, A. P., Jr. 1967. *My years with General Motors.* London: Pan Books.

Smith, C., and G. Gemmill. 1991. Change in the small group: A dissipative structure perspective. *Human Relations* 44, no. 7:697–716.

Smith, K. K., and D. N. Berg. 1987. *Paradoxes of group life.* San Francisco: Jossey-Bass.

Snow, C. C., R. E. Miles, and H. J. Coleman, Jr. 1992. Managing 21st century network organizations. *Organizational Dynamics,* winter, 5–20.

Sombart, W. 1969. *The Jews and modern capitalism.* New York: Burt Franklin.

Sommer, R. 1969. *Personal space.* Englewood Cliffs, New Jersey: Prentice-Hall.

Speer, A. 1970. *Inside the Third Reich.* New York: Macmillan.

Springer, S. P., and G. Deutsch. 1989. *Left brain, right brain.* New York: Freeman.

Stacey, R. D. 1991. *The chaos frontier.* Oxford, England: Butterworth-Heinemann.

Stayer, R. 1990. How I learned to let my workers lead. *Harvard Business Review,* November–December, 66–83.

Steele, F. 1983. The ecology of executive teams: A new view of the top. *Organizational Dynamics* (spring):65–78.

Strasser, J. B., and L. Becklund. 1991. *Swoosh: The unauthorized story of Nike and the men who played there.* New York: Harcourt Brace Jovanovich.

Takeuchi, H., and I. Nonaka. 1986. The new product development game. *Harvard Business Review* 64, no. 1:137–146.

Tao te ching. 1982. Translated by Ch'u Ta-Kao. London: Mandala Books, Unwin Paperbacks.

Terborgh, J. 1992. *Diversity and the tropical rain forest.* New York: Scientific American Library.

Terry, T. R. 1964. *Principles of management.* Homewood, Ill.: Irwin.

Therrien, L. 1992. Savvy consumers keep PC makers hopping. *Business Week,* 2 November, 151.

Thompson, J. D. 1967. *Organizations in action.* New York: McGraw-Hill.

Tichy, N. M., and R. Charan. 1989. Speed, simplicity, self-confidence: An interview with Jack Welch. *Harvard Business Review,* September–October, 112–120.

Tichy, N. M., and S. Sherman. 1993. *Control your destiny or someone else will.* New York: Doubleday.

Tillich, P. 1948. *The Protestant era.* Chicago: University of Chicago Press.

Toynbee, A. J. 1947. *A study of history.* Abridgment of vols. 1–6 by D. C. Somervell. New York: Oxford University Press.

Trinder, B. S. 1981. *The industrial revolution in Shropshire.* London: Phillimore.

Trist, E. 1981. *The evolution of socio-technical systems.* Occasional paper 2. Ontario: Ontario Ministry of Labour, Ontario Quality of Working Life Centre.

Tsoukas, H. 1991. The missing link: A transformational view of metaphors in organizational science. *Academy of Management Review* 16, no. 3:566–585.

Turnbull, C. M. 1968. The importance of flux in two hunting societies. In *Man the hunter,* edited by R. B. Lee and I. DeVore, 132–137. New York: Aldine

Tushman, M. L., and E. Romanelli. 1985. Organizational evolution: A metamorphosis model of convergence and reorientation. In *The evolution and adaptation of organizations,* edited by B. M. Staw and L. L. Cummings, 139–190. Greenwich, Conn.: JAI Press.

Tushman, M. L., and W. L. Moore, eds. 1988. *Readings in the management of innovation.* Cambridge, Mass.: Ballinger.

Ulanowicz, R. 1987. Growth and development: Variational principles reconsidered. *European Journal of Operational Research* 30:173–178.

Utterback, J. M. 1994. *Mastering the dynamics of innovation.* Boston: Harvard Business School Press.

Vaill, P. B. 1989. *Managing as a performing art.* San Francisco: Jossey-Bass.

Valente, J., and C. Duff. 1993. Trickle-down pain: Demise of the catalog hurts small businesses that counted on Sears. *Wall Street Journal,* 2 March, A1.

van Creveld, M. 1983. *Fighting power: German and U.S. Army performance. 1939–1945.* London: Lionel Leventhal.

Van der Post, Sir L. 1988. *The lost world of the Kalahari.* London: Chatto & Windus.

Van de Ven, A. H. 1992. Suggestions for studying strategy process: A research note. *Strategic Management Journal* 13:169–188.

Vinnicombe, P. 1976. *People of the Eland.* Pietermaritzburg, South Africa: University of Natal Press.

Watzlawick, P., ed. 1984. *The invented reality.* New York: Norton.

Watzlawick, P., J. H. Weakland, and R. Fisch. 1974. *Change.* New York: Norton.

Webber, A. M. 1990. Consensus, continuity, and common sense: An interview with Compaq's Rod Canion. *Harvard Business Review,* July–August, 115–123.

Weber, M. 1947. *The theory of social and economic organization.* London: Free Press of Glencoe, Macmillan.

———. 1976. *The Protestant ethic and the rise of capitalism.* New York: Scribner.

Weick, K. E. 1976. Educational institutions as loosely coupled systems. *Administrative Science Quarterly* 21, 1–19.

———. 1979. *The social psychology of organizing.* 2nd ed. Reading, Mass.: Addison-Wesley.

———. 1990. *Obstacles to renewal.* Paper presented to the Academy of Management, August 14.

Weick, K. E., and P. W. Van Orden. 1991. Organizing on a global scale. *Human Resource Management* 29, no. 1:49–61.

Wheelwright, P. 1962. *Metaphor and reality.* Bloomington: Indiana University Press.

White, L. 1962. *Medieval technology and social change.* London: Oxford University Press.

Whitehead, A. N. 1978. *Process and reality.* New York: Free Press.

Whorf, B. J. 1982. *Language, thought, and reality.* Cambridge, Mass.: MIT Press.

Whyte, W. F., and K. F. Whyte. 1988. *Making Mondragon.* Ithaca, N.Y.: ILR Press.

Wilshire, B. W. 1971. *William James: The essential writings.* New York: Harper Torchbooks.

Wilson, E. O. 1975. *Sociobiology.* Cambridge, Mass.: Belknap Press.

Windsor, D. B. 1980. *The Quaker enterprise.* London: Frederick Muller.

Wolf, W. B. 1974. *The basic Barnard.* Ithaca, N.Y.: Cornell University, New York School of Industrial and Labor Relations.

Womack, J. P., D. T. Jones, and D. Roos. 1991. *The machine that changed the world.* New York: HarperCollins.

Woodburn, J. 1982. Egalitarian societies. *Man,* n.s., 17:431–451.

Worthy, J. C. 1984. *Shaping an American institution.* Urbana: University of Illinois Press.

Wren, D. A. 1979. *The evolution of management thought.* 2nd ed. New York: Wiley.

Wright, H. A., and A. W. Bailey. 1982. *Fire ecology, United States and Southern Canada.* New York: Wiley.

Yates, F. E. 1987. *Self-organizing systems.* New York: Plenum.

Yellen, J. E. 1990. The transformation of the Kalahari !Kung. *Scientific American,* April, 96–105.

Yoshino, M. Y. 1968. *Japan's managerial system.* Cambridge, Mass.: MIT Press.

Zak, M. J. 1981. *Evans Carlson and the Carlson Raiders.* Case 9-481-193. Cambridge, Mass.: Harvard Business School.

Zaleznick, A. 1977. Managers and leaders: Are they different? *Harvard Business Review,* May–June, 67–78.

Zimmerman, Brenda J. 1991. Strategy, chaos and equilibrium: A case study of Federal Metals, Inc. Ph.D. dissertation, York University, North York, Ontario.

———. 1992a. Chaos and self-renewing organizations: Designing transformation processes for co-evolution. Working paper, 29–92. Faculty of Administrative Studies, York University, Ontario, Canada.

———. 1992b. The inherent drive towards chaos. In *Implementing strategic processes: Change, learning and cooperation,* edited by P. Lorange, B. Chakravarthy, A. Van de Ven, and J. Roos, 373–393. London: Basil Blackwell.

———. 1993. Chaos and nonequilibrium: The flip side of strategic processes. *Organization Development Journal,* 11, no. 1:31–38.

Zimmerman, Brenda J., and D. K. Hurst. 1993. Breaking the boundaries: The fractal organization. *Journal of Management Inquiry* 2, no. 4 (December):334–355.

Zuiderhout, R. W. L. 1990. Chaos and the dynamics of self-organization. *Human Systems Management* 9:225–238.

Name Index

Endnotes are referenced in the index by page number(s) on which they occur followed by *n.* (for one note) or *nn.* (for two or more) and the note number(s) or span of numbers.

Abernathy, W. J., 185n. 19
Agassi, Andre, 40
Allison, Graham, 171n. 9
Argyris, C., 177n. 16
Arieti, S., 193n. 28
Arnheim, Rudolph, 172n. 13
Arnst, C., 185n. 21
Arthur, M. B., 192n. 13
Ashton, T. S., 179nn. 2, 3

Bailey, A. W., 184n. 8, 190n. 36
Barbour, H., 93, 180nn. 9, 10, 182nn. 24, 29, 30
Barclay, Robert, 77, 92, 94, 112
Barnard, Chester, 170n. 3
Bartlett, J., 180nn. 11, 13, 181nn. 15, 16
Bateson, G., 194n. 28
Becklund, L., 175nn. 2, 6, 178n. 25
Berg, D. N., 192n. 12
Berger, P. L., 178n. 24
Blumenschine, R. J., 173n. 2

Boleyn, Anne, 77
Boughey, J., 182n. 26
Boulding, Kenneth, 188n. 14
Boulton, Matthew, 90
Bowerman, Bill, 34, 35, 36, 38, 39, 114, 167, 175n. 3, 185n. 30
Brinton, H. H., 180nn. 10, 12, 14, 181nn. 17, 20
Brittain, J. W., 183nn. 3, 7
Brubaker, R., 171n. 12
Buber, Martin, 81, 181n. 21
Bulkeley, W. M., 185n. 25
Burke, J., 170n. 8
Burns, J. M., 191nn. 5, 6
Burrell, G., 172n. 12
Buxton, J., 185n. 22

Caldwell, Philip, 127–128, 189n. 21
Cameron, K., 184n. 14, 189n. 28, 190n. 37
Canion, Rod, 107, 108

Carroll, G. R., 187n. 6
Catharine of Aragon, 77
Cather, Willa, 27
Cavallo, J. A., 173n. 2
Champy, J., 190nn. 41–43
Chance, M. R. A., 13
Chang, David, 176n. 12
Chappell, Tom, 181n. 22
Charan, R., 113, 185n. 29
Charles I (king of England), 76
Charles II (king of England), 180n. 9
Christensen, C. R., 175nn. 2, 5, 176nn.
   9, 12, 14, 177nn. 18, 20
Cohen, M. D., 171n. 8
Cromwell, Oliver, 79

Dalton, John, 92
Daft, R. L., 193n. 27
Darby, Abraham, I, 84–85, 86
Darby, Abraham, II, 87, 88
Darby, Abraham, III, 87, 89–90
Davis, T. R. V., 195n. 32
Deckop, J. R., 191n. 1
Delacroix, J., 187n. 6
Deming, Edwards, 121, 130
Depke, D. A., 185n. 21
Deutsch, G., 194n. 28
DeVore, I., 13, 173nn. 5–8, 174n. 16,
   195n. 36
Dill, William, 191n. 2
Diorio, S. G., 191n. 3
Dowson, T. A., 13
Drucker, Peter, 119, 147, 176n. 14, 186n.
   4, 191nn. 7, 8
Duff, C., 184n. 10
Duguid, P., 196n. 47
Dumaine, B., 191n. 4
Durant, Bill, 125, 126
Dyer, D., 188n. 14
Dyer, J. H., 194n. 31

Eccles, R. G., 178n. 29, 185n. 21, 194n.
   30, 195n. 37
Eisler, R., 184n. 11
Eldredge, N., 187n. 5
Elizabeth I (queen of England), 76
Emden, P. H., 180n. 10
Emery, F., 179n. 5, 185n. 26, 188n. 13
Etzioni, A., 188n. 14

Follett, Mary Parker, 148, 149–150, 165,
   189n. 28, 191n. 9, 192n. 14, 196n.
   43, 197n. 50
Ford, Henry, I, 125
Ford, Henry, II, 127

Ford, Richard, 86, 87
Forest, S. A., 185n. 21
Foster, Peter, 55, 56, 58, 68
Fox, George, 77, 78, 80, 94, 112, 180nn.
   11, 13, 181nn. 15, 16
Francis, B., 185n. 21
Freeman, J. H., 171n. 7, 183nn. 3, 7
Freud, Sigmund, 193n. 28
Friedman, Milton, 104, 185n. 15
Frost, J. W., 93, 180nn. 9, 10, 182nn.
   24, 29, 30
Frye, Northrop, 21, 170n. 2, 174n. 13
Furcy, T. R., 191n. 3

Galbraith, J. R., 178n. 26, 196n. 44
Gandhi, Mahatma (Mohandas), 148
Gersick, C. J., 187n. 5
Gladwin, D., 182n. 26
Gleick, J., 184n. 12
Goggin, W. C., 196n. 44
Goodstein, J., 187n. 6
Gore, Bill, 196n. 44
Gould, S. J., 187n. 5
Granovetter, M. S., 176n. 10
Gregory, K. L., 193nn. 18, 19, 23
Greiner, L. E., 184n. 14, 187n. 5

Hadfield, C., 182n. 26
Halberstam, D., 127, 188nn. 15, 20,
   189nn. 21, 22
Hammer, M., 190nn. 41–43
Hampden-Turner, C., 180n. 6, 187n. 8
Hampton, W. J., 189n. 23
Hannan, M., 171n. 7
Hassard, J., 180n. 10
Hayes, Del, 37, 176n. 9, 177n. 20
Hayes, R. H., 185n. 17
Hedberg, B. L. T., 178n. 27
Henry VIII (king of England), 77
Hitler, Adolf, 147, 148
Hoerr, J. P., 185n. 23
Hofer, C. W., 191n. 2
Holling, C. S., 97, 182n. 1
Honda, Soichiro, 122
House, J., 192n. 13
Huey, J., 191n. 7
Hurst, D. K., 13, 53, 96, 172n. 14, 185n.
   27, 190nn. 39, 40, 191n. 9, 196n. 45,
   197n. 52

Iacocca, Lee, 128, 151
Ibarra, H., 183n. 4
Imai, K., 193n. 26
Ivey, M., 185n. 21

Raistrick, A., 180n. 10, 182n. 25
Reynolds, Richard, 88, 89
Reynolds, William, 89, 90
Rikert, D. C., 175nn. 2, 5, 176nn. 9, 12, 14, 177nn. 18, 20
Rittel, H. W. R., 176n. 7
Roberts, M. J., 175n. 2, 177n. 20
Roethlisberger, Fritz, 178n. 2
Rogers, E. M., 193n. 18
Romanelli, E., 187n. 5
Roos, D., 188nn. 10, 15
Rosenbluth, H., 196n. 48
Rothenberg, A., 193n. 28
Rowlinson, M., 180n. 10
Russel, Archie, 54–55, 56, 58, 68
Russel, Guy, 54–55

Saxenian, A., 193n. 22
Schendel, D. E., 191n. 2
Schon, Donald, 119, 171n. 10, 177n. 16, 186n. 5
Schumpeter, Joseph, 184n. 9
Seely Brown, J., 196n. 47
Senge, P. M., 189n. 26
Shamir, B. R., 192n. 13
Sherman, S., 137, 138, 141, 145, 154, 189n. 30, 190nn. 33, 38, 192n. 10, 195n. 39
Shipper, F., 196n. 44
Shkut, Al, 59
Silberbauer, G. B., 174nn. 11, 12
Simon, H. A., 171n. 6, 177n. 19
Sloan, Alfred, 126, 188nn. 15, 17
Smith, K. K., 192n. 12
Sombart, W., 193n. 17
Sommer, R., 195n. 32
Speer, Albert, 120, 187n. 7
Sperlich, Hal, 127–128, 189n. 21
Springer, S. P., 194n. 28
Stalin, Joseph, 147, 148
Starbuck, W. H., 178n. 27
Stayer, R., 196n. 46
Steele, F., 157, 195n. 33
Stein, B. A., 171n. 11, 185n. 18
Steinberg, Sam, 186n. 3
Stephenson, George, 91
Strasser, J. B., 175nn. 2, 6, 178n. 25

Takeuchi, H., 193n. 26
Terborgh, J., 183n. 5
Teresa, Mother, 148
Therrien, L., 185n. 21
Thompson, J. D., 197n. 53
Thompson, J. Walter, 92

Tichy, N. M., 113, 137, 138, 141, 145, 154, 185n. 29, 189n. 30, 190nn. 33, 38, 192n. 10, 195n. 39
Toynbee, Arnold, 193n. 17
Toyoda, Eiji, 122, 123
Trinder, B. S., 182n. 25
Trist, E. L., 179n. 5, 185n. 26
Trompenaars, R., 180n. 6, 187n. 8
Tudor, Mary (Bloody Mary), 77
Turnbull, Colin, 173n. 5
Tushman, M. L., 171n. 11, 176n. 15, 187n. 5, 197n. 55

Umehara, Takeshi, 187n. 8
Useem, M., 186n. 1
Utterback, J. M., 185nn. 19, 20, 188n. 18
Uys, James, 174n. 14

Valente, J., 184n. 10
Van der Post, Sir Laurens, 172n. 1
Van de Ven, A. H., 184n. 14
Van Orden, P. W., 193n. 27
Vinnicombe, P., 13

Waters, J. A., 171n. 8
Watson, Thomas J., 151, 192n. 16
Watts, James, 87, 90
Webber, M. M., 176n. 7, 185n. 21
Weber, Max, 75, 76, 171n. 12, 172n. 15, 179n. 4
Weick, Karl, 170n. 1, 171n. 8, 177n. 16, 183n. 4, 193n. 27
Welch, Jack, 112–114, 138–139, 141, 148, 151, 185nn. 28, 29, 190n. 38, 192n. 10
Werschkul, Rich, 176n. 12
Wesley, John, 180n. 5
Wharton, Joseph, 91
Wheelwright, S. C., 185n. 17
Whyte, K. F., 193n. 17
Whyte, W. F., 193n. 17
Wilke, J. R., 185n. 25
Wilshire, B. W., 184n. 13, 191n. 5
Wilson, E. O., 183n. 6
Windsor, D. B., 180n. 10, 182n. 25
Wolf, W. B., 170n. 3
Womack, J. P., 188nn. 10, 15
Wood, Robert E., 176n. 14
Woodburn, J., 173n. 3
Woodell, Bob, 176n. 9
Worthy, J. C., 176n. 14
Wright, H. A., 184n. 8, 190n. 36

Yellen, J. E., 13, 24
Yoshino, M. Y., 187n. 9, 188n. 12, 194n. 28

Zaleznick, A., 191n. 5

Zimmerman, Brenda, 96, 136, 172n., 14, 189n. 27, 190nn. 39, 40, 196n. 45, 197n. 52

Subject Index

Endnotes are referenced in the index by page number(s) on which they occur followed by *n.* (for one note) or *nn.* (for two or more) and the note number(s) or span of numbers.

Conventional organization life cycle
  conservation phase in, 108–109,
    185nn. 23, 24
  crisis destruction phase in, 109–111,
    185n. 25
  instrumental rationality in, 105–108,
    185nn. 19–22
  nature of, 104–105, 185nn. 16, 17
Cookworthy china, 91
Corning Glass, 156
"Counter Revolution" (Economist), 187n.
  6
"Cracks in Quality, The," 189n. 24
Creative destruction phase of ecocycle
  of forests, 100–101, 184nn. 9–13
  of organizations, 109–111, 185n. 25
"Creative stall," 70–71
Crisis
  constraints promoting, 123–124, 136,
    188n. 14
    automotive parts company, 133–134
    in computer software company,
      131–133, 189n. 25
    in steel distribution company,
      134–135
    in U.S. auto industry, 124–131,
      188–189nn. 15–24
  in ecocycle organizational model,
    100–101, 110–111
  Hugh Russel's takeover, 57, 68
  management action in, 136–143,
    189–190nn. 26–43
  need for creation of, 118–123,
    186–188nn. 3–13
  in renewal process, 1, 9, 10, 117–118,
    186nn. 1, 2
Crossfield chemicals, 91
Cross-functional project teams
  in crisis situations, 60–63, 69
  learning in, 163–164, 196n. 47
Cyclical climax, 99

Darwinian gradualism, 186n. 5
Dialogue, 155–158, 193–194nn. 27–38.
  See also Communication
Diggers, 77
Dissenters, 76, 77, 79, 80, 179n. 2
Dominant design, 106–107, 108, 185nn.
  19, 20
Doublethink, 195n. 41. See also Think
  double
Downsizing, 72–73
DuPont, 196n. 44

Ecocycle organizational model, 10
  conservation phase of, 108–109,
    185nn. 23, 24
  conventional life cycle and, 104–105,
    185nn. 16, 17
  creative destruction phase of,
    109–111, 185n. 25
  crisis creation in, 117–123,
    186–188nn. 1–13
    constraints promoting, 123–136,
      188–189nn. 14–25
    management of, 135–143,
      189–190nn. 26–43
  derivation of, 96–97, 182n. 1
  of forests, 97–102, 182–184nn. 2–13
  instrumental rationality phase of,
    105–108, 185nn. 19–22
  key features of, 102–104, 184n. 14
  perspectives on management of,
    115–116, 117–118, 186n. 1
  renewal phase of, 111–115, 185nn.
    26–30
Ecology (defined), 10
Education, in-house, 158–160, 195nn.
  39, 40
Egalitarianism
  assertive, 165–166, 167, 197n. 50
  in leadership, 146, 147–148, 153–154
  of Quakers, 79–80
Electric-powered vehicles, 125, 188n. 16
"Eliminating Paper and the Organiza-
    tional Structure" (Oticon), 195n.
  38
Emergent management action, 6, 7,
  171n. 8
Emerging organization. See Learning
  organization
English Civil War, 119
English industrial revolution, 9
  economy, society, and science during,
    91–93
  effects of canals, bridges, and railroads
    on, 88–91, 182n. 26
  effects of Coalbrookdale on, 83–87,
    182n. 25
  effects of steam engines and trams on,
    87–88
  nature of, 75–77, 179–180nn. 4–9
English Reformation, 77
English Restoration, 79
Entrepreneurship
  in renewal cycle, 113–115, 185n. 30
  success of, 41, 176n. 14
  See also Leadership

in hunter-gatherer structure, 16, 173nn. 4–6
leadership and, 146–147, 153–154
in maturing organization, 43–44, 177n. 19
in shift from performance to learning organization, 60–63, 69, 70, 72
See also Organizational structure
Honda, 120, 130, 131, 154–155, 193nn. 25, 26
Horizontal organizations, 160–162, 195–196nn. 42–45
Hugh Russel Inc., 178n. 1
 emergence and growth of, 54–57
 hostile takeover at, 57, 160–161
 new corporate culture at, 69–71, 178n. 2
 renewal cycle at, 71–73, 139, 140, 149, 165–166
 shift from performance to learning at, 58, 67–69
  networks in, 63–64
  recognition in, 65–66
  roles in, 58–60
  strategy in, 66–67
  teams in, 60–63
  transformation of people in, 64–65
 See also Russelsteel
Hui, 181n. 23
Hunter-gatherer culture
 absence of hierarchy in, 16, 173nn. 4–6
 communication in, 18–20, 173nn. 7–9
 cooperative values in, 17–18
 emergent strategy in, 16–17
 in modern organization, 27–28, 174n. 15
 nature of, 13–16, 22, 172–173nn. 2, 3
 renewal cycle in, 28–31, 174n. 16
 shared vision in, 20–21, 173n. 10, 174nn. 11, 13
 in shift to herder culture, 26–27
 stability of, 21–22, 174n. 12
 See also Learning organization
Huntley and Palmer foods, 91
Huntsman steel, 91
Hutterites, 195n. 36

IBM, 150, 192n. 16
Icarus paradox, 185n. 24
I.C.I. (company), 94
Ignatius of Loyola, 11
"I-It" relationship, 81, 180n. 22
Immediate-return economies

egalitarianism in, 165–166
 mutual dependence and open territories in, 164–165
 nature of, 162–163, 196n. 46
 self-direction in, 163–164, 196nn. 47, 48
Infinity loops, 97, 104–105, 111, 184n. 14. *See also* Learning loops; Performance loops
Information
 in emerging organizations, 37–38, 176nn. 10–12
 in maturing organizations, 44–45, 177–178nn. 21–23
 in shift from performance to learning organization, 63–64, 68
 syntactic and semantic, 177n. 21
 See also Communication
Innovation, 119–120, 186–187nn. 5–7, 192n. 17
Instrumental rationality
 at Compaq, 106–108, 185nn. 21, 22
 nature of, 105–106, 118, 127, 185nn. 19, 20, 186n. 2, 197n. 55
Intel, 153, 193nn. 23, 24
International Motor Vehicle Program (IMVP), 187n. 10. *See also* Lean production system
Iron
 Coalbrookdale production of, 83–85, 182n. 25
 continuous production of, 85–87
 steam engines and trams in production of, 87–88
 transportation of, 88–91
"I-Thou" relationship, 81, 180n. 21

Japanese auto industry, 193nn. 26, 28
 reinvention of, 120–123, 187–188nn. 8–13
 U.S. auto industry response to, 124, 129, 130, 131
Japanese culture, 187nn. 8, 9, 188n. 12, 193n. 28
Japanese executive offices, 195n. 34. *See also* Physical spaces
Jesuits, 11–12
Johnsonville Foods, 163, 164, 196n. 46
Joint ventures, 130
Just-in-time system, 122–123, 190n. 37
J. Walter Thompson, 92

Kanban, 122–123, 163
K-selection, 106, 145

rationality in process of, 7–8, 171nn.
10–12
rhythms of, 167–169
in shift from herder to hunter culture,
28–30, 174n. 16
values in process of, 11–12
Retrospective sensemaking, 42, 177n. 16
Rewards
compensation systems as, 45, 65–66
in emerging organizations, 38–39, 40
"Rocket" locomotive, 91
Roles
in emerging organizations, 35–36, 39,
40
in established organizations, 42–43
in shift from performance to learning
culture, 58–60
Rosenbluth Travel, 164, 196n. 48
Round tables, 165–166, 197n. 51
Rowntree foods, 91
r-selection environments, 99, 183n. 6
r-strategists
nature of, 98–99, 109, 182–183nn. 3,
4, 6
at Nike, 105–106
in U.S. auto industry, 126
Run for Your Life (Bowerman et al.),
175n. 3
Russelsteel, 54, 70, 71, 119. See also Hugh
Russel Inc.

S.A.E. standards, 125–126
Salaries. See Rewards
San, meaning of, 13, 172n. 1. See also
Bushmen
Sears, 176n. 14, 184n. 10
Self-direction
economics of individual, 163–164,
174n. 16, 196nn. 47, 48
of Quakers, 82–83, 182n. 24
Self-organizing behavior, 97–98, 182n. 2,
184n. 11
Semantic information, 177n. 21
Seven Years' War, 88
Silicon Valley, 83, 152–154, 192–193nn.
17–24. See also Coalbrookdale
Social fusion, 80–81, 173n. 10
Social systems
in ecocycle organizational model, 112,
114, 117–118, 185nn. 26, 30,
186n. 1
ethical anarchy and crisis promoting,
145–146

in Japanese auto industry, 123, 188n.
13
Society of Friends. See Quakers
Society of Jesus, 11–12
Soft matrix organizations, 160–162,
166–167, 196n. 44
Soviet Union, 187n. 6
"Spirit of Capitalism" (Weber), 75
Steam engines, 87, 90
Steel industry
crisis creation in, 134–135
success and decline of U.S., 109, 115,
185nn. 23, 24
See also Hugh Russel Inc.
Stockton and Darlington railroad, 91
Strategy
within all levels of organization,
166–167, 197n. 52
in compensation and career planning,
45
in defining tasks, 42–43, 177n. 18
in defining teams, 43–44, 177nn. 19,
20
emergence of, 41–42, 176–177nn.
14–17
information defining, 44–45,
177–178nn. 21–23
instrumental rational, 105–108,
185nn. 19–22
people in defining, 46, 178nn. 24, 25
in shift from performance to learning
organization, 66–67
Study of History, A (Toynbee), 192n. 17
Substantive rationality, 171n. 12. See also
Value-based rationality
Syntactic information, 177n. 21
Systems thinking
in crisis creation, 131–137, 189nn.
25–28
of hunter-gatherer culture, 21–22,
174n. 12

Tanomoshi, 181n. 23
Tasks
in performance organization, 42–43
in shift from performance to learning,
58–60
See also Roles
Teams, 9
as element of organizations, 36–37, 39,
40
in Japanese auto industry, 123, 188n.
12

About the Author

David K. Hurst is currently a research fellow at the University of Western Ontario's National Centre for Management Research and Development. He is also a reflective management practitioner, speaking and consulting around the world to organizations undergoing radical change. He has taught business policy and organizational behavior at several of Canada's business schools and was an operating manager in diversified companies for twenty-five years. David Hurst has written articles for various management journals, including the *Harvard Business Review.*

David Hurst was born in England and grew up in South Africa. He has lived in Canada for eighteen years.